CAPTURED
BY THE
ENEMY

A WWII Story
of Determination,
Endurance and Hope

THE TRUE STORY OF POW CARL LEROY GOOD

CAPTURED
BY THE
ENEMY

CRYSTAL ACEVES

Copyright © 2015 by Crystal Aceves

All rights reserved. No part of this publication may be reproduced, distributed, or transmitted in any form or by any means, including photocopying, recording, or other electronic or mechanical methods, without the prior written permission of the publisher, except in the case of brief quotations embodied in critical reviews and certain other noncommercial uses permitted by copyright law.

Ordering Information:

Quantity sales. Special discounts are available on quantity purchases by corporations, associations, and others. For details, contact Crystal Aceves at kansasgold@gmail.com.

Printed in the United States of America

First Printing, 2015

ISBN-13: 978-1512083330
ISBN-10: 151208333X

www.crystalaceves.com/

CONTENTS

Notable List of Photos vii
Prologue: How It All Began xi
Author's Note xxi
Chapter 1   GETTING HOME 1
Chapter 2   BROKEN PROMISES 15
Chapter 3   SPINNING BACK IN TIME 27
Chapter 4   ROUGH LANDINGS IN AFRICA 44
Chapter 5   PUSHING FORWARD 67
Chapter 6   CORK OAK FOREST 81
Chapter 7   1943 106
Chapter 8   CALL OF TUNISIA 124
Chapter 9   EX AFRICA SEMPER ALIQUID NOVI 144
Chapter 10   CAPTURED BY THE ENEMY 165
Chapter 11   LIVING HELL 183
Chapter 12   NARROW ESCAPE 206
Chapter 13   COLD 229
Chapter 14   TAKING A CHANCE 251
Chapter 15   HEALING 283
Chapter 16   A LIFE WELL LIVED 311
Works Cited 321

NOTABLE LIST OF PHOTOS

Figure 1:   Two pictures of the Jefferson Barracks in 1944 3
Figure 2:   Emporia Livestock Company sales barn in the 1940s 12
Figure 3:   Carl in his uniform and the 3rd Division patch 24
Figure 4:   Close up of the *USS Tasker H. Bliss* 28
Figure 5:   Map of Mediterranean Sea 33
Figure 6:   Major General George S. Patton 34
Figure 7:   General Patton (on L) and Admiral Hewitt (on R) aboard the *USS Augusta* 46
Figure 8:   U.S. Navy Task Force, carrying General Patton's Western Task Force 52
Figure 9:   Map of Morocco 54
Figure 10: Original flag armband worn by Carl upon landing 56
Figure 11: Center transports off the coast of Fedala 59
Figure 12: The unloading of a jeep in Fedala in calm waters 63
Figure 13: Lost landing craft and equipment cover landing Beach Red 3 64
Figure 14: The sprawling city of Casablanca 72
Figure 15: Rodeo Buddies 78
Figure 16: Pen/pencil Carl bought at the market in Casablanca 86
Figure 17: North African graves 92
Figure 18: Actual censored letter sent to Carl from his mother from later in 1943 95

Figure 19:	Troops and tank of the 7th Infantry, 3rd Division, inland of Fedala	96
Figure 20:	Map of Morocco	97
Figure 21:	Cork oak tree bark	98
Figure 22:	The original New Testament given to Carl by the chaplain in 1942	104
Figure 23:	Map of North Africa	113
Figure 24:	Map showing distance from Arzew to Kasserine Pass	123
Figure 25:	Goat skinned billfold Carl bought while in North Africa	132
Figure 26:	Map that shows Tunisia, Sicily, Sardinia, Greece, Italy, Corsica, and France	141
Figure 27:	LCT	143
Figure 28:	Post card sent to Carl's mother to tell her that Carl had gone MIA	182
Figure 29:	Map that shows Sicily and Naples, Italy	193
Figure 30:	Camp 59 near Servigliano, Italy	205
Figure 31:	The hole in the wall from which Carl and his group escaped Camp 59	213
Figure 32:	Map showing their starting point near Servigliano	214
Figure 33:	View of Monte San Martino landscape in 2015	216
Figure 34:	Photo of the Monte San Martino landscape	227
Figure 35:	Leader of Gruppo 1 Maggio, Decio Fillipponi	234
Figure 36:	Landscape looking away from the Funari house 2009	236
Figure 37:	Pictures of the Funari house 2015	259
Figure 38:	Map that shows Monte San Martino, Rome, and Terni	263
Figure 39:	Map that shows Ascoli	272
Figure 40:	Postcard Carl picked up from Ascoli when he made it back to Allied lines	275

Figure 41: Map that shows Ascoli and Bari 277
Figure 42: Supplies that were given to Carl by the 12th Air Force after he made it to Allied lines 280
Figure 43: Post card sent to Carl's mother to inform her that he had made it to Allied lines. 281
Figure 44: List of escapees to be sent back to Oran 282
Figure 45: Scanned pages of booklet for Camp Myles Standish 290
Figure 46: Picture of the Hays Tavern from 1943 293
Figure 47: Picture of Carl and Nadine on their wedding day 297
Figure 48: Medals Carl earned in WWII 298
Figure 49: Carl's discharge paper from the United States Army on October 12, 1945 312

PROLOGUE

HOW IT ALL BEGAN

LET ME GIVE you a quick prelude into the early life of Carl Leroy Good, a strong, silent hero. You might ask, "How can he be a hero? I've never heard of him before."

It's true. He's not in the history books, he's not on television, and he doesn't play sports, but he's a different kind of hero. He's the kind who quietly walks among us, but has only been discovered by a few. The kind who if found can teach us through wisdom and experience. Yes, heroes are all around us if we take the time to look and that is how Carl became mine. To understand the middle and the end, you must first start at the beginning.

Carl's life began on July 3, 1919. He was the third of what would be eight children born to Furrel and Lillie Good. Upon looking at a map, if you are lucky, you might see a small dot in Kansas called Parkerville about eighteen miles northwest of Council Grove—that was where he was born. Furrel farmed the Kansas soil just outside of town.

When Carl was three years old, they moved to Bartlesville, Oklahoma, with only a small wagon and two teams of horses. The trip was grueling for Lillie with four young children—George, Edith, Carl, and Emma (not even a year younger than Carl.) Not long after they moved, a traditional Thanksgiving dinner turned into heartbreak when five-year-old Edith caught a cold that progressed

One of the last pictures taken of Edith

into pneumonia. She passed away two days before Christmas on December 23, 1921. Her mourning family took her little body back to Kansas for burial and then returned to Oklahoma.

Furrel continued to work the oil fields with his horses for a couple more years, but had little success. Where was all the money everyone was talking about? He thought hauling coal might be better, but it wasn't long before he went back to doing what he knew best—farming. Although he loved farming, it was getting harder for him to provide for his growing family, which now included two more boys, Clarence and Bert.

However, a small window of opportunity opened for them when Lillie's brother, a foreman at the Chevrolet factory, talked them into moving to Flint, Michigan. He promised a booming economy and a solid job for Furrel at the factory. So they sold out, packed up their belongings and five young children, and made the long, hard trip to Michigan. They floated on a ray of hope that it was finally their turn to get a small piece of the American Dream. After all, they were in the Roaring Twenties—a time of economic growth and wonder.

Carl was quick to make new friends as he started the second grade in Flint. He loved the cold winters of Michigan and spent hours ice-skating across the large, frozen river of Flint. For a little over five years, life was good as Furrel worked in the Chevrolet factory. They bought a new five-room bungalow on Cass Avenue and began to save money for a rainy day.

Unfortunately, when that rainy day came, it didn't only rain—it poured. The Great Depression set in with the complete crash of the Wall Street market on October 29, 1929. Like a row of falling dominoes, things quickly collapsed. Sure enough, one gloomy morning in 1930 it happened to them. That was the morning Furrel went to work as usual, but instead of finding the factory opened, the workers in his division found great big chains and a padlock around the entrance. That was it for them—the end of the American Dream and the beginning of The Great Depression. They

Ten-year-old Carl

used their savings while searching for something else, but there was nothing.

However, struggling did not mean they would lose heart. That was not who they were or who they would become. Carl's parents made that clear when they saw a neighbor kid searching their trash for scraps of food. Although they didn't have much to offer, Carl was sent over with a small wagon of food to share.

Before long, they had to let their new home go back to the bank, but they didn't give up. In hope and strength, they rented some farmland 80 miles north, near Standish, Michigan. By the spring of 1931, they were determined to try their hand at farming once again—this time in the soil of Michigan.

Although they had limited means, Furrel found a way to make things work to provide for his family. He let the neighbor use part of his pastureland in exchange for use of teams and machinery. He planted potatoes, beans, melons, corn, and cucumbers—selling the cucumbers to a nearby pickling factory. When he found five acres of sugar beets, he contracted them too. Everyone in the family worked together to ensure a successful harvest that year. Carl was in the eighth grade, and he was old enough to work outside in the fields along with his older brother, George. Many hours were spent on their hands and knees as they thinned plants by hand.

There were also two little ones now, Ruby and new baby John, who were born into the family while in Michigan. Come what may, they weren't going to sit by and let the depression destroy them. They did everything they could to move forward, but Furrel unexpectedly got sick in November 1932. He had an emergency operation, but it was too late—his appendix had burst. Sadly, it didn't take long for the dreaded and deadly gangrene to set in.

Carl (back middle) with his brothers and sisters (except baby John.) Late 1932/Early 1933.

Carl's world fell apart when the hospital called the family at 2:00 A.M. and told them they had better go and say goodbye. They stood by Furrel's side and

xiii

he tenderly kissed each one of them. He pulled Carl and George close and whispered that they would need to take care of the family since he wouldn't be with them for a while. There were many tears and shortly after saying their goodbyes, Furrel passed away. Carl was only thirteen, and this left Lillie to care for seven children on her own. Family from Kansas took Furrel's body back for burial and the young family was officially left fatherless and mourning.

There was no time for Carl to finish the eighth grade. George and he needed to run the farm until all the loose ends were tied. Three months later in February 1933, they said goodbye to the neighbors who had so graciously helped with the younger children each day and were on their way home—back to the support of close family in Kansas.

They took their meager possessions and moved to Council Grove to live with Furrel's mother, Sarepta. Furrel's father, Peter, had passed away less than a year and a half earlier from a heart condition shortly after losing everything he had worked so hard for in the cattle and ranching business. Buying purebred bulls, cattle, and horses by the trainloads had brought him success, but he lost his fortune nearly over night when retail prices hit rock bottom.

Lillie was grateful for Sarepta's help, but she couldn't wait to get back on a farm. She had a small amount of Furrel's life insurance money left, and it was just enough to rent a small farm ($5.00/month) outside of Wilsey, Kansas, and buy two milk cows. They were only about twelve miles west of Sarepta, and Furrel's sister, Linnie, lived on a farm nearby with her husband, Howard, and two young children, Lawrence and Margie. Linnie helped whenever she could and provided extra love and support. Carl was able to finish the 8th grade there, but then took on the responsibility of making sure the family needs were met.

It helped that an abundance of rabbits made food obtainable. In fact, rabbits were so plentiful Carl crouched low by the barn with his rifle and easily shot over a dozen rabbits in less than half an hour. He carefully cleaned and dressed them and sold them at ten cents apiece. It was easy money for him, and he sold at least two every week to the local hotel and an additional three or four to other people in town without a problem. Whatever rabbit meat he didn't sell fed the family. Anything extra beyond that was canned for the hard winters ahead.

Besides rabbit hunting, Carl also found work nearby as a hired hand for anyone who could afford to pay him a wage, including his Uncle Howard. He started at sunup and ended at sundown as he tirelessly labored every day. Furthermore, whenever eligible, he enrolled in government-sponsored programs such as the Civilian Conservation Corps (CCC) for six-month intervals throughout 1936-1938. These programs were available due to the difficulty of finding work during the depression. He took whatever they offered him, including projects in soil erosion control, soil conservation, and road construction throughout Council Grove and in the state of Washington. Although the program covered his housing and food needs, he went home in the evenings to help with the farm when he was close enough and gave most of his earnings of $30.00/month to his mother. He knew she needed it more than he did.

Carl and CCC living quarters

From the age of sixteen, between the intervals of working with the CCC, he started working for Clyde Varnes and learned how to run his successful ranching business. The Great Depression was winding down and WWII was getting started. The farming industry was turning around and hope began to emerge like the sun on a rainy day. Clyde wanted to retire and was ready to put everything he had into Carl's hands.

Carl had been dealt a difficult hand in life, but things were slowly turning around for him. Through hard work, diligence, and persistence, he was doing the things he loved. When he wasn't working, he filled his life with rodeo, friends, and horses. He met and dated a girl from around the area and when he asked her to marry him, she accepted.

However, as good as everything was headed in one direction, the war began to pull on the other. All of Carl's buddies began to be called away and shortly after, he received his "Greeting" from the U.S. Draft Board as well. He knew farmers could be excluded, but duty called and he was bound to participate like everyone else. Therefore, on April 21, 1942, he left the opportunity that had begun to shine around him and entered the U.S. Army.

He was to serve in a war that would forever change his life. In this book, I hope to share only a sliver of his courage, integrity, honesty, dedication, bravery, and so much more that comes from experience and hardship. As you read above, he wasn't new to the difficulties of life, and perhaps that is what made the difference between being a person who gave up and one who kept going even when it seemed impossible. This book was written so his actions, and those of so many others, are not forgotten. Yes, I found my hero right next to me—for Carl is my granddad.

Once I discovered him, I wanted to know more and took the opportunity to interview and record him for a paper I was writing for college in 2007. Even at the age of eighty-eight, my granddad kept plenty busy and I had to schedule in a time to meet with him and his second wife, Katherine. I drove from Emporia to Council Grove with my three young daughters and a tape recorder in tow and started the first of what would become many recordings.

I walked in the front door of his dark pink house and it was like being transported back twenty years to the Christmas gatherings I attended as a child. Everything was familiar as I went into the dining room and sat at the wooden table across from my granddad. The sun shone through the two side windows and the room hadn't changed much even though my uncle and aunt lived there now. Even some of the furniture was the same with the curio cabinet and familiar knickknacks standing in the corner between the living room and the hallway.

The sentiment of past family gatherings was so strong I could almost smell the Christmas ham baking in the oven and hear my grandma's laugh as she joked in the kitchen. In reality, those moments had long passed. My granddad was noticeably older, I was older, and my grandma's laugh was only a desired memory since her death in 1987.

Nevertheless, now was my chance to ask those questions that had been bouncing inside my head since I first read my granddad's war memoir as a young child. My maternal grandma, Velna Lindquist, had transcribed the hard-to-read, handwritten copy to a legal-sized, typewritten copy as a gift for my dad, David. In doing that, she opened up a story that at one time was a forbidden subject that transported unforgettable memories to the forefront and still haunted my granddad all those years later. It was a subject that my dad knew to avoid as a child. After all, the memory of watching his dad "stuck" in a haunting flashback as the local doctor was called was enough to keep anyone from being a trigger.

Yet as the years passed, it almost was as if the memories held captive so long needed to be free. He needed to tell the story that haunted his being for so many years. I looked at him sitting across from me at the dining room table and I began to record. He looked at me with aged eyes that had now changed from dark brown to a dark gray with blue outlining and said, "Oh, I didn't do nothing special. I was just one of the boys."

I probed for more as he took off his beige Stetson cowboy hat and set it on the table. Little specks of orange wood shavings stuck to his thinning, gray hair. He had finished fixing a door and the proof remained. His aged hand, spotted with sun marks and time, ran through his hair. When he looked at me, there was a gleam in his eye and a *you won't believe it* tone in his voice, "I didn't have nothing to do with making it home; the Good Man Upstairs sure took care of me. Many men died and they are the ones who deserve the glory. I didn't do nothing special."

His face was soft, clean shaven, and showed the marks of experience and age. Sixty-five years had passed since he started his Army journey, yet the stories held captive for so many years began to spill out one by one. His memory was fresh and polished. I sat forward in my chair and listened intently. Amazed at the clarity and preciseness of dates, names, and places, a picture effortlessly began to form in my mind as he shared his amazing story with me.

So you see, my hero was an ordinary person who honorably survived the scars war left on him. He chose to keep going even when it was easier to give up. He proved that life was worth living no matter what curve balls were thrown his way. He never quit, he fought to survive, and with his wife, Nadine, they taught their six kids the true worth of hard work and high values. In my eyes, those things are what make him a hero.

Open your eyes to the everyday heroes around you whose quiet acts are unknown. Your hero could be sitting next to you, but you haven't taken the time to find out. With that said, here is only a small part of the pain my granddad shared with me to write his remarkable story, *Captured by the Enemy.*

LONG FAREWELL FOR SELECTEES

More Than 400 People Gathered to See Soldier Boys Start for Military Camps——Wilsey Near Top of List

Scores of well-wishers remained up all night to see another contingent of Morris county selectees started safely to Ft. Leavenworth this morning. Gene Boudeman, draft clerk, reports that at 4 o'clock this morning, the inductees were still dancing in the high school gymnasium. One observer estimated the number of friends and relatives who gathered for the farewell party at more than 400.

Wilsey and Council Grove sent the largest number of draftees, the former having eight and the county seat nine on the roster. Among those called into military service were: LeRoy Marvin Hodson, Delavan; Allie Albert Brundage, Wilsey; Alfred Alexander Swann, Wilsey; Ira Everett Welch, Wilsey Lloyd Scott Irwin, Wilsey; Rome Roland Goodman, White City; Howard Samuel Andrews, Delavan; Howard Chester Stewart, Delavan; Robert Ernest Lee Dunlap; Russell Louis Herpich Delavan; James William Maloney Skiddy; Verlen William Barnhart Council Grove Carl Leroy Good, Wilsey; Sylvester Frederick Rial, Dwight; Leslie Leroy Schultz, Council Grove; Dea Whitt Cheatham, Council Grove; Edwin Fred Krause, Latimer; Edward Daniel Hoffman, Council Grove; Edwin Lyle Williams, Council Grove; Maurice Cashman, Council Grove Donald Lowell Miller, Delavan; Wayne Everett McDougal, Wilsey; Linus Albert Burnett, Council Grove; Curtis Wayne Hougland, Wilsey; Earl ...ner, Council Grove; W... Young, Council Grove Jackson Campbell, Wilse...

COUNCIL GROVE YOUTH MISSING IN ACTION

Special to The Gazette:

Council Grove, Aug. 30.—Mrs. Lillie Good, widow living in East Council Grove has received news through the United States War department that her son, Pvt. Carl Good, enlisted from Morris county, has been missing in action since July 17. He was last heard from in the North Africa area.

Mrs. Good, who has five younger children at home, has another son, Clarence Good, who is with U. S. troops in Australia.

The family came to Council Grove from Wilsey.

CARL GOOD MISSING

Pvt Carl Good of Wilsey is missing in action in the North African area. A telegram from the war department to his mother Mrs Lillie Good informs her that Carl has been accounted for since July 17. The last the family heard from the soldier he was in Tripoli. The meager information furnished leaves the family hopeful that Carl may be a captive.

HOME ON FURLOUGH

Pfc. Carl Good, who has been overseas for 21 months in the European theater, is due at Jefferson Barracks, Mo., Thursday on a furlough home. He has been with the 7th Infantry, and will spend his furlough period with his mother, Mrs. L. M. Good.

World War II POW
Carl Good On Run From Germans For Nine Months

AUTHOR'S NOTE

I WOULD LIKE to express my thanks to the many people who have helped me with this project. My husband, Ali, and four awesome kids, Elicia, Brianna, Isabelle, and Tristan, were patient and supportive with the endless hours I spent on research and writing. My granddad talked to me and let me record him whenever I got the chance. And of course, as my granddad would say, the "Good Man Upstairs" helped me make it to the end in every aspect.

I also thank the many knowledgeable people who answered my questions and gave me permission to use their photos. Each one of these people helped support this project in different ways—Melinda Haney, David, Evelyn, Steven, Michael, CJ, and Rebekah Good and their families, Tabitha Tatman, Carla Stone, Cheryl and Doug Bibens, Rebekah Fuller, Dennis Hill, Ricardo and Vanesa Funari, Antonio Millozzi, John Simkins, Ian McCarthy, Derek Murphy, and photographer, Ibrahim Malla. To all of you, I say thank you!

This project is very dear to my heart for many reasons:

- Number one, it is an amazing story. There are no other words to describe how I feel when I read my granddad's memoir and talked to him about his experiences.
- Number two, my granddad deserved the proper honor of being recognized as a survivor. His story should not be hidden. I am proud of his service to our country.
- Number three, he received an injury in a POW camp, but he didn't get his Purple Heart because he lacked paper proof of

the injury. Nevertheless, I hope this will be a way to honor him in a different way.

All the facts, history, and places in the book are real, and any error due to faulty research or misunderstood concepts should in no way affect the trueness of *his* story. War is an extremely complicated time and there is a lot of confusion and differing information as it progresses. I followed his role in the 3rd Division, 7th Infantry, Cannon Company, but I could not specify every detail of every group involved. Although all divisions and infantries played an important role, I followed his. This does not make any one group more important than another. However, it does allow me tell my granddad's true story based on history, not write a history book.

I chose to write his story as creative nonfiction (also known as literary or narrative nonfiction). This means that his story is 100% true, but creative elements, such as conversation and characters, have been added to help recreate the event. I have noted which characters are real in the footnotes. I wrote his story through extensive historical research, Army reports, other personal accounts, and a memoir he wrote in 1945. I interviewed him for many hours, and he patiently answered my questions. He truly went through these things and even some of the dialogue is directly quoted from him.

You may notice I wrote this book without excessive profanity, much to the dislike of General George Patton, I'm sure. Although associated with war, profanity generally wasn't tolerated by the average American "Citizen Soldier" during that time. When profanity was used, it was used to get attention or by those who were in the Army as a career choice (like General Patton.) I hope this can be read by anyone wanting to learn more about WWII. With or without profanity, I can still share this amazing story about my hero.

Lastly, I worked on this project for eight years, but I continually learn new things. I have done my best to take all the many stories and put them together into one that follows a timeline. However, I wasn't there. Therefore, if you find a mistake, feel free to leave me a message at kansasgold@gmail.com. I am sure I will continue to learn.

I wrote this book with great honor and pride for my granddad—Carl Leroy Good.

Crystal Good Aceves

Author with her family

xxiii

Chapter 1

GETTING HOME

AN INTERNAL BATTLE raged inside Carl as he stood waiting for the train near Boston. The train whistle loudly echoed through his mind and numbed his body as it approached. Trains hadn't bothered him before, but now he had a new memory associated with them. Being in a train meant being in an enclosed, hot piece of metal that was a sure target for bombs with little chance for escape.

The stench of his recent past had contaminated his thoughts with fear. His body wanted to run—to get away from the threatening situation, but he convinced himself he would be okay. He was back in the States now, and there were no bayonet-carrying guards to push him along and watch him cling to the last strings of life.

A nudge from behind made him jump as an unknown voice said, "You going?"

Carl hadn't realized he was holding up the line. He looked at the empty space in front of him and something from deep within moved his feet forward. Sweaty, pale, and shaking, he quietly made it to an empty seat and sat down. He refused to let this new fear take hold. If anything, he would do it in spite of the enemy—to prove to them that they had not won him over.

When his eyes adjusted to the darkness of the train car, he slid his finger across the bottom of the window and watched as the dust effortlessly lifted into the air and silently landed around him. *If only readjusting to life was so simple*, he thought as another soldier sat down beside him. He was in no mood to talk, but he used the last of his energy to force a polite smile.

He felt and heard every movement as the first car started down the tracks. Hands tightly clasped in his lap, the other cars jolted into motion behind it. Out the window, the tall, green trees and the beautiful, rolling hills of the United States passed by as the train picked up speed on the way to their next stop 1200-miles away—the Jefferson Barracks.

Once they were moving, he tried hard not to fall asleep even though he was tired. Unwillingly nodding off, his head jerked up with the sound of the train whistle as they approached a small, tucked away town—again. He had decided it was better that way as he fought to push the blackness of the memories away that sometimes seeped in with sleep.

Yet try as he might, involuntary flashbacks slid in like an unwanted stranger with the clickity-clack of the train as it rolled over the tracks. Desperately trying to wake up from the nightmare as it replayed in his head, he couldn't shake the vision of lying in a dark, airless car with others crowded around him as he struggled to stay alive. Transported like animals to the next hellhole, he was too weak to move and his throat was sore and swollen. He felt like he was suffocating. Trying to catch his breath, he moaned.

The soldier next to him softly nudged him and asked, "You okay?"

Carl jumped in his seat and instinctively looked around him for a weapon. His surroundings slowly brought him back to the present. He closed his eyes and took a deep breath. "Huh? Oh, sorry. Yeah, I'm fine."

He sat back and wondered what exactly he had done to make the soldier ask if he was okay. He must not let those thoughts consume him. That was over... or was it? The memories seemed as if they would haunt him forever—slowly consuming him from the inside out like maggots eating rotten flesh to the point of exhaustion.

And it was exhausting—mentally and physically. In his heart, he still wanted to be the trusting, soft-spoken, charming, go-getter who had left for war two years ago. Now, he was left as a suspecting, nervous, quiet, and guarded wreck of a man who could trust no one. The war had transformed him into a person he didn't like, and he could only hope time would heal all things.

Chapter 1 – GETTING HOME

After a long trip, they made it to the Jefferson Barracks, ten miles south of St. Louis, Missouri, and above the bluffs of the Mississippi River. Gratefully stepping off the train, he stretched his achy bones and looked around him. His mind moved in a blur from exhaustion, but he noticed there were so many others—dark shadows standing close by watching, too weak and tired to move, but unwilling to give up. They were more like empty shells rather than men—war had destroyed them from the inside. He was not alone.

Walking across the grounds, he wondered how long he would have to stay there—one week... maybe two. God knew he only wanted to be on his way home. Until then, he would either be staying inside the barracks or outside in the tent camps set up for extra space.

The only problem was the anxiety that came from being on the run for so long. There were people around him all the time. He would have felt right at home before, but that was before. He wasn't ready to trust people yet, and getting assigned to the old barracks reminded him of the prison camps.

Every night he spent there dragged on as he desperately tried to ignore the stains of death said to be permanently marked across the 118-year-old barracks. His recent brush with death was still a tender, oozing wound filled with anger, hurt, and hate. He knew it would take years, or maybe even his whole life to heal.

His thoughts wildly swirled with the bleak tales of death and pain of soldiers dying where he lay. The red brick walls didn't hold in the heat and the small potbellied stoves placed in the 240-foot

Figure 1: Two pictures of the Jefferson Barracks in 1944
(Permission granted by Jefferson Barracks, St. Louis County Parks Dept.)

3

barrack were no match for the damp, frigid winters of Missouri. As a result, death came in the forms of pneumonia or soldiers freezing to death. He was glad he didn't have to worry about that now—he knew what it was like to be cold.

He pushed those thoughts aside and took a deep breath. He only wanted to rest. Was that too much to ask? However, when he closed his eyes, it felt like the spirits said to be left behind quietly tiptoed behind him into his dreams. Never-ending darkness surrounded him. "Get that black scarf away from me," he moaned into the night. "God help me!" he yelled, sitting straight up in his bunk. His hand shook as he wiped his sweaty forehead. Why did these night terrors continue to plague him? He had already lived through it once.

Every morning, he hoped to hear his papers had gone through. He hoped to hear it was his turn for furlough—his turn to go home. When they hadn't, he took a walk outside. The bright sun, fresh air, and a warm, summer breeze made it somewhat bearable as he waited. He looked up at the clear blue sky where long, white wisps of clouds effortlessly crossed it. How was it possible for a sky that peaceful to be the same one that rested above so much pain and misery a continent away?

There were never answers to those questions, but he couldn't help but wonder as he impatiently waited. After a week, the news finally came. Papers in hand, he got ready to leave. His dark brown eyes scanned his area to make sure he wasn't leaving anything behind.

He stopped when he saw a young soldier lying on his bunk glaring a hole into the wall with a scowl across his thin lips. Surprised, Carl squinted over at him and asked with a slight nod of the head, "Hey soldier, what in the world are you doing in bed? Aren't you going home?"[1]

Before answering, the soldier looked around to make sure he was talking to him. Then, chewing his lower lip, he answered, "I can't."

"Well, why can't you?" Carl asked as he took a step closer.

Without looking back up and staring straight ahead, the solider mumbled, "I don't have any money. They messed my payroll up, and they didn't give me my money."

---

[1] True conversation as told by Carl.

Chapter 1 – Getting Home

"Heck, I'll let you have some money. Where you living?" he asked without thinking twice about what he was saying.

The soldier's head snapped up in surprise as he answered, "Iowa."

Slightly smiling, Carl said, "Well, I'll give you some money and when you get home, when you get it, you can send it to me."

The soldier sat up and Carl could feel his light blue eyes staring at him before saying, "Oh, you wouldn't want to do that, you don't know me."

"I don't got to know you. We got a deal."

Slowly, the soldier stood up, "My name is John, and I promise you, you'll get your money. We have money at home. Give me your address and I'll get you your money back."

Automatically, Carl reached for his billfold in his back pocket. He had always carried it there—before. He stopped short when he remembered he no longer had it. His face reddened as a twinge of anger rushed through him. He remembered the German officer going through it and then tossing it to the side—confirming his loss of identity as a prisoner.

He tried not to think about that as a surge of hate passed through his body. He wouldn't let the hate overtake him. He was better than that. He didn't need to live off his surroundings or depend on a humble meal given out of complete kindness anymore. The enemy hadn't made him a faceless soldier like they had hoped. The war may have conditioned him to be tough, but in his heart there was still a piece the war couldn't take over—he wouldn't let it.

Carl pulled out a small wad of bills from his front pocket instead. Moments earlier, he had received his pay, so he handed John $100.00 and said, "That should do it. Go get home."

With a big, brotherly hug, John thanked him and ran down the hall. If Carl had it his way, he would always help people. He may not trust them, but he was born with a giving soul. Luckily, that part hadn't been affected by the war. It felt pretty darn good being on the giving side again.

After John was gone, Carl looked back down at the ticket in his hand. In bold type, Emporia, Kansas, was written as the place of destination. Although Emporia wasn't home, he would be within thirty-five miles from it, and that was close enough. Just thinking about getting on the train made him sweat, but he knew he could do it this time.

Once he was on, he picked a seat by the window again and tried to stop his legs from shaking as he sat down. He hoped he would get to sit alone this time. With no such luck, he looked at the man who sat down beside him. The man was an older gentleman, probably in his late sixties. Although he had a newspaper in his hand, he looked at Carl and started a conversation, "Have you been home long, soldier?"

He didn't mind talking this time around, but he didn't want to talk about the war. "Made it back August 2," he said, keeping it simple.

The white-haired man reached out his hand, "I'm Stan Emmetts[2]. Welcome home, soldier." Then, pointing to the newspaper in his lap, he added, "You boys are doing a mighty good job out there."

Carl wondered what information was written in the newspaper. Was the paper full of propaganda like he had seen firsthand in the other countries? No, he didn't want to know until he heard the words *the war is over and we have won*.

Still, being respectful, he responded, "Thank you, sir."

"Call me Mr. Emmetts, if you will. What is your name, son?"

"Carl Good."

"Well, Carl, you got any plans for when you get home?"

He had been thinking about that and answered, "I'll be seeing my family first, but then I'll go see my girl[3]."

"How long has it been since you've seen her?"

Carl stayed vague with the times as he answered, "Oh, a couple years. My last night home with her we had a big dance[4]. There was lots of us boys leaving from the areas around my small town in Wilsey and—"

"Wilsey? Now, where's that?" Mr. Emmetts interrupted.

"It's a tiny town not too far from Council Grove."

---

[2] Character added for dialogue and information
[3] Real character
[4] Dance was in a newspaper article with Carl's name listed in it

"Council Grove, huh? Now, there's a town full of history. Why, I remember…"

Mr. Emmetts went on talking something about the Santa Fe Trail and his voice slid into the background as Carl thought about that last dance before he left. He remembered that night as if it were yesterday.

There he was dancing and singing the night away with his fiancé, Helen, until the wee hours of the morning. Wiping his sweaty head with the sleeve of his shirt, he grabbed Helen's hand and said, "It's hot in here. Let's step out for some fresh air."

The redness of her cheeks told him she would welcome a break. They stepped out into the early morning air and his face tightened as the sweat disappeared into the misty coolness. Suddenly, the front door swung open and he turned to shield her from being hit. Startled, his buddy looked over at them and said, "Oh, sorry. I didn't see you guys there. What you two lovebirds doing out here in the rain?"

Carl looked out, "It ain't raining, just a light mist is all. Where you headed?"

His friend looked at him as he walked backwards down the front steps and said, "Home. I haven't got much done and we'll be leaving soon."

Carl stood closer to Helen and listened to the music as it flowed into the stillness of the spring night. Looking down at his watch, he said, "He's right! I wish the time would slow down just for tonight."

Pulling her sweater tighter around her shoulders, Helen asked, "Why? What time is it?"

"Nearly 3:30 in the morning," he reluctantly replied. The inside lights threw a yellow tint over her as he continued, "You know I'll wait for you. We'll get married as soon as I get back."

The glassy look in her eyes told him she was holding back tears—she didn't want him to go. He knew she wouldn't try to hold him back, but it was hard. She pulled out a small picture from her hand purse and said, "Remember me while you're gone, and I'll be waiting when you get home."

She lightly placed her lips on the picture before handing it to him. He promptly put it in the safety of his billfold. In the darkness, he felt her warm hand on his arm and he knew it would be all right.

Gently pushing her hair back, he leaned in and kissed her forehead as he said, "Wait for me and life will be good for us."

She nodded, "I know. It'll only be the two of us, and Clyde[5] already said he'd give you the ranch as soon as we're married."

"Yep, over 400 head of cattle, a big beautiful house, a great barn, and everything else we'll need on the ranch," he said as he squeezed her hand and gently pulled her toward the front door to enjoy their last minutes of the dance together.

Thinking about that night made him more anxious than ever. Suddenly, he realized Mr. Emmetts had stopped talking and was looking at him. "Sorry. What'd you say?"

"I asked if you got a job lined up yet," Mr. Emmetts repeated.

"I only got about three weeks at home, and then I got to go to Texas to finish my time in the Army. But I left with the deal of a lifetime, so I hope I can make that happen."

"That's good. Can I ask what the deal of a lifetime would be?"

He looked at Mr. Emmetts and thought, *Boy, he sure asks a lot of questions.* However, he respected the older generation and knew it was only a friendly conversation. There wasn't anybody here trying to get secure information or trying to trip him up. Still, he carefully chose his words, "Well, I'm a farmer by blood and before I left, I helped a good man with his ranch. He was like a father to me really. He told me when I got home, he'd retire and I'd keep the ranch going. He'd leave it all to me, and we'd split it down the middle—fifty/fifty."

"Sounds like you got it made there," Mr. Emmetts said with a smile.

He sat back in his seat as Mr. Emmetts picked up the paper and said, "I'm going to catch up on the latest news here."

It wouldn't be long before Carl could restart the life he had left behind. He was ready and he knew he could trust Clyde. He had worked for him on and off since he was sixteen.

Once again, the train whistles interrupted his thoughts and he slightly jumped in his seat. He was still plenty jumpy. As he looked

---

[5] Clyde Varnes—real character and Carl's good friend who was going to have Carl take over his ranch

Chapter 1 – Getting Home

past Mr. Emmetts, he noticed all the strangers around him, but this time he saw something different.

Every person held secret shadows of pain deeply etched into his/her eyes. It passed through eyes of all colors and circumstances like the thump of a heartbeat with blurs of blue, green, and brown. He wondered what his pain looked like from the outside. He could hide some of it, but he knew it had changed him. Circling back through time, he knew from firsthand experience that pain had no preference. Rich, poor, old, young—it didn't matter. Every person carried an unseen cross, but some could hide it better than others.

Finally, they arrived in Emporia, Kansas, and stepped off the train at the grand depot of the Atchison, Topeka & Santa Fe Railway. Mr. Emmetts was in front of him, but turned back to say, "This is a great depot Emporia has here."

The huge brick structure was a welcome sign and a grand sight in the growing town of Emporia. The sun shone through the heavy clouds and the wind blew by them like a welcome from a long lost friend. Carl turned his face toward the sky and took a deep breath of fresh Kansas air. "It sure is swell to be so close to home," he said as they walked away from the busy tracks.

A man in blue overalls and work boots hurriedly passed by them and nodded a quick hello. It took him a minute to realize the man wasn't walking toward him, but to a 1939 Chevrolet pickup truck parked nearby. Carl half smiled as he nodded his head in the direction of the truck and said, "You see that huge dent in his door? I bet it's sprung from a conflict with an angry, runaway bull." From experience, he knew the familiar groan the door would make as the man opened it.

Mr. Emmetts smiled, "I don't know much about that."

Carl watched as the man stepped onto the thick, dirt-caked running board and sat down next to a young woman. When he pulled away, Carl caught a glimmer of green paint shine out from under the heavy dust. The wind blew through the open windows of the truck and the loose strands of the woman's brown hair blew around her thin, pale face.

That's a life I'm ready to have back, he thought as Helen's image flashed through his mind.

Walking a little ways across the depot with Mr. Emmetts, he couldn't help but hear the hum of mixed news. The January old news about the death of William Allen White still buzzed throughout the town, making sure to reach every unsuspecting guest. He felt the glances of many as he walked through in his Army uniform. The war was a common topic updated daily in the Emporia Gazette, but that was something he already knew plenty about.

"Where you going now?" he asked Mr. Emmetts.

"I have a friend who will be picking me up. I have a couple meetings here before heading back to St. Louis."

They stopped walking to wait for a couple casually strolling by arm in arm. The rushing wind took advantage of the war-shortened outfits[6], and he noticed how the woman's modern clothes screamed, "Conservative!" as she pushed her knee-length skirt to her legs. A second later, a woman's hat tumbled by them in the wind and he reached over and gently caught it. A woman wearing a matching dress ran up to him and reached out her hand. Smiling, she said, "Thank you, soldier!"

They walked on, but after a bit, Mr. Emmetts stopped and said, "This is as far as I go. Where are you going from here?"

"Oh, I figured I'd walk to the sales barn[7]," Carl answered, adjusting the bag he was carrying. "It'll be my best bet in finding a ride back to Council Grove. If I'm not mistaken, there should be a livestock auction going on about now."

"Do you want a ride?"

"Nah. I'll be all right. It's a straight walk down the side of these here tracks," he said, looking toward the dirt road. Then he shook Mr. Emmetts's hand and said, "It was nice talking to you, sir. Have a good trip."

---

[6] Due to the ration of fabric in WWII from the War Production Board, outfits became shorter and simpler than ever before. Nylon, silk, leather, and rubber were all needed for war efforts and severely limited. Even common materials as wool and cotton were to be used for military uniforms. Anything extra on an outfit was considered unpatriotic.

[7] Emporia Livestock Company sales barn was the true location as told by Carl

Chapter 1 – Getting Home

Mr. Emmetts waved at him as he headed down West 3rd Avenue. There were only a few houses built here and there along the other streets going north, but heading west, there wasn't a single one. Carl leaned over, scooped up a big handful of rich, brown Kansas dirt, and sifted it through his fingers. It silently blew back into the wind. One thing was for sure—he was almost home. He was so close he could feel it float across the Kansas air and push him along his path.

It was a little under a mile, but it felt longer. His nerves were shot, and every noise sounded louder than it really was. He looked over his shoulder for the hundredth time. Why did it still feel like he was being hunted? This little walk should be nothing. He had been walking for months and not along a peaceful, dirt road as he was on now, but through the rugged, Italian terrain. He didn't need to look over his shoulder or hide in the brush because there wasn't anyone out looking for him, but he couldn't help it.

Somewhat isolated along Albert St., the Emporia Livestock Company sprawled across the western limits of Emporia. From Funston St., he turned north and walked along the pen area to the main building and entrance. The familiar wooden structure looked the same—old and worn from the many years in business. Yet it glowed with experience and a hard earned reputation built by trust and loyalty. He had gone there many times with Clyde when working at the ranch, and he knew he could trust the people inside. The loose dust fell off his boots as he shook them off before walking in the door.

Once inside, it took a second for his eyes to adjust to the darkness. His shirt was wrinkled from the trip and he tried to smooth it out with his hand. The smell of cigarette smoke drifted heavily from the door on his left. He cracked the door a bit and saw an office with a small, wooden radio on an old, dusty desk stacked with papers. Quiet music drifted to where he was standing and he instantly recognized the voice of Gene Autry singing *The Last Round-Up*. He took a deep breath—he hadn't heard that music for a long time!

The notes created a tunnel in time, and the music seemed to pick him up and carry him back to when he was finishing the eighth grade in Wilsey. He remembered leaning against the side of his desk and entertaining his classmates as he sang and yodeled. He smiled at the thought. Some of the kids had even started calling him Gene Autry—saying he sounded just as good.

Now, he quietly mouthed the words to the second verse as it played, "I'm heading for the last roundup to the far away ranch of the Boss in the sky. Where the strays are counted and branded there go I. I'm heading for the last roundup."

Gosh, he loved that music. When the chorus started next, he tried softly to sing along, "Git along little doggie, git along, git along..." but the words no longer had a clear outlet. His throat and vocal chords couldn't handle the trauma from the blast. It could have been worse. He could still talk, and he was grateful for that. It was another memory he'd have to lock in a silent chest of time along with all the others, but how he wished he could sing again.

Smoke rising from the unattended cigarette in the ashtray by the door grabbed his attention. There wasn't anybody in the office, so he closed the door. Not a smoker himself, he welcomed the strong, pungent odor of livestock that stung his nose as he continued down the hall. Even with his loss of smell, he could smell that. Yes—it was the smell of life before the war.

The circular auction room was crowded as large fans moved the August air around. Since cattle were needed for the war effort, mostly horses and mules were being auctioned off. Bidders, sellers, and spectators crowded around the sale ring, or sat in a tier of wooden seats that went three-quarters of the way around it, but he didn't see

Figure 2: Two pictures of the Emporia Livestock Company sales barn in the 1940s (Permission granted by Vic Peak)

12

anyone he recognized. In the front, there was an elevated box with more people, including the weight master.

Tired and hopeful, he made his way through the crowd to where the auctioneer was standing in the ring and called over to him, "Sir, I'm trying to find a ride back to Council Grove. Can you ask if there's anybody headed in that there direction?"

Looking Carl over as he stood there in his uniform with his small bag of possessions hanging over his right shoulder, the auctioneer said, "Son, looks like you've had a mighty long trip. Let's make an announcement and get you the rest of the way home."

The announcement was made and he waited to see if fortune was on his side. He was relieved when he saw a man stand up from the back of the crowded room. The man wore dark work jeans, brown cowboy boots, and a felt cowboy hat that fit squarely on his head. His face was not tan from working in the sun, and although he wore leather gloves, his hands were not those of a farmer. Carl recognized the man from the Council Grove grocery store—Mr. Roberts[8], if he remembered correctly.

"Al be danged! One of the Good boys," Mr. Roberts said as he got closer.

"Yes, sir."

Mr. Roberts looked him over, "I heard you were alive and coming home, but I didn't imagine I'd be the one to finish taking you there. Boy, you're looking real thin. I bet you're glad to be back home for some good ole cooking."

Carl slightly pushed the side of his mouth into a smile, "Yes, sir, can't wait."

Mr. Roberts shook his head at the sight of seeing him standing there thin and quiet. "Well, let's get going. I'm done here today. I was here to check out prices anyway. I reckon your family's waiting for you. Boy, am I glad to see you make it home! Not everybody's been so lucky."

---

[8] Real character who took Carl the rest of the way home to Council Grove (Carl remembered name as Roberts)

"Yes, sir," Carl said as they walked out, "I'm mighty glad to be home myself."

The sales barn had brought in quite a crowd and they had to walk a ways to get back to the car. Carefully parked off Highway 50, a black 1940 Ford Coupe sat waiting. The flat-topped hood dominated the front, and although Carl was impressed with the style, he secretly preferred a good old farm truck for himself. The afternoon light shone off the chrome of the grill, and his first thought was the danger of the reflection.

He hoped he could stay awake the rest of the way home as the V8 engine roared to life and they headed west out of Emporia on Highway 50. The seats were clean and comfortable and he could tell Mr. Roberts took great pride in taking care of his car. It wasn't like the farm trucks that had a gunnysack on the seats for protection against the wear and tear of country life.

Mr. Roberts filled him in on a few things going on around Council Grove and Carl listened. Even though he had lived in Wilsey before leaving for the war, he had worked around Council Grove and could follow what Mr. Roberts was talking about. Small towns usually had a connection with the ones around them, and he was grateful for that now as they headed in that direction.

He was glad Mr. Roberts didn't ask him many questions as the dry, hot, August wind blew through the open windows. The gathered hay neatly stacked in the fields reminded him of those in Italy, and the hands of the past reached toward him. He could almost hear the screams of burning escapees fill his mind.

Chapter 2

BROKEN PROMISES

NONE TOO SOON, Council Grove came into view. Suddenly, a surge of excitement passed through the darkness Carl had felt only minutes earlier—he had finally made it! In a few minutes, he would be getting out of the car and seeing the beautiful face of his mother—something he had convinced himself he wouldn't see again. He had been told one too many times he would never go home, but somehow… he was there.

A quick scenario played out in his head. He would get out and… wait… He had been gone for over two years. His mother had moved to this house in town while he was away because she couldn't manage the farm without her boys there to help. It was her home, not his. Should he knock patiently on the front door, call out to his mother from the porch, or just open the door and walk in? Maybe his mother would be outside hanging laundry to dry or…

Before he could think any longer, Mr. Roberts stopped in front of an old two-story house at 417 Union. "I believe this is it."

"Thanks for the lift," Carl said as he got out of the car.

Mr. Roberts smiled, "Welcome home. We're glad to have you back."

Although the house was old with cracked, white paint and had an overgrown lawn, he realized home, no matter where, was a beautiful place. It was even more beautiful after chasing the dream for so long that someday he would be standing there again. He hesitated as he looked at the old house directly sitting in front of him. Mixed feelings fluttered through his stomach. Nerves and excitement stirred together as if making a lethal concoction deep inside. He had returned a different man and a slight fear of rejection began to creep up and add to the mixture.

Suddenly, the front door swung open and his mother came running down the porch steps. "Carl! Oh Carl! You're home!" she screamed.

Her long, dark hair was pinned on her head in a bun and her dress flapped against her legs as she ran down the sidewalk toward him. She wrapped her arms tightly around him, spun him around, and then put her head in his boney shoulder. The color of his shirt darkened from her tears and he felt his eyes burning. A few hot tears escaped down his face—tears he didn't know he still had. He had held it in for so long! There never was enough energy to waste on feeling sorry for himself—there was only enough energy to survive. It was a day-to-day battle to stay alive. Looking up at him, his mother said through her tears of joy, "God has answered our prayers."

No other words were needed as he thought to himself, *Yeah, and He has answered a lot of mine too.*

Standing there, he looked over to see his sister, Emma, and her four-year-old son, Jerry, come out the front door toward him. Not far behind, came his younger sister, Ruby, and his youngest brother, Johnny. Boy was he glad to see them all! He leaned over and picked up Jerry. "Last time I saw you, you was just a baby." He smiled at Johnny and Ruby and added, "No hugs from you two?"

As they stood in a group hug on the sidewalk, he felt safe for the first time in a long while. Of course, they didn't know that. He had always been their protector. Since their dad had died over ten years ago, Carl had stepped up to help care for them—all of them. Whether they needed discipline or love, he had been there. Not to mention, the financial support he provided. They looked up to him and respected him in return. And although he looked a lot thinner, he was back home, and they were sure glad to see him.

Once inside the old house, his mother silently followed as Ruby excitedly gave him a tour and showed him a small room upstairs that was for him. Sitting on the small bed against the wall, he thought, *I'm home now. I'm really home.* He tried to internalize he didn't have to

Chapter 2 – Broken Promises

hide anymore. He was a free man again. He was done being chased, and now he could chase his own dreams. Yet deep inside, he knew it wouldn't be that easy—his mind wouldn't let him forget.

His mother sat down on the bed next to him. He looked over at her and realized her face was a little more worn and a little older than he had remembered, but he had greatly missed her. "We're sure glad to have you home, Carl," she said. "Is there anything you need?"

"Not right now. I think I'll rest a bit and then go over and visit Helen and Clyde in the morning," he said.

He heard his mother take a deep breath and knew bad news was coming. "Oh Carl, you didn't get my letters?"

Already knowing what was coming, he asked, "What letters?"

"The ones I sent you to the prison camp," she reluctantly replied.

"I wasn't in the camps as long as I was on the run. I didn't get your letters," he quietly said, looking down at the scratches in the wooden floor.

"Oh Carl, I'm sorry. I thought you knew. Clyde done sold the ranch and Helen didn't wait. Why, she…"

Suddenly, she stopped talking as if she didn't want to upset him more. She leaned over and hugged him, but he stayed as stiff as a board. The news shattered his thoughts. Both things he wanted most were suddenly gone. His hopes and dreams of making it home to find success and happiness had vanished within one sentence. To say he was disappointed was an understatement, but keeping his emotions in check, he said, "Well, I've had a heck of a day. I think I'll hit the sack."

He really just wanted to be alone, but he could tell his mother didn't want to leave him as she changed the subject. "You sure you don't need something? We'll have some family over tomorrow. Your Aunt Linnie and your cousins, Lawrence and Margie, can't wait to see you."

Taking off his boots, he stretched out on the bed. With his head buried in the pillow, he made it obvious he was done talking. Before leaving, his mother bent down and kissed the back of his head. He wondered if she could feel the despair that settled over him.

There was only so much he could do to hide the whirlwind of pain and hurt that still ran through his veins. He knew they would catch

17

glimmers of it, just as he had caught the glimmer of green on that dusty truck earlier, but he would do his darnest to protect them from the hell he had lived. His way of spitting in the enemies' faces had been to survive. Now he needed to finish the deed by letting go and living, even if he couldn't control the damage that had already been done.

The next few days passed and he felt like a misshaped puzzle piece that no longer fit exactly where it should. He didn't want his family to get him wrong. It was wonderful to be home and he loved them, but he had lost the feeling of security and safety he once had taken for granted. He was more distant and quiet—a silent figure standing against the wall trying to find his place in a different world.

Listening to everyone talk, he could not be broken open. The pain was still too fresh. It didn't matter, though, because the war was still going on and he was limited by what he could say anyway. He didn't want to put the ones still fighting in jeopardy. That was made clear before he left the Jefferson Barracks, and he had signed a paper stating he understood what it meant.

However, it was better that way because he desperately wished he could bury the memories and continue as if the war hadn't existed. Unfortunately, that wasn't an option. He was left with the stress and trauma of a war that did exist.

His family completely avoided the subject if he was anywhere near, but occasionally, concerned aunts and uncles whispered with his mother. Without going into detail, she always ended the conversation in the same way, "Keep him in your prayers." She didn't share the details about his screams that broke through the stillness of night as the memories of death reached toward him, or the moments when flashbacks, as real as the skin on her face, carried her boy off into the distant memories of horror. She didn't tell them the fear of losing him, even though he was home.

Like his family, most people got it, but there were always the select few from whom Carl had to use every ounce of self-control to excuse himself. He really wanted to yell and curse at them and say, "What the heck is wrong with you? Don't you understand? War is not a game! In one way or another, it kills every single person who serves in it. Look at what it's done to me!"

He didn't understand how people could think war was good. It may be necessary, but he felt the only people who wanted war were the ones who hadn't been in it. He had seen firsthand the catastrophic side of war and he only wanted it to end.

It was different with Jerry, and Carl had more patience for him. At four-years-old, Jerry didn't understand what had happened, but he remembered his Uncle Carl and loved him. Yet being young and inquisitive, he asked all kinds of questions—most of which went unanswered. Since Jerry's father, Jack, was also fighting in the war, Jerry lived at the house with them and was always around. Sometimes he could feel Jerry's little eyes watching him from inside. If he looked closely, he could see Jerry's head pressed against the warm glass of the living room window watching him as he worked.

There was plenty to do to clean up around the outside of the house. Since there were no grown men left at home, there was a lot of neglected work. Carl didn't mind because it temporarily kept his mind at peace. However, a sudden noise behind him made him grab the pitchfork and run toward the barn[9].

Jerry saw him and ran to where his Grandma Lillie[10] was washing dishes in the old sink hanging on the kitchen wall. "Grandma?" Jerry asked.

With soap dripping from her wet hands, Lillie looked at him standing there pulling the front of his overall straps as he waited for her to answer him. Jerry's blue eyes looked at her, and he slightly turned his head up in her direction and repeated, "Grandma?"

"Yes?"

A beautiful reddish color tinted Jerry's sandy blond hair as the sun shone through a section of the kitchen window. In his sweet child's voice, he asked, "Why does Uncle Carl get the pitchfork and run to the barn?"

---

[9] True story remembered by Jerry
[10] Carl's mother

Lillie's usual sternness left for the moment as she looked at Jerry standing there waiting for a reply. How she loved that little boy. They had formed a close bond as she watched him every day while his mother taught classes at the school. Pulling him close to her, Lillie kissed him on his fair-skinned forehead and whispered to him softly, "Jerry, do you love your daddy?"

Jerry looked at her with a confused expression. "I love my daddy, but he's went away."

Lillie smiled, "Where'd he go, Jerry?"

"Daddy's fighting far away. Someday I will be big enough to go, right? Like my daddy, Uncle Carl, Uncle George[11], and Uncle Bert[12], too."

Lillie's heart almost broke in half as she suspected he probably would[13]. It was in his blood. She knew the benefits of the military, but she also knew the heartache. She thought about what to say as the words slowly came out of her mouth, "Maybe Jerry, but right now we gotta pray for your daddy and uncles to come home safe. See, your Uncle Carl has done come home."

"Should we pray for Uncle Carl, too?" Jerry innocently asked.

"The good Lord brought him home, but we need to pray for him too, Jerry." Then, changing the subject, Lillie added, "Jerry, are you done with what you were doing in the other room?"

Smiling shyly, Jerry slowly turned around and ran back to the window. His Uncle Carl was working out under the sun again as if nothing ever happened. Jerry looked over at the little lamp table and saw Carl's picture in the paper. Grabbing it, he sat on the floor to look at it. He thought about what his grandma had told him, and said, "God bless my daddy and bless my Uncle Carl too."

Although he was too little to understand the true horrors of the war and the flashbacks that would haunt Carl for the rest of his life,

---

[11] Carl's older brother who was in the war also.
[12] Carl's younger brother who was still stationed in the U.S.
[13] Although she didn't know it at the time, Jerry's memory and attention to detail would place him in a specialized section of the military that required top-secret clearance. Later he would go on to be a foreign liaison for the State Department. Information about Jerry from his sister, Jackie.

he was always proud of him. "That's MY Uncle Carl," he said as he pointed to the picture.

Lillie was glad Jerry hadn't asked more. She knew she hadn't answered his question, but she didn't know what else to tell him. She wasn't sure, but could only assume the reason was from an unexpected sound that triggered a sudden flashback for Carl as he worked outside. He had been on the run for so long, he had to use whatever was around him to protect himself—even if there was nothing there. She was slowly learning this from little episodes that lugged him off into the depths of unforgettable memories. At those moments, he shared a smidgen of why his scars from war were painfully deep.

Right now, Lillie knew he needed the love and support only family and close friends could give. He needed to readjust to the life he had once left behind. Most of all, he needed his nerves to calm down and to get rid of the memories holding him captive, even though he was free. He was still the same kind and giving person—only scarred and hardened by the atrocities of war. They would do whatever it took to make him feel safe.

After being home for almost a week, Carl went downstairs and told his mother, "I'm going for a drive this afternoon."

She looked at him and asked, "You going by to see your Aunt Linnie?"

He knew she wouldn't approve of what he was about to say, but he told her anyway, "No, I'm going by Helen's house."

The angry squint in his mother's eyes told him everything she was thinking. He was sure she knew more than he did, but it didn't matter. He only wanted to hear it for himself and say goodbye. The shock was gone and he wanted to close the door and move on.

When he got to her house, he began to think that maybe his mother was right. What was he doing? However, he had gone too far to turn around, so he went ahead and knocked on the wooden door. He didn't say anything for a moment when she opened it. Caught off guard by the feelings that flooded over him, he could only stare at her.

He knew by the way she pressed her lips together and looked at him that she was also unsure of what to say.

There was no way she had missed the news he was back, but he could tell she hadn't expected to see him at her house. After what felt like minutes of silence, he told her what he had planned to say, "I know you've moved on with your life and that's okay because I'm not interested nomore. You didn't keep your end of the bargain and I don't want nothing like that."

She reached out and touched his arm. "I didn't know if you were coming home. I'm sorry."

It was hard to walk away from her, but there was nothing left for them. He pulled his arm away and said, "Goodbye, Helen."

She leaned against the doorframe and he could feel her watching him as he walked back to the car. Quietly, under her breath, she said, "Bye, Carl," but he didn't hear her.

He drove along the gravel roads to clear his head and decided to run by Clyde's ranch before going home. The drive would give him time to think. The rumble of the small rocks beneath the tires and the ping as they hit the bottom of the car brought back a flood of memories. He thought back to the day when he had received his draft letter from the United States Army:

His name and order number were neatly typed along the top and it read:

> *Greeting: Having submitted yourself to a local board composed of your neighbors for the purpose of determining your availability for training and service in the armed forces of the United States, you are hereby notified that you have been selected for training and service in the* <u>*Army*</u>*.*
>
> *You will, therefore, report to the local board named above at...*

With a date, time, and place, he knew his time working for Clyde was limited. He quickly headed over to show Clyde the draft letter.

"Don't worry," Clyde said. "Farmers can get out of it. You stay here and help me, and you'll be okay."

Chapter 2 – BROKEN PROMISES

Then, looking for support, Clyde skimmed through the bottom of the letter aloud:

> ...You will there be examined, and, if accepted for training and service, you will then be inducted into the stated branch of the service... some instances may be rejected for physical or other reasons... Willful failure to report promptly to the local board at the hour and on the day named in this notice is a violation of the Selective Training and Service Act of 1940, as amended, and subjects the violator to fine and imprisonment.

Clyde handed the letter back to him without the support he'd hoped to find and said with a smile, "Well, at least it says there is a possibility for rejection."

They both knew he wouldn't be rejected—not a hard working farm kid like him. Then getting serious, Clyde continued, "Well, even though it don't say it there, I know there is an exception for men in occupations that are important for the war effort. Farmers will qualify. Let me get you out of this."

His mind was already made up. "I can't. I need to go. All my buddies are leaving or have already left. I'd just get called by a second draft anyway."

Clyde shook his head in disappointment, "Do what you have to do, but you better hurry. I'm getting too old to run this ranch by myself. I want to retire."

Carl nodded his head. It wasn't that he didn't want to stay, but he needed to fulfill his obligation with his country first.

"You just bring yourself back alive," Clyde added, "and it's yours like we talked about. You run the ranch, and I'll help you out while I can. It'll be fair for you, and I'll treat you right. You're a good worker, my boy. I'll really miss ya."

They shook hands on it, and he left for his induction into the United States Army on April 21, 1942, in Fort Leavenworth, Kansas. Weighing in at nearly 175 pounds and with a height of 5'9 ½", he had no problem meeting Army requirements. Strong and tanned from hard physical *labor, he prepared himself for what was to come because he knew once the ball started rolling it didn't slow down.*

And he was right. Only a few days later, he left for Camp Roberts in California for a grueling thirteen weeks of basic training before being sent over to Fort Ord[14] to be assigned to an Army division. He was excited to be placed in the 3rd Division[15] led as a whole by Major General Jonathan W. Anderson.

Prestige and high expectation were associated with the 3rd Division. But it was more than wearing the blue and white shoulder patch edged in dark Army green thread; it was maintaining the honor of soldiers who had proved themselves many times in the past. With that knowledge, he went on to receive his full assignment to be a driver for the 3rd Division, 7th Infantry, Cannon Company.

He felt proud and up to the challenge. He had farming background and plenty of experience driving light trucks and tractors. Plus, he had learned how to be resourceful and make minor repairs to equipment and buildings. Those skills made him a prime candidate for the job. He felt somewhat confident in his new assignment and was ready for what was to come.

A big bump in the road shook the car. It was interesting how things had changed. Had he been prepared like he thought he was? Really, how do you prepare for something as awful as war? He knew now—there was

Figure 3: Carl in his uniform and the 3rd Division patch (only picture that didn't get destroyed)

---

[14] Fort Ord was also in California
[15] As simple as the word "division" may appear, it is the beginning of a complex and organized structure of the Army. It had been changed and adjusted for the new war and the 3rd Division broke into three infantry regiments: the 7th, 15th, and 30th. Each infantry regiment had 1st, 2nd, and 3rd battalions and each of those battalions divided into four companies. The Cannon Company was also a part of each regiment and would serve the regiment as a whole where needed, but customarily was grouped with the supporting artillery battalion.

Chapter 2 – Broken Promises

no way to prepare for war. In fact, it hadn't taken him long to learn his skills were only a fraction of what determined whether he kept his own life. And he had—barely. But what about the lives of the others, the ones who didn't make it home? Didn't their life mean something? Could he have saved any of them by doing something different? Should they have come home in his place?

Those thoughts were still running through his mind when he stopped in front of Clyde's house at the ranch. Facing his second big disappointment, he looked at the old rocking chair on the wraparound porch. He'd heard Clyde sold the ranch when he received an offer too good to pass up. He fully understood everyone thought he had been killed, but it didn't make it easier to accept his dreams had been completely crushed.

The big house (that should have been his) was dark and silent. He didn't have to get out of the car to tell there was nobody home. It hadn't been mentioned, but he wondered if Clyde and his wife had already moved to Wichita. It would be easy enough to find out in such a tiny town, but he didn't care to do it today. His head ached and he was ready to get back home. It was harder to close those pages on his life than he had thought.

On his drive home, his thoughts were consumed by what should have been. In fact, he hardly remembered the drive as he sat in the car for a minute and looked at the old house that had become home for the past week. Sometimes things in life were unfair—he knew that from experience. Once again, things had not gone in his favor. To add to it, he felt guilty he had made it home when so many others hadn't.

He slammed the car door harder than he realized as he felt the disappointment and anger from the day starting to gnaw on his nerves —what nerves he had left. If only he could go back in time and replace all the heartache and anger, but he knew better than that. When he walked in the house, his mother was in the kitchen cooking. He gave her a quick kiss on the cheek before heading upstairs. As he walked away, she called to him, "Carl, aren't you going to eat with us tonight?"

"I got a headache and I'm really tired. I think I'll rest," he said as he headed to the narrow stairway.

He felt her eyes follow him as he walked. He knew she was worried, but he didn't feel like eating or talking, and he was in no mood to pretend that night. He knew he had come home different, but it was painful to know everyone else knew it too. He really only wanted to be alone as the anger inside him was building like a thick cloud of black dust bellowing from his soul.

He didn't notice Ruby was sent upstairs to check on him. Quietly peeking through the cracked door, she saw as the flashbacks of war, disappointment, and the impossible to answer questions all rolled together like feathers on hot tar and tore her brother apart. He wanted to scream, but silence was the only answer. Grabbing the pillow off the bed, he pressed his thin fingers into the outer softness. The small feathers inside pricked him as he shredded it with his bare hands. Within minutes, there were only scraps of material and small, white feathers silently floating to the hard, wooden floor[16].

Then, flinging his blankets off the bed, he rested on the bare mattress. Limp and lean, his body was silhouetted in the moonlight shining through the small bedroom window. Ruby quickly ran back downstairs. As a teenager, she understood war was painful, but she didn't know how painful it would be to watch the brother she loved suffer the trauma left behind.

His eyes fluttered shut, and he began to wander into the nightmares of his past—forcing him to relive something he was trying so hard to forget. He'd already destroyed every photo he could find, what else did he need to do to rid his mind of those relentless memories? Yet the sounds, colors, struggles, and deep pain began to replay in his mind as they slowly returned like a translucent ghost floating through the dark shadows to drag him back through the night.

---

[16] As remembered by his sister, Emma

Chapter 3

SPINNING BACK IN TIME

SUDDENLY, CARL OPENED his eyes. He looked around him in the darkness as a glimmer of white caught his attention from the calendar hanging on the wall. He could barely see the large 1944 in the darkness. Had he fallen asleep?

Something didn't feel right. Confused, he stared at the old calendar across from him. As he watched, an invisible wind began to tear away the pages one by one. He looked at the window—it was closed. Yet he saw the loose pages picking up speed as they swirled across the floor.

In panic, he watched as a funnel formed and the violent winds ripped through his room, picking up the few things he had. Tightly holding onto the bed, he felt as the winds sucked at him and dared him to let go. Finally, unable to resist the pull, his fingers slipped loose, and he disappeared into the swirling blackness.

There was no way this was happening! He knew he was dreaming as he spun back to the beginning of his nightmare, but he couldn't wake himself up. Instead, the dream continued as the funnel dropped him free in a place he had been before almost two years earlier on October 22, 1942.

Vivid and crisp, he found himself getting off a train onto a pier in Norfolk, Virginia. Worn-out from completing a couple weeks training in Camp Pickett, Virginia, he slowly walked along the pier and talked with a small group from his company. "For being half an hour 'til midnight, there is sure a lot going on around here," he mentioned as essential loading lights pierced through the night and illuminated the large, gray transport ships in the Hampton Roads port.

The hum and clatter of the winches stopped once the final cargo was loaded. Now the transports waited for the most important part—the 3rd Division. He stopped walking as they approached a large ship with a big, black 42 on the side. He was standing at the *USS Tasker H. Bliss*, and it looked like that was his stop.

The ship hadn't been a Navy transport long. In fact, this was the first scheduled trip under its newly called position in the Navy. Until August, it carried the name *SS President Cleveland*, but it was quickly converted for the war effort.

The fall breeze blew cool and fresh. It was nearly midnight now. Unsure of how long it would be before his name was called out from the sailing list, he yawned and sat down on the cold concrete. Leaning back against his bag, he closed his eyes. It crossed his mind he might be waiting for a while—maybe all night. His body twitched as it started to relax, and then he heard his name.

He jumped up and brushed himself off. There was a short check-in line before being able to cross the thick gangplank onto the steel deck of the ship. Steel stairs descended to the troop compartment below, and a blast of hot, moist air met him as he went down.

Figure 4: Close up of the USS Tasker H. Bliss. Taken Oct. 8, 1942.
(U.S. National Archives)

The stacked bunks were four high with a canvas in between. He didn't even have to get in one to know they were uncomfortable. There was so little room between the canvases that anyone who got anything but the top could hardly turn over without hitting the bunk above. Needless to say, unless he was sleeping, he'd try his darnest to avoid his bunk.

Glad to see the soldier already in the bunk above him was several inches shorter than he was and just as thin, he introduced himself, "How'd you get lucky enough to get a top bunk? I was hoping, but looks like it ain't meant to be. By the way, I'm Carl Good."

"How-do? I can tell ya I ain't that GOOD, but the name's Kyle Bellis[17]. And don't ya go a-worryin' cause it don't matter where ya at, it's all uncomfortable down here."

Carl immediately noticed the strong Southern accent and guessed Bellis was from somewhere near Alabama. He laughed. Everyone always thought the "Good" jokes were original, but he had already heard them all—several times. "Well, at least we got a place to rest. I'm beat."

"Well, good luck with a-gettin' rest down in here," Bellis said, pushing his dark glasses up on his nose. "With no cool breeze and the extra body heat in these tight quarters, it's hotter than a goat's butt in a pepper patch."

Carl laughed at the expression. Undoubtedly, Bellis was right though—it was hot and muggy, and sweat was already starting to roll down the side of his face. He realized he might not get as much rest on the ship as he thought. There was still a lot of movement as bunks were filling up around him. Lying down, he called up to Bellis, "It's not only the heat, but the noise is unreal! How in the world do we sleep with all this racket?"

Bellis didn't answer, but Carl figured it was because he couldn't hear him over the running ship. Covering his ears with his arms, he closed his eyes. Luckily, he was tired enough that he did get some sleep after a while, but the next morning came way too early.

The first challenge of the day was to slip out of the bunk and get ready. Personal space was nonexistent and it was a matter of trying not to step on anybody else. Bellis was nearby and Carl called over to him, "Well, we made it our first night, but I don't think the ship moved an inch."

"I didn't get a lick of sleep." Bellis said with a yawn. "I'm a-thinkin' we still in Hampton Roads. I heard something about a-leavin' at different times, but I don't know nothing about that."

---

[17] Character added for information and dialogue

* For reading purposes, only a few characteristics of a Southern accent have been added

It turned out the submarines had been sent out a few days earlier, and the Northern and Southern Attack Groups were leaving later that day after a last minute shore conference for the commanders. With over 100 ships in their convoy, it was important they left at different times and places and headed in different directions to avoid any unwanted attention.

After a day of introductions, he learned what was expected of them. There were many rules which included a schedule of what they were allowed to do and when they could do it. Ship duties were assigned and it was another night in the hot troop compartment.

The next morning, the ship came alive with movement extremely early. This was the day they would leave for an unknown adventure with the remaining transports from *Task Force 34*[18]—commanded by Navy Admiral Hewitt. It was October 24, and with two silver blimps and the *USS Augusta* (an eleven-year-old cruiser as the flagship) proudly leading the way, the convoy was ready to move out by the intended 0800[19] hours. Headed northeast, the plan began to unfold with a disguised trip to the United Kingdom.

He talked to a group of new buddies that morning, but the conversation was quieter than usual. He figured everybody was thinking about the gloomy reality of leaving home. Yet the sooner the adventure started, the sooner it could end. None of them had any idea of the great mission that loomed in front of them, but there was no turning back. This was the real deal. They were leaving the U.S. and meeting the enemy soon. Where? Nobody knew.

So great was the secrecy of their true destination that even the officers of the Naval Task Force were kept in the dark until they were fully embarked on their journey. In fact, the commanding officers had only found out at the shore conference the day before when Admiral Hewitt calmly went over the plans with a reasoned statement and purpose. That certainly explained why there were so many speculations flying rampant among the troops. Everybody thought

---

[18] Also known as the *Western Naval Task Force*
[19] 0800 represents the time 8:00AM. Time is written with the 24-hour clock, often referred to as military time. It is more exact and leads to less errors when stating times.

he had figured it out. Carl didn't know, but he listened to the many theories being tossed about.

"Look at what we were issued. We're headed somewhere warm."

"What about France. We need to help them out."

"It's gotta be in the South Pacific? We got amphibious training. There's gonna be water nearby."

"Japan has it coming. The Marines struck at Guadalcanal a couple months ago. Maybe we're the second rounds."

"What about Hitler? Who's gonna stop that German S.O.B.?"

"Why even guess? We could be going anywhere."

That was true—it could be anywhere. Since the U.S. declared war on Japan in response to their surprise attack on Pearl Harbor on December 7, 1941, he heard a lot of speculation gravitating toward a large-scale landing in the South Pacific. It sounded like a logical place because everyone knew Japan had made a personal threat to the safety and security of the American people.

However, it wasn't that simple. After declaring war on Japan, the war had quickly escalated when Germany and Italy defended their Axis[20] partner and officially declared war against the United States only four days later. That opened up the landing possibilities in so many directions.

Like it or not, they had been drawn into the middle of a second world war, and now there they were in the midst of a mighty armada of ships. Taking it all in, Carl told Bellis, "Everything has happened so fast. Four months after Pearl Harbor, I was drafted. Now, five months later, look where we're at."

"Oh, I hear ya," Bellis agreed. "Reckon we might ought expect it though. Great Britain been fighting the war with Germany for some three years[21]."

"Well, I really thought we'd[22] get our way and not get involved in a European conflict," Carl said. "Well, until Pearl Harbor happened anyway."

---

[20] The Axis powers were Japan, Germany, and Italy
[21] Since September 1939 when Germany refused to withdraw troops from Poland
[22] The people of the United States

A nearby soldier, Al Schondermier [23], was listening and joined in on their conversation. "Oh, it was bound to happen. It was only a matter of time. Why, President Roosevelt knew what was happening. He respected other opinions, but saw the bigger picture and had already been supplying the Allies with arms and supplies so they could stay in the fight. Now, we will shortly join them."

Carl looked at Schondermier. He seemed to keep quiet unless it had to do with history, and then he became a know-it-all. Not only was he educated, but he also sought up to date information even while they were on the ship. He looked too serious and uptight to joke with, but it was nice to know what was going on.

"There's nothing to argue about there," Carl said when Schondermier finished. "Good thing is we haven't hit any resistance out here in the water. So far, guard duty out here has been easy."

It had been, but it was hard work keeping it that way. With the greatest fleet ever sent out by the U.S. in route, they had to stay in low profile. That meant taking every precaution to prevent detection. With the help of the submarines, refueling in route, radio silence, and avoiding all ships, it was working.

What their role was as part of that great fleet, he didn't know, but it wasn't too long before they were out far enough that finally some of the landing objectives could be shared. They appeared to be in a safe place—a place in the middle of the Atlantic Ocean where the words that were spoken could not get leaked back to the enemy. When the highly anticipated briefing began, he stood in surprise. He could tell by the stir that he wasn't the only one who didn't make sense of the highly debated location. "North Africa?" he repeated. He could hear the low hush of other such questions from around him.

"How was North Africa a threat?"

"How did that even relate to the Axis powers of Japan, Germany, and Italy?"

The briefing continued and the quiet whispers stopped. Everyone intently listened to understand a little more about why the landing would be in North Africa. The first part made sense. The greatest

---

[23] Character added for information and dialogue

threat needed to be handled first. That meant Great Britain and the U.S. had made a "Germany First" policy. But how did that tie into North Africa?

The answer was through the French. What many people didn't know was that the French controlled parts of North Africa. With the fall of France to Germany in 1940, Germany gained control of the French Empire in Africa, including the French Fleet. If the Axis powers gained complete control of the French Fleets, there would be no stopping them. They would control every transatlantic harbor from the North Cape to the Gulf of Guinea, with an exception of only Great Britain (located above France), Portugal, and Spain (that played neutral, but favored the Axis powers.)

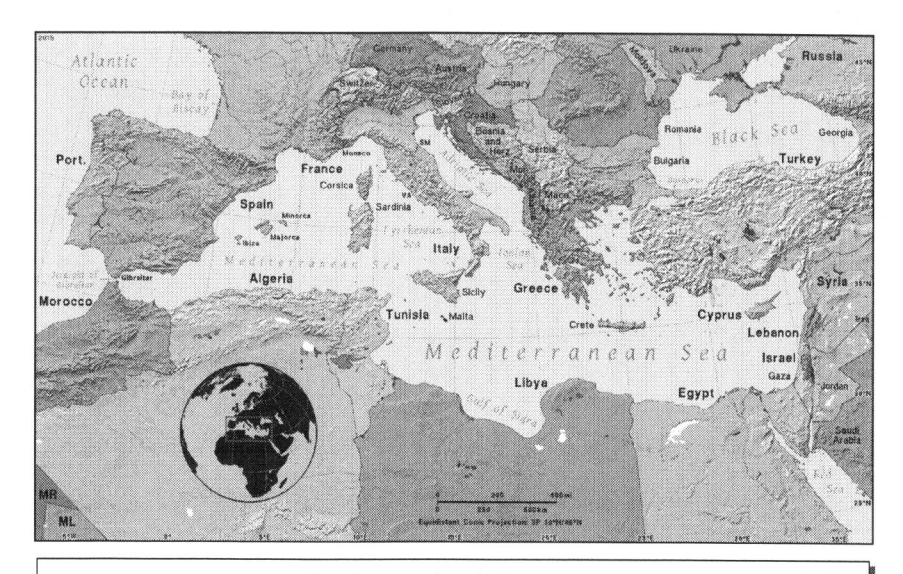

Figure 5: Map of Mediterranean Sea (PAT public domain maps)

If Germany held onto this power, even with the British Army fiercely fighting back in Egypt, they would gain an ultimate and dangerous advantage. However, the French had always been loyal Allies. The hope was if the French were freed from German power, they would join in the fight with the Allied powers and help gain the needed control of major ports and airports. Success meant the Axis forces would not overtake North Africa and access to the

Mediterranean Sea would remain open, providing a door for a Southern Europe invasion next.

They were only the first step in a multi-step approach with the operation as a whole conveniently code-named *Operation Torch*. Major General Dwight D. Eisenhower had taken charge of the military buildup since June, and the 3rd Division reinforced, along with four other U.S. divisions, were part of three major task forces (Western, Center, and Eastern)[24] created in the attack plan.

Commanded by Army Major General George S. Patton, Carl was only one soldier of about 35,000 sent to do the job in the all American Western Task Force. Being further divided into sub-task forces, the 3rd Division was placed in the Center Attack Group—the largest division in the Western Task Force with slightly under 20,000 Army officers and troops. Led by General Patton himself, they were code-named *Operation Brushwood*. Their mission was to gain control of the powerful forces in Casablanca, French Morocco. There was no doubt that General Patton planned to do exactly that. If all three landings in the Western Task Force were successful, communication lines and ports would be secured for all French Morocco.

Figure 6: Major General George S. Patton (Public domain)

With the main points passed along at the briefing, Carl talked it over with Bellis, Schondermier, and a few other buddies later that morning. "That was not what I expected, but at least we know where we're headed. Explains some of them immunizations before leaving though."

"Sure thing, I hated all them dadgum shots," agreed Bellis.

---

[24] The Western Task Force (all American), the Center Task Force (British ships/American Army), and the Eastern Task Force (British and American ships/British and American troops)

"I got tough, hardened skin from working in the sun all the time," Carl said. "Shot giver didn't like that much because it bent his danged needle. I heard him mutter under his breath, "Damn farm boys." Made me laugh though. Poor city boy—probably never worked a full day in the sun."

"The same happened to me," added Eli Lewis[25] with a laugh. Then, going back to the subject at hand, he added, "We'll get more information as we get closer. I'm not sure how I feel about landing in Africa. I guess I don't know much about it to be honest."

Carl enjoyed talking to Lewis. Seemed like a good guy all around—plain and honest. In fact, most of the guys he talked to were. A lot of them were civilian draftees and there wasn't much swearing or crazy behavior among them. They were all different, but in general, they were hardworking citizens called to duty.

Occasionally, he ran into the rude, obnoxious guys who only dreamed of women and beer and had nothing decent to say, but even so, these were the men he was sent to fight with and he respected their differences. In one way or another, they were all his Army brothers. With them, he would fight until the end. After all, that's what a soldier did, and that's exactly what the senior officers who had studied the operation expected them to do. The senior officers knew this operation was extremely risky. Not only was it the first amphibious operation so far from base, but it was also undertaken at night after crossing 4,000 miles of ocean. It was risky and it had to play out as planned.

It was quiet for a moment as everyone thought about what they had been told. Lewis broke through the silence again. "All I know is we've been placed on the fine line of living or dying for the country we love. Where it'll take us? It's hard to say."

Bellis chimed in with his strong Southern accent, "The heck of it is that we'll be a-creatin' justice and freedom for people we won't never know while perhaps a-gettin' ourselves sent home in a wooden box."

"But is death so bad if it's standing against the greater evil?" asked Schondermier, looking specifically at Bellis. "Somebody's got to stop it before it gets worse. You have to understand what's going on to get it."

---

[25] Character added for information and dialogue

By the look in Bellis's eyes, Carl knew Schondermier shouldn't have added that last part. Before Carl could say anything, Bellis looked at Schondermier and made a quick Southern insult, "No, I get it, but you the reason we say Yankees are like hemorrhoids—pain in the butt when they come down and always a relief when they go back up."

Schondermier opened his mouth to say something back, but Carl interrupted, "Right now, it's not about death, it's about the fight."

But really, that depended on whom you asked. General Patton knew and expected many soldiers to die. It wasn't that he wanted them to die, but it was a natural consequence of war in accomplishing their missions, and he was going to accomplish his missions no matter what it took. If *Operation Brushwood* failed, the whole expedition was at risk of failure. However, failure wasn't part of General Patton's vocabulary, and he wouldn't allow it to be used by his men either.

"Well, boys, Good is right," said Lewis. "We've come here to fight and death isn't an option. So, let's get ready because the training doesn't end."

That was true enough—the training dragged on and on. Huge rope nets set up from one end of the ship to the other verified that. Throughout different times of the day, Carl was sent with other troops to practice climbing up and down them.

It was hard not to step on fingers or bump others who were descending, but he was up for the challenge. He could lighten the mood with a quick joke or encouraging word, but he still took the training seriously. If he couldn't climb down these rope nets and feel secure while doing it, he would be stuck on the transport—it was the only way to get onto the landing craft that would take him to shore.

That night Carl got a few minutes to talk to the guys and they started laughing about good times from home. When the subject of school came up, he laughed, "That reminds me of the times my teacher asked on me to write sentences on the blackboard. I could write with both my right and left hand, but she wouldn't allow us to use the left hand at school. She'd call me up there and I'd start with my left hand, then switch the chalk to my right hand, and finish up without ever moving. Her face would turn red and she'd get mad, but everyone else would quietly snicker. I'd smile as I went back and sat down. That never got old."

"Oh, let me tell y'all. I hated my teacher," said Bellis, his blue eyes shining bright behind his glasses. "She was crazier than a road runnin' lizard. I reckon she kept the wooden paddle ready only to find excuses to use it on me... and I was the good kid."

Carl laughed. "The good kid, huh?"

"Save that for Good, here," Lewis chimed in as he bumped Carl's shoulder, "He's the "good" kid around here." Of course, everyone thought the joke was funny and laughed. Sometimes Carl laughed—not because it was funny to him, but because it was ridiculous that everyone else thought it was funny.

The stories continued and they all laughed until Schondermier suddenly changed the tone. "Speaking of school and the such, I studied a lot of history. Does anyone know why we're being sent without really being ready? I mean, look around. We are in route for our landings and we're still training."

The question was unexpected and nobody said anything for a moment. This was the first thing Schondermier had said all night. Then Schondermier answered his own question, "Time! The answer is time."

Not sure where Schondermier was going with it, they waited for him to continue. While the rest of them were talking and having a good time, he must have been lost in thought about the trainings and landings. Finally, he continued, "Well, it reminds me of a British campaign from WWI. There was a principle amphibious operation called The Dardanelles Campaign[26]. It had been postponed for over six weeks so the men would be well trained and prepared for the landing. However, the postponement gave the Turkish time to prepare for an expected land assault and created a slaughterhouse in return."

---

[26] Referring to this very incident, Admiral Sir Andrew Cunningham of the British stated: "No officer commanding a unit will ever be satisfied that he has had adequate preparation and training until his unit is trained and equipped down to the last gaiter button. There are times in history when we cannot afford to wait for the final polish. I suggest that it should be made widely known to all units that for "Torch" particularly we could not afford to wait, and that the risk of embarking on these large-scale operations with inadequate training was deliberately accepted, in order to strike while the time was ripe. We must now push forward our training so that such a situation cannot again arise." (Morison, 1984)

After a moment, Bellis looked at Schondermier and said, "Ya gotta be kiddin'. Ya done ruined the mood."

Schondermier smiled and exposed a large gap in his two front teeth. "Sorry. I've been thinking. I mean, why are we in such a hurry? What is it that we don't know?"

When Bellis answered with a flat and drawn out, "Ever-thing," the conversation quickly turned back to funny stories and Schondermier stayed lost in thought. Nobody wanted to think about that right then. But whether Schondermier knew it or not, he was right.

A little training was better than the alternative of landing in winter conditions on the beaches, where surf often ran up to fifteen feet high with few days of calm. With the Moroccan winters lasting from November to February, waiting would mean postponing the landings until next year—1943. The landings had already been pushed back from October 30 to November 8, which was the final day a landing at that time could be risked.

By waiting until 1943, it would be too late—too late to stop the Axis from completely gaining control of the Mediterranean. The Axis powers were well on their way, gaining strength quickly, and they had to be stopped—now! There was absolutely no more time. Their training was inadequate, but if they could catch the opponent in a state of surprise, it would be sufficient. Therefore, trained or untrained, they were well on their way to North Africa on a full and tight schedule.

Although plenty busy with training and his other Army duties aboard the ship as the days passed, Carl took advantage of some scheduled free time to go on deck to savor the bright autumn sunlight and to breathe in the fresh air. As he went up, he saw Lewis's short, dark, curly hair from behind. Giving Lewis a light pat on the upper back, he said, "Gosh, this fall weather has been beautiful so far. I wonder how much longer it'll last."

Lewis looked up at the blue sky. "I hear you there. I hope it lasts a good time more."

"You know, after spending most my life outside, I sure miss the wind when we're down in the cramped quarters. Makes me feel shut in without it," Carl said, looking out at the water.

Chapter 3 – Spinning Back In Time

"You're from Kansas, right?"

Carl thought about what to say before answering because he was born in Kansas, but had moved to Oklahoma as a toddler. Then they had moved to Michigan when he was in the 2nd grade. When he was in the 8th grade, his dad unexpectedly died and his mother moved him and his six siblings back to Kansas to be near family[27]. Thinking of the easiest way to put it, he said, "Well, I'll claim Kansas. That's where I've been most of the last ten years."

Lewis nodded. "I got family nearby there in Colorado. Too cold for my blood, I was raised in Arizona."

"The cold don't bother me none. I'd miss it if it was gone. Even when I lived in Michigan, I was always outside. I'd ice skate on the Flint River for hours. I missed that when we left there. Of course, after my dad died, everything changed. I was only thirteen, but I knew I needed to step up and help my mother."

"I can relate," Lewis said. "My dad passed when I was eight. Grew up around my grandpa on a ranch though. I still had to work hard, but it was nice having him around."

That must be the reason he liked talking to Lewis. It turned out they had a lot in common. "So you know what it feels like when the wind blows through an open field. We may not got a field here, but being out here in the open like this makes a trapped man feel free."

"That's for sure," agreed Lewis. "Well, as free as you can feel standing on deck with three large guns looming on the stern and the ship so full of supplies and troops you can hardly move."

Carl looked around him. He had noticed it before, but it sure was packed solid, no doubt about that. Looking at the Welin davit (a large, solid, crane-like structure used for moving heavy equipment,) he knew that in a few days it would be lowering a LCV (Landing Craft Vehicle) with his jeep over the side of the ship and into the water.

As he thought about it, he heard two of the deckhands talking as they stopped by where several of the lifeboats had been replaced with LCVs and a couple LCMs (Landing Craft Mechanized) for the

---

[27] More detailed information about his life in the foreword

landing. "I still can't believe the conversion yard got all those changes done in less than thirty days," one said to the other in awe.

"Priority pays," was the quick and snide reply.

Not losing momentum and pointing to the davit by where Carl was standing with Lewis, the first continued, "Yeah, but adding eight of these Welin davits, making all that extra storage for thirty-four landing boats plus two tank lighters, and replacing all the life boats—that's awful fast. I mean, how can they get all that done with all the other ships needing work too?"

Obviously not as interested in the conversation, or how it got done so fast, the other replied, "Darn it, James[28]. I don't care!" Then promptly he added, "Probably government. They get what they want when they want it."

Smiling as he heard that last response before the two men walked on, Carl laughed. Looking over at Lewis, he asked, "Was you there when Schondermier brought up history the other day? Well, this guy here and Schondermier would make quick friends."

Lewis nodded with a laugh as he ran his hand along the cool, smooth railing, "Schondermier can get on the nerves, but he's about as smart as they come. I'm not sure how he ended up out here."

Carl looked down at the glassy, green water as the immense 535-foot long ship effortlessly glided across it. Yet with conflicting reality, the size of the ship also felt insignificant compared to the great and mighty ocean below. He hadn't been around an ocean much, but he knew it was a bold demander of respect.

Another soldier stopped and looked over the rail not too far from them. Carl didn't recognize him and didn't think he had ever talked to him before. The soldier looked over at him, and Carl saw a boy's face marked with worry. At the same time, he also saw a gleam of excitement dancing bright and alive in the boy's green eyes.

The boy's enthusiasm for this trip was obvious, but his face was young and inexperienced as he said with a nod, "How's it goin'?"

"Not bad," Carl said as he shook the boy's hand. "The name's Good, and this is Lewis."

---

[28] Character added for dialogue and information

Chapter 3 – SPINNING BACK IN TIME

Lewis was busy talking to somebody else who had come up and didn't hear him, so Carl moved a step closer as the boy introduced himself, "I'm William Smith[29], but my friends call me Billy. I just as well prefer that anyway, too danged many Smiths walking around here."

He looked at Billy, "I have a younger brother and you look about his—"

Before he could finish, Billy interrupted, "Good, ya remind me of my older brother, Paul. I trust ya. Can ya keep a secret?"

Unsure what he was getting into he said, "Sure, Billy. Why?"

Billy slyly grinned, highlighting a profound dimple on his left cheek and shared what he couldn't hold in any longer, "Well, I couldn't wait to get in the Army, but I was only sixteen. My brothers were all goin' and I wanted to go too. It didn't take much to get through those paper checkin' ladies."

"How'd you do that?" Carl asked.

"I'm tall so I only changed my age a little on them papers. Nobody bothered double-checkin' it. I honestly don't think they cared—takin' anyone goin' through that door. But I gotta say… I can't wait to get out there and fight!"

"Well, you're as tall as me, but you still got that baby face," Carl said with a laugh. "I turned twenty-three in July."

Billy's stared out at the water. Suddenly, his tone changed as he asked, "Think we'll be the ones to make it home again?"

Slightly squinting his eyes, Carl thought of what to say to him. He knew the reality. He knew it was going to be a long trip that would take some of them away forever. Their departing port in Virginia was to become a distant memory just like everything else. Of course, he wasn't going to tell Billy that. "Well, Billy… I'd say we definitely—"

Billy must have realized his question made him sound weak and he quickly interrupted, "I'm not afraid of it, ya know. I can do double the work and stay alert better than any soldier I know!"

---

[29] William Smith has been added to recreate the attitude of a young soldier. Many soldiers joined before they were 18 and their ages were not double-checked. He has been added for dialogue and information, but his attitude would have been similar to a young soldier.

Carl smiled. "I don't doubt that one bit, Billy."

Still, having slightly floundered for a moment, Billy laughed it off and said, "Well, I got two brothers and they'd be calling me a sissy 'bout now. I'm gonna show them. I'm not always gonna be on the bottom rung of their jokes, ya know. I miss them at times, but I guess I can credit them for makin' me tough."

Then, quickly changing the subject, Billy asked with a half-smile, "So whatcha gonna be doin' out there?"

"Driver," Carl answered. However, there was so much more to it than that. In his head, he thought of what being a driver meant. At first, being a driver didn't sound as dangerous as it really was. Not only would he drive and make minor repairs to light and heavy trucks while transporting material, merchandise, equipment, and personnel, but he also would have to drive in combat areas, over rough roads, and under black out conditions. Much of the time, he would be sent out alone with only his passenger and guard. If he were to make a delivery and ended up in the wrong place, get shot at, or run into the enemy, there was no one around to back him up. He was also well aware the enemy knew that as a driver he would have information they could use. It didn't take much of an imagination to know an enemy stops at nothing to get want they want. In training, he learned what to do if he ever ran into a bad situation like that, but he hoped he wouldn't have to use it.

Interrupting his thoughts, Billy asked, "So they got ya in a tank?"

"Nope… jeep driver—mainly of personnel is what I'm told, but I'll drive whatever they give me."

Billy looked down at the water, "Well, maybe I'll see ya out there somewhere when we get landed." Then looking back up, excitement came into his voice as he said, "It'll be a hell of a day! Nobody beats the 3rd Division."

"That's right," Carl said with a smile.

Well, I'm gonna get goin'. I'm sure I'll be seein' ya around," Billy said as he turned to leave.

"See ya around, Billy."

There were more ships gathering. Carl felt the glory of being part of something big and important, but he also knew the reality—not everyone was going to make it home. Sometimes the truth hurt. However, knowing that did not prevent the steam turbine from pushing its way ahead, and he had no idea what the landing had in store for him—none of them did, but at least they were all in it together.

Chapter 4

ROUGH LANDINGS IN AFRICA

CARL COULD SEE more and more ships gathering as they trained on the deck. "You think those are the same ships that all left at different times for different places at departure?" he asked Bellis.

"Not sure," Bellis said. "Ya know, sometimes ya hear stuff around, but truth be told, we all out here a-goin' off half-cocked[30]."

However, Carl's assumption was correct. The time had come for *Task Force 34* to start gathering in the middle of the Atlantic. Proudly displaying their glory upon the water's surface, they covered a section of ocean about twenty by thirty miles. The dark silhouettes of destroyers, attack transports, light and heavy cruisers, cargo transports, oilers, battleships headed by the *USS Massachusetts,* and aircraft carriers headed by the *USS Ranger* were what they were seeing.

Carl had one more question for Bellis, "If the convoy of over 100 ships *is* meeting together, don't you think it would start calling enemy attention?"

"The enemy don't know where we headed. Heck, when I heard, I was so surprised you coulda knocked my eyes off with a stick." Bellis replied.

"That's true," joined in Lewis. "But what about out here on the water? I hope those aggressive patrolling German submarines... what are they called..."

"U-boats," Schondermier chimed in.

---

[30] Going off half-cocked is to move ahead without knowing all the facts

44

"Yeah, I hope they don't detect us out here. They could definitely stir things up in a hurry."

"I'm sure we got our own submarines out and on high alert for that," Carl said as he thought of what damage the U-boats could do to them while they were in the middle of the ocean.

Lewis added, "I heard there haven't been any U-boat sightings and nobody's quite sure why. Guesses range from them being busy checking out a British convoy to us just being plain lucky."

"Either way, sounds like a good sign for a peaceful landing," Carl said, crossing his fingers.

He wasn't the only one hoping that. In the middle of it all, aboard the *USS Augusta*, Rear Admiral Hewitt and General Patton were making sure everything was in order and ready to go. Between the two of them, they were smooth working and efficient, but ever so different with no unity of command until the expedition got underway.

In fact, with General Patton's strong ego in the Army, he had blazingly announced in the shore conference with Admiral Hewitt that he fully expected the Navy's intricate landing plans to be broken down within the first five minutes, but the Army would then take over. Such a comment validated the concern of having the Army and the Navy work together as General Patton continued his insult:

> "Never in history has the Navy landed an Army at the planned time and place. If you land anywhere within fifty miles of Fedala and within one week of D-day, I'll go ahead and win . . . We shall attack for sixty days and then, if we have to, for sixty more. If we go forward with desperation, if we go forward with utmost speed and fight, these people cannot stand against us."[31]

Such words were not unusual for General Patton. Born into a strong military family, he had an impressive Army career and was known for his eccentricity, controversial gruffness, and profanity. He

---

[31] (Morison, 1984)

had earned the name Ole Blood and Guts for a reason, and he wanted people to remember him as a rugged, colorful commander.

On the other hand, Admiral Hewitt had been active in the Navy for thirty-five years, and he was especially selected to solve the difficult administrative questions involved in this landing. Being experienced, organized, and tactful, he did his best with the physical material given to him, thus inspiring loyalty, confidence, and affection.

Figure 7: General Patton (on L) and Admiral Hewitt (on R) aboard the *USS Augusta* off the shores of North Africa (Public domain)

If anyone could pull off a joint operation with General Patton, Admiral Hewitt could. However, truth being told, even with the best commanders, nobody was sure of what to expect upon landing. There was a lot more to it than that.

Schondermier kept them filled in about the history of the French, who were now under Vichy control, saying, "France has always been Allies with the U.S. The only reason they collaborated their government with Axis powers was to keep from dividing in 1940 when Germany defeated them. That collaboration of government became the Vichy regime, and Germany keeps them in tight command. That's what we're up against."

Although they sometimes laughed at Schondermier and his history-filled comments, it was nice knowing some of the whys of what they were doing. That explained *why* the French reaction was as unpredictable as ever. That explained *why* the American flag was plastered over everything in hope the French would defy their German commanders and choose not to fight. That explained *why* the operation was a risk as thousands of U.S. troops were propelling across the Atlantic waves together.

Yet the profound sense of loyalty and pride pushed them along as they waited for their landings. The energy of anticipation built up and whirled around the ships as morning and night came and went. Perhaps some of the anticipation came on November 3 when the following letter from General Patton was read:

> Soldiers: We are to be congratulated because we have been chosen as the units of the United States Army best trained to take part in this great American effort…
>
> It is not known whether the French African army, composed of both white and colored troops, will contest our landing. It is regrettable to contemplate the necessity of fighting the gallant French who are at heart sympathetic toward us, but all resistance by whomever offered must be destroyed. However, when any of the French soldiers seek to surrender, you will accept it and treat them with the respect due a brave opponent and future ally. Remember, the French are not Nazis or Japs…
>
> When the great day of battle comes, remember your training, and remember above all that speed and vigor of attack are the sure roads to success and you must succeed—for to retreat is as cowardly as it is fatal. Indeed, once landed, retreat is impossible. Americans do not surrender.
>
> During the first few days and nights after you get ashore, you must work unceasingly, regardless of sleep, regardless of food. A pint of sweat will save a gallon of blood.
>
> The eyes of the world are watching us; the heart of America beats for us; God is with us. On our victory depends the freedom or slavery of the human race. We shall surely win.[32]

After that, they all knew the landing was close. Carl could feel it creeping toward them like an unseen sniper. Standing next to Bellis, he said, "Gosh, I know the landing is coming, but not knowing what to expect when we get there makes me ready to get there and get it over with. All this waiting is the hard part."

---

[32] The Patton Papers: 1940-1945 (Blumenson, 1974)

"Ya ain't kiddin'. The anticipation is a-killin' me," Bellis agreed.

However, the next day, November 4, brought an unexpected twist as the wind picked up in the northwest and the ship began to bounce ruthlessly through the rough water. It was no wonder the weather finally decided to challenge them. After all, they were given the first ten days of crisp, wonderful, autumn weather at no cost. Now it was apparent exactly how fast the calm of the ocean could so quickly change to fury.

Down in the quarters on the second day of the storm, Carl could hear the loud clashes ring across the ship as the LCVs blew outside in the wind and banged against the side of the ship. With training out of the question, he went to his bunk. He saw Bellis in the top bunk with his hands over his stomach. "You okay?" Carl asked.

"I ain't been laid up this entire trip, but I feel like the underside of a turnip green. I don't know if I can stomach the ship a-divin' through the waves like this," Bellis answered, grabbing at the sick bucket he kept at his side.

"Yeah, I kinda feel nauseous too," Carl admitted. "This storm makes the two meals we get a day sound like plenty."

Bellis agreed and closed his eyes.

Carl felt a little queasy, but not that bad. Pulling out a few of the letters he had gotten from home before leaving, he looked at the one from Helen. The cursive writing on the envelope matched her personality, but he tried not to think about what he was missing as he put it down again.

Even with the loud noise of the engine room, the thunder made its presence known. Great, deep, rumbling roars from the heavens shook the ship from the outside in. BOOM—the sounds of the storm brought back memories. A particularly vivid memory replayed in his mind as he lay staring blankly at Bellis's bulk in the canvas above him. He saw it fresh in his mind as he closed his eyes.

He was walking through a row of tall, green stalks in an open cornfield. Suddenly, the bright morning sun was replaced with dark storm clouds as they silently rolled in. Hearing a low rumble of thunder in the distance, the smell of fresh, wet dirt clung to the air as the oncoming storm moved closer. As the heavy air darkened before his eyes,

Chapter 4 – Rough Landings In Africa

it was as if God had dimmed the lights and was showing His natural power.

Lightning boldly flashed above, but the deafening clash of thunder had stalled for more than a few seconds and meant he still had time to get indoors. He didn't mind a good Kansas storm—after all, it was what made the grass and fields grow. Nevertheless, he always kept an open eye on the lightning. He knew better than to underestimate its blazing power. He knew it could pass through a glass window and strike, as it had to his younger sister, Emma. He definitely didn't want to be caught in an open field.

The first giant drops of rain began to fall, and he decided to make a run for the barn. With the cool wetness pelting through his long sleeve western shirt and blue jeans, the lightening shattered through the darkness. Mud splashed off his cowboy boots as he ran faster, and the windblown stalks of corn reached out and scratched at him. Rain rolled off his cowboy hat and dripped down his face, and he felt the excitement in the air—almost like an unseen force of electricity as the storm moved in closer.

The same electrifying stormy air was around him when he opened his eyes to his current reality. He longed to feel the cool rain on his face and to hear it ping and pang off an old tin roof. Instead, he found himself enclosed on a rolling ship under the control of the mighty, deep ocean. He knew going outside now would lead to getting washed overboard and most likely death in a watery grave. But seriously, he needed fresh air—this storm had been going on for two days straight.

Rolling over and off the bunk, he got up. Bellis was still sick and said, "Dang, Good, a-havin' them landings come early don't sound too bad right now."

"You're not the only one thinking that. I saw some men who were literally green with seasickness. It's like the storm is following us," Carl said as the man next to them threw up in a bucket.

Talk of the storm blew around them like the storm itself. As the rumors flew, the best information always came from hearsay of the ship workers. A speculation of a delay loomed in the air like the thick rain clouds above.

Schondermier shared what he had heard. "The reports are forecasting the landing with surfs at fifteen feet high!"

"That would make landings impossible. If they move forward as planned, they could kill us before we even get a chance to fight," Lewis remarked in disbelief.

"Who gets to make the decision if we live or die then?" Carl asked.

Schondermier repeated what he had heard. "Admiral Hewitt, but he has no time to think about it. Tomorrow morning the other task forces will begin to divide."

Time was running out. Many lives were in the hands of Admiral Hewitt, who had to make the correct decision based on his best judgment. His weather officer had suggested moving ahead with hopes the storm would actually minimize the high swells and surfs at the landing points.

After a pause, Schondermier added, "And I heard he's going to go for it. We're already here and he's afraid to delay the landings a day longer."

"Well, let's get this ball rolling then," Lewis said, rubbing his hands together as he looked around at them.

And Admiral Hewitt was precisely doing that. He made a risky bet with fate and decided to proceed as originally planned. The next day, November 7, they would separate into their assault positions.

Back in his bunk, Carl desperately tried to ignore the smell of feet and sickness around him. After several days in such tight, closed quarters down in the hold, the smell was strong and pungent. As sick as Bellis was, he couldn't resist calling down one of his signature expressions to Carl, "It smells bad enough down here to gag a maggot."

Carl laughed and then heard a voice yell across the quarters, "Hey, Good. Come play some Craps with us!"

He recognized the voice from training. It was Mike Garretts[33], but everyone called him Big Red. Although a little on the wild side, Carl enjoyed training with him for the most part. Like the color of his red hair, he also had a fiery personality. Being over 6 foot tall and probably 260 pounds, Garretts could get away with it.

Carl got up and headed over to the small, tight group of bored men who had formed a circle in a small section of open floor. Taking

---

[33] Character added for information and dialogue

advantage of the free time, they huddled together to prevent being thrown off balance. He heard the whoops and hollers of a winning roll, meaning the dice were still able to roll on the floor of the storm-ridden ship.

He wasn't a bit surprised to see Billy tightly squeezed in the middle. Billy was young and he liked the excitement of something different. He nodded his head up at him, "Hey there, Billy. Winning much?"

Billy grabbed the dice and thrust them over to him, "Your turn, Good. Let's see what ya got!"

The dice felt hot and alive in his hands. He wasn't a big gambler and he didn't have any extra money to spare. Handing them back with a smile, he said, "Nah, I don't got the money to lose."

Garretts retorted by giving him a light push on the arm, "You could make some if you got real lucky."

"Or lose it all," Carl replied with a laugh.

He wasn't afraid to say he didn't gamble. This wouldn't be the first time he was the only one doing something different. He was not a simple follower. Stubborn and determined, yes, but he didn't do stuff because everybody else was.

"So, you winning much, Big Red?" he asked.

Black-framed glasses sat low on his freckled nose as Garretts tightly held onto his winnings and laughed, "Well, I plan on it. You have to keep playing until it's all gone if you want to win big."

Carl laughed and continued to watch the game as the ship wildly rolled in the mighty ocean. Before long, Garretts lost all his money in one crazy roll. Slowly getting up, he smiled and said, "And now I'm done."

Carl was glad he hadn't played. Tomorrow was almost the day of landings, and it wouldn't be a game anymore. They needed all the luck they could get.

That night as he tried to get some sleep, he turned onto his stomach and buried his face into the canvas of his bunk. It was hard to ignore the movement of the ship, the sounds of sickness, and most of all, the smell. Tomorrow they would see if Admiral Hewitt had boldly made the right decision to move forward as planned.

Thankfully, Admiral Hewitt had—the storm calmly retreated sometime during the short hours of the night, and only a moderate ground swell remained that morning, November 7. A cool, autumn breeze welcomed Carl when he got a chance to go up on deck. The sky was gray and overcast, and the 68-degree weather and fresh air felt amazing after being down in the troop compartment during the storm.

Although refreshing, the fact remained that the landings were silently approaching—hour-by-hour, minute-by-minute. The day went on as last minute preparations and new instructions were given. Lewis handed Carl a circular and said, "Here, read this. It's some information about Moroccan customs."

"The local population will respect strong, quiet men who live up to their promises. Do not boast or brag, and keep any agreement you make," he read under his breath. Then looking at Lewis he said, "Well, I don't know about you, but it sounds like common sense to me."

"That's what I thought," agreed Lewis.

"My mother was pretty strict with us kids," Carl said as he passed on the circular. "I don't blame her. Since my dad died at the beginning of the Great Depression, it was rough. She took on what she could, but you had better not do anything to flare her temper. You know what though… she taught me the difference between right and wrong, and I respect her for that."

Figure 8: U.S. Navy Task Force, carrying General Patton's Western Task Force, approaches the coast of French Morocco. (National Archives)

"I hear ya. Speaking of right or wrong, did you ever hear if ships had separated from the convoy this morning at the break of dawn?" Lewis asked, looking at Schondermier.

Chapter 4 – Rough Landings In Africa

"When I was on deck this morning, I heard there was a big section of them that broke off around that time, but I couldn't get the exact details," Schondermier answered.

They didn't know that Southern Attack Group had left and was headed for a landing in Safi. Nor did they know that at 1600 hours, the Northern Attack Group would also separate for a landing in Mehedia-Port Lyautey, leaving their Center Attack Group to travel on to Fedala alone. But first, before the Northern Attack Group separated, they all listened to the awaited "skipper" speech from Admiral Giffen at 1415 hours.

Being a naval tradition for as long as anyone could remember, it was done before going into any battle. With no loudspeaker systems to broadcast the speech to every ship, each commanding officer repeated the speech for his men. He listened as the following was read:

> The time has now come to prove ourselves worthy of the trust placed in us by our Nation. If circumstances force us to fire upon the French, once our victorious ally, let it be done with the firm conviction that we are striking not at the French people, but at the men who prefer Hitler's slavery to freedom. If we fight, hit hard and break clean. There is glory enough for us all. Good luck. Go with God.[34]

Those words ran through their minds, and it was hard not to feel the anticipation again as the clock brought them closer with each ticking minute. Having zigzagged at fourteen knots during the day, their true destination had been concealed from the enemy. At night, they had steamed along in a straight course, thus meeting the important time objectives. All the zigzagging added an extra 500 miles to the 4,000-mile trip, but time wise they were right on schedule.

This came into play now, as every Attack Group was expected to arrive to their positions a few minutes before or exactly at midnight on those dark shores of North Africa. Five landing beaches stretched between the rough reefs and barriers, but only four of them would be

---

[34] (Morison, 1984)

used due to the proximity to enemy artillery. Even with all the beaches being subject to numerous fixed and mobile shore batteries, this was the best plan. Attacking any closer to the Casablanca Harbor was suicidal due to even higher defense and protection. After all, it was the only large harbor on the coast of Morocco.

One thing was for sure—time did not stall for anyone. In fact, it appeared to pick up speed as midnight snuck upon them. Although neat

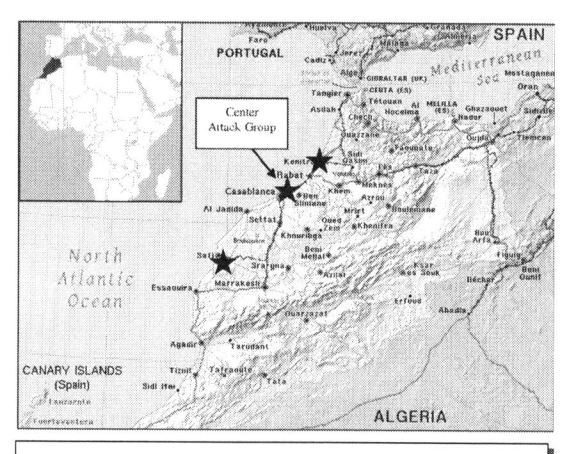

Figure 9: Map of Morocco (PAT public domain maps)

and orderly landings were exhaustingly planned, the pitch darkness, inexperience, and a northeasterly set of currents made many of the ships lose track of locations. They quickly tried to correct the mistakes, but the initial landing times were pushed back. Had this landing not come as a complete and total surprise, this could have been a deadly mistake.

Down in the quarters, there was a sleepless night in store. Right before midnight struck, Carl stood in line for his last sure meal—breakfast. Standing with Bellis, Lewis, and Schondermier, they watched as a couple soldiers pushed through the line laughing.

"Geez, are you kidding me? Here we are on the last day and they can't even be civil," Schondermier muttered.

"Don't get your knickers in a knot, Schondermier," Bellis said. "In the end, them boys won't have a chance if they keep it up."

Carl laughed, "Gosh, I'm going to miss you boys when we get out there. We'll be all going in different directions, but I won't forget you guys."

"You right, Good. We'll a-getting' off at different times, but I'll have all y'all's back," Bellis said.

"Absolutely," they all agreed and hoped they'd see each other again.

After they finished eating, order and organization were of the essence as darkness masked the ships. Giant chains loudly rattled as the anchors splashed deep into the darkness of the ocean below. Shortly after, for the first time, total blackout was enforced. With it, all noise came to a halt and complete silence ensued. It was unnaturally eerie, like death waiting quietly to claim its share. The hum of the motors and other noises of the last few weeks were gone. There was nothing to help calm the nerves.

Down in the dark hold, the void of ship noises was quickly replaced with new sounds as the Navy prepared for the landings topside. Loaded in a more complicated combat style, it made landing in hostile conditions easier as troops could be unloaded with the crucial equipment, vehicles, and supplies in the order it was needed. However, that didn't prevent the Navy from angrily kicking gear around as they stumbled over it and cursed landlubbers[35] to no end.

It wasn't long before the thick rope nets they had used in training were thrown over the sides of the ship. The sound of changing bells mixed with the loud whir of power winches that lowered landing craft down into the water. Once a LCV was lowered for Carl's jeep, he would be headed to the beach earlier than most of the infantrymen on his ship.

The time was near. Carl could feel the energy from fear, excitement, and the unknown all mix in the air. It was like a tornado forming to hit an unsuspecting city—which is exactly what they planned to do early that Sunday morning, November 8, 1942. Strangely enough, there also came with it a new and strange thrill of carrying the American flag into battle in Africa.

There wasn't time to worry. Adrenaline, like a natural drug, pumped through Carl's body as he prepared in the stuffy hold below. Checking his equipment in the dim blue lamplight, he tried to put it on without bumping into someone else. Hardly able to move, he worked his way to the steel steps leading up to the deck and waited in a sea of men.

---

[35] Someone unfamiliar with the sea or an inexperienced sailor

In the darkness, he could vaguely see the roughness of the off-white armband pinned onto the left sleeve of his green, herringbone twill uniform. On it, the American flag proudly displayed thirteen stripes and forty-eight stars[36]. There was one stripe for each of the thirteen original states and one star for each current American state. He was hopeful the flag would give the Vichy French one less reason to fire at him. Only time would tell, and now came the hard part—waiting without knowing for what.

Figure 10: Original flag armband worn by Carl upon landing

Like a bull being ushered through a cattle pen, he went up the narrow steps to the deck with only the aid of a small, blue light. Tightly crammed and pressed together, his chest bumped against the soldier ahead of him as he was being pushed on from behind. Grabbing the handrail, he pulled himself up. With the pull of the extra weight of his equipment, he tried to keep it tight as to not hit anyone in the face with his hanging canteen. From the top, he could hear officers urging, "Come on." "Keep it moving." "Let's go."

The darkened deck area was packed with both silent soldiers and irritated sailors. Carl's senses heightened in the veil of blackness as the vague scent of charcoal smoke floated across the dark night reminding him of the reality of what was about to take place. They were so close to land he could actually smell it.

---

[36] In 1942, Hawaii and Alaska had not yet become states of the United States. Therefore, there were only 48 states.

Chapter 4 – Rough Landings In Africa

They waited on deck when suddenly a bright searchlight in Fedala cut through the starless sky. Within seconds, a second one shone brightly upwards as well. "That can't be good," he muttered.

"Don't worry," replied a sailor who happened to be standing nearby. "Earlier this morning, the president gave a short message and then General Eisenhower broadcasted for the Vichy French to shine their searchlights vertically as a token of welcome. Since our first assault waves landed an hour and a half late and in short number, this is good news."

Those sentences changed the mood around Carl, until he heard someone grumble in the darkness, "Whatta ya know, they ain't gonna fight."

It had to be an act. Fear dominated combat and only a liar or a fool would fail to admit it[37]. Most of the men breathed in a sigh of relief. In Carl's mind, the less fighting, the better. There would be plenty of time for fighting—he was sure of that. They had come to fight the Germans and Italians, not the French. In fact, they wanted to free the Vichy French from the grip of the Axis. In return, they needed their support to help enter Tunisia where the British had been bitterly fighting for months.

Then with contradicting theory and quickness, the searchlights shot downwards where they penetrated holes through the darkness. Not expecting this sudden change, his heart pounded—they had been discovered! The lights silently moved through the blackness and carefully rested upon a landing boat, and then ever so silently proceeded to another object. After about five minutes, machine gun fire from an armed support boat accompanying assault waves to the beaches broke through the hushed silence.

The searchlights went out. Confusion from the mixed signal lingered in the air for a moment. Nobody said a word as silence returned. However, it didn't last long when the sound of gunfire brilliantly rang out in the distance.

It had appeared the Vichy French were initially welcoming them, but maybe it was a mistake. Perhaps the searchlights were directed

---

[37] Haunted (Ells, 2005)

upwards as they looked for the sound of plane engines, not the first U.S. boat waves moving in. Nobody knew the broadcast hadn't even been heard. It had been repeated every half hour since 0130 hours, but nobody of importance appeared to have received it, including none of the officers on the French ships. Apparently, they didn't know who was attacking them and were caught in a total state of surprise.

The Cannon Company's mission was to provide timely and effective fire support in close liaison of the attacking infantry. Carl knew he would be going in soon, especially since he was driving a 2nd lieutenant radio operator and his equipment. Communication was essential to the attack plan. But the landings had become more complicated with the break out of shooting in the distance. By 0620 hours, there was plenty of firepower on the beach, and it didn't look like it would be stopping anytime soon.

Although he didn't know what he'd have to go through to get to shore, he wasn't underestimating the situation. The landing beaches and offshore water were covered thoroughly. Well prepared and organized for defense, four large batteries were placed strategically around the beaches along with antiaircraft machine guns and gun pits. Ten to twelve miles of offshore water was covered as well. Some of the batteries had a range of up to 18,000 yards, and the unfinished French ship, *Jean Bart*, had full use of the fifteen-inch guns and modern range-finding equipment onboard. *Jean Bart* was harbored in Casablanca, but was easily able to reach the Fedala area only twelve nautical miles away.

Then as some men worked faster and others stayed guard, a couple guys ran out from the ship's bridge and said, "Captain Emmet just boomed over the radiotelephone PLAY BALL!"

"What? Only ten minutes earlier, the code word BATTER UP was signaled. What does PLAY BALL mean?" he asked to no one in particular.

Nobody answered. There was no time to explain that BATTER UP meant there was local resistance to the American forces, and PLAY BALL was the next step—the war was on and the attack plan was to be put into full effect. Things were quickly progressing and there was no stopping it.

Chapter 4 – Rough Landings In Africa

The hazy light of dawn was still faint. Looking into the gray, cloudy sky, Carl said a silent prayer. Since the LCV only carried one jeep and they needed jeeps on shore, he wouldn't have to wait and face the chaos of finding and getting on one of the landing crafts that had been delayed by inexperienced crews working in the dark.

Not only that, but he heard the deck crews complaining there weren't enough landing craft to send the planned amount of men ashore. The front rows of ships were trying to borrow landing craft from the lines behind, and there was utter chaos and confusion. Not to mention, the orders of sending out fifty landing craft was anything but possible when each ship only had an average of thirty-two. Although the landing craft could make multiple trips, many of the craft making it to the beaches weren't making it back. He heard an earful about that as he waited his turn to go.

He got it—frustrations were high. Every mistake cost immeasurable amounts at this point. They had to get landed and help secure the beach however possible. Men were dying and time was running out as the sun began to shine the light of day through the gray covered sky.

Figure 11: Center transports off the coast of Fedala (Public domain)

Targets were easier to see the later it got, and the Vichy French were firing from everywhere: land batteries, naval ships, and they even had their fighter planes strafing the beaches. It was estimated there were 168 French planes in airfields close to the landing beaches and in operational condition, and they had to be stopped. The *USS Ranger* and four other essential air supports flew into action, but even the quick reply in fire support did not prevent bullets from giving the sting of death to their next American victim.

Even with visual glimpses of the red path from tracer bullets[38], he was unable to wait any longer. Under attack or not, he had to go. Driving for 2nd Lieutenant Radio Operator Ralphston[39] for the Cannon Company, it was imperative they got to shore earlier than the rest. Since the davits hadn't been properly tested for significant amounts of weight and the LCVs were not designed to be lowered when loaded, his jeep was lowered into the 36'3" LCV first.

To reach his jeep, they had to climb down the rope net thrown down the side of the ship. He had trained for this and he went over the rail with three others. Confidently, he felt for a place to put his feet and grabbed onto the thick ropes. The net violently swayed as he held on for dear life. *This is different from the trainings*, he thought as he took a deep breath. Instantly, he regretted it as the smells of wet rope and salty ocean penetrated through his lungs nearly making him gag. As the day wore on, the smell would only become more unbearable and disgusting from those who descended in fear as bullets flew through the area.

Like the rest of the troops, he was overburdened with guns, ammunition, food, water, equipment, and supplies. Rung-by-rung he silently cursed the Army's choice of necessary equipment strapped to his lean body, making descent twice as hard. The extra sixty pounds felt mighty heavy, especially when climbing down a swaying net to get onto a pitching LCV he hoped was waiting in the right position.

More than halfway down, the wind caught the net and smashed him against the rough, steel, barnacle-encrusted side of the ship. His knuckles scraped along the side, becoming raw and bloody. Getting

---

[38] A tracer bullet has a small pyrotechnic charge in the base that burns brightly and allows the shooter to see the route of the bullet

[39] Name changed, but real character

Chapter 4 – Rough Landings In Africa

his hand smashed against the ship was a bitter reminder he needed to hurry, but without getting careless.

Carelessness meant a fall into the water and he knew what would happen then. As far as he was concerned, the gas inflating rubber life belts they had been given were useless—the extra weight he was carrying was still too much. Unless the extra cargo was quickly ditched at the last minute, nearly an impossible task, he would drown. Although this sounded dramatic, he knew it could happen. In fact, it did happen when one of the nets from the *U.S.S. Jefferson* got carried away by the wind, flinging the descending soldiers into the deep water below.

Almost to the bottom, Lt. Ralphston hollered in a quiet, but gruff voice from below, "Come on Good. Get the hell down here!"

Ha, he thought. He wasn't far behind the lieutenant, but he knew better than to say anything. Before he could even sit down in the jeep, Lt. Ralphston hastily called out, "Let's get a move on it. We've got an objective to meet!"

He hadn't even started driving for Lt. Ralphston, and he was already getting tired of him. "Ready, Sir," he replied as he bit his tongue to prevent himself from saying more.

The heavy packs and equipment made a loud thump as he sat down in the driver's seat. He had returned to his comfort zone as a driver where he knew what to do and how to do it. The steering wheel was positioned high and fit snugly against his lower waist. The flat white paint of the star on the hood of his jeep popped out from the olive drab green. Near the second point of the star, a lengthened piece of pipe about three feet long created an intake snorkel. It was carefully placed directly over the carburetor to protect his jeep from the water. He hoped his jeep would withstand the waterproofing measures and prayed they would make it to shore without getting hit by enemy fire.

The coxswain[40] stood in the small area at the back and started the LCV's engine with a whir. Lightly accelerating the motor, the coxswain cleared the side of the ship before pressing the gas harder. Across the waves the engine loudly whined as they headed toward Beach

---

[40] A sailor who navigates or steers a boat, or in this case, the LCV

Red 3—the beach that had the most problems that morning and was constantly harassed by nearby batteries.

Before long, they connected with other loaded craft and were on their way to the beaches 4,000 yards away to provide needed support. They bounced across the waves of the water with his jeep tightly sitting between the engine compartment and the exit ramp of the LCV. With calmer than usual surf for this time of year, the unyielding waves still hit at close intervals. He tried not to shiver as the ocean spray fell silently into the craft like a cold spring rain. The salt from the water burned the freshly opened skin on his bleeding knuckles, but nothing much was said as they traveled in silence.

He tried to forget about the war zone ahead as the landing zone got closer. Instead, he waited for the LCV to position so he could drive into the water once the ramp was opened. Unlike some of the other jeeps, his engine roared to life when he started it. It needed to be warm, but not too hot to protect it from the cool ocean water. His tires were fifty percent deflated so he could drive over the beach sand, and he was as ready as he could be. He ran through the rest of protocol in his mind and waited for it to play out.

Before the LCV was correctly positioned, it suddenly stopped[41]. He took a deep breath when he realized he was going to have to improvise. It appeared the craft in front of them had a deeper draft[42] and got caught on a sandbar that blocked his straight exit onto the beach. Not being able to go any closer and without being able to go straight ahead, he prepared a plan in his mind.

He couldn't make it to the beach unless he went in the shape of an upside down L—that was sideways first and then turn to drive straight in. It would be a little tricky to beat the waves, but it looked like his only option. When the ramp dropped, he would be ready.

Pulling the choke out a fourth of the way so it would compensate for the cooling effect of the water, he put his jeep in first gear and waited. The wheels were positioned to make the turn, but he cautiously watched as a huge wave raced toward them from behind.

---

[41] Landing story as told by Carl
[42] Draft is the term used to describe how deep a boat sits beneath the water line

Chapter 4 – Rough Landings In Africa

He marveled at its size and said, "By gosh, that wave gots to be at least ten feet high!"

He wasn't sure if the lieutenant had heard him or not, but the words from his training loudly echoed in his head—*don't go in that high water.* He stalled a moment and prepared to go as soon as it passed by them. This would also allow him the extra time he needed to cut back into the beach and prevent a sure loss of his vehicle.

Lt. Ralphston's voice abruptly broke through his thoughts, "Let's go, let's go, let's go!"

He couldn't believe what he was hearing. He knew he couldn't make it through that wave—it was almost on them! He might be able to make it if he drove straight into it, but he had to turn first to miss the other landing craft stranded in front of them. He figured Lt. Ralphston was speaking from excitement and fear and yelled back to him, "I can't go. There's too much water. We won't make it!"

Figure 12: The unloading of a jeep in Fedala in calm waters. Unfortunately, Carl did not get this luxury, as he landed under attack. (Public Domain)

Angrily, with a slur of cursing, Lt. Ralphston demanded again, "I said let's go! LET'S GO!"

Obeying orders, he increased the engine speed to three-fourths of a throttle. He slammed his right foot on the accelerator pedal, and they went under the massive wave. Pressure built up in his lungs as the wave slowly passed and the jeep rested on the sandy bottom. The cool water receded and he grabbed a quick breath of air before the next wave came. One thing was for sure—he had no plans of dying this early in the game.

Desperately, he tried to start his jeep again. They weren't in too deep, but the unforgiving waves continued to pound over them. Water had gotten into the carburetor and as many times as he tried, the engine would not come to life as they held their breath and hoped it might start on the next try. He kept trying until he heard the battery click. *Great,* he thought sarcastically, *now we got a dead battery!*

Lt. Ralphston heard it too and yelled out, "Let's get to the beach! Grab what you can and forget the vehicle or we're going to drown. Just let 'er go, let 'er go!"

Angry at leaving his jeep behind and irritated with Lt. Ralphston, Carl climbed out from behind the steering wheel. Adrenaline pumping, he grabbed what supplies he could and jumped into the water. The waves took side with the enemy, pushing and pulling on him as he attempted to make it to shore. With his helmet tightly strapped to his lowered head, he had almost made it out of the water—tired, wet, and cold. He looked back, but didn't see Lt. Ralphston. *What in the world happened to him?* he wondered as he moved forward into an unexpected chaos.

When he noticed the streaks of bloody redness floating out to greet him, he wanted to vomit. He knew he had been loaded for burial, but there in front of him was something he would never forget—wrecked or stalled landing craft that never made it back for the next group, lost equipment, supplies, and worst of all—bodies. His buddies, brothers in the Army, lay dead and injured along the beach… and it was still early.

Carl's heart sank as he moved forward. Death was everywhere—in front of him, behind him, and beside him. Some had drowned from the heavy weight of the load on a surf-swept beach—being swept off their feet by rolling waves and unable to regain them due to the extra weight. Some had crashed into the jagged rocks and reefs. Many had been shot.

Time felt like it had stopped. He was running forward, but it was as if he wasn't moving. His vision was blurred and noise penetrated through every

Figure 13: Lost landing craft and equipment cover landing Beach Red 3 off Fedala by 1100 hours (Public domain)

thought in his mind as gunshots echoed through the air. He could feel them closing in on him as he moved forward. The further he moved up the beach, the louder and closer they got. He heard a voice yelling from somewhere, "Take off your flag band! Take it off! It's a danged target! Get it off!"

On the coolness of the beach, he stumbled and fell to his knees. Foxholes frantically dug into the sand by troops earlier that morning still remained, but didn't guarantee anything with the enemy's fighter planes strafing the beaches from above. Flying sand stung his face as unknown defenders tried to kill him off with live ammunition.

Hastily, he took off the American flag he had on his arm, stuffed it into his pocket, and struggled to get back up in his water soaked clothes. Out of the corner of his eye, he noticed something a few feet to his right. Everything was a blur. Blinking his eyes, he saw a body—bloody and lifeless.

In a half crawl, half run, he kept down and quickly moved in that direction. He stopped at the motionless form whose helmet was knocked to the side. Unable to see the face clearly, he flipped the body onto its back. Green eyes, once full of life, were slightly opened and stock-still. The dimpled smile was gone. Having been shot, more than once, thick, crimson blood oozed out of his mouth and onto the sand of a country he didn't even know. The blood-covered shirt displayed a hole that penetrated through his chest.

As Carl looked around him at the death-covered beach, an angry beast began to rise from deep within him. It wasn't supposed to happen this way. Somehow, they had found Billy first—a young boy full of life, blown away like ash on a cold winter breeze. With his American flag band still tightly pinned around his left arm, he died alone as a brave American soldier. Billy's words from that day on the ship rang through his head, "I can't wait to get out there and fight!"

Blood, thick and crimson, began to dry on Carl's tightly clenched fist as he punched the sand. This war had only begun. It wasn't a matter of survival anymore. He was mad and ready to get even. A bullet hit the sand a little too close and time returned as he jumped up with new meaning. His buddies were dead and injured in the sand and the enemy relentlessly kept firing.

A medical worker ran by dragging a moaning body up the beach behind him. Right then and there, Carl decided if they wanted him dead, they would have to try harder than that. Suddenly, the most grievous crime of killing another human being became a necessity, and the trigger on his gun was a little easier to pull as he ran up the beach.

Chapter 5

PUSHING FORWARD

FURTHER UP THE beach, a temporary shelter for a first aid station was already set up. This surprised Carl, but he was even more surprised by the number of soldiers who were already there. A soldier covered in oozing blood from deep lacerations on his face and body gazed at him as he passed. It looked like the soldier must have collided with the sharp, jagged rocks and reefs upon landing. A shudder passed through Carl's body at the eerie sensation of seeing men so close to the edge of death.

Out of the corner of his eye, he saw Lt. Ralphston limping toward the shelter with his jacket tightened around his right thigh. Blood seeped through the light colored material and dyed it red. He quickly helped him over to the shelter. "What happened to you?"

Grimacing in pain, Lt. Ralphston stuttered, "I…I…I…caught my leg or something on my way in." His former demeanor of being in command disappeared as he closed his eyes and continued to talk low and slow, "Don't know how it happened… somehow I tore through my upper thigh. I tried to grab some of the radio equipment from the jeep, but barely made it myself… lost it all."

Before Carl could say anything in return, a low flying plane made him look for cover. Unexpected beach strafing from enemy planes had already caused many to lose their lives. However, a quick glance upward through the haze of the day made his pounding heart slow down when he vaguely saw the markings of a white star instead of the French's red, white, and blue bull's eye used on some of their fighter planes. Indeed, it was heartening to see American planes above rather than those with the unforgettable markings of the enemy.

A slight bump from behind made Carl turn around as a man stumbled into the shelter. The pale man's arm was raw, bloody, and loosely hanging as he collapsed into a heap inside. First aid helpers rushed over and immediately began assessing the situation. Something was said about a definite amputation.

He hadn't seen anyone else from his company. Where was everyone? He knew he had to keep moving. Not too far away, he found an area to assemble and reorganize. With a landing of this size, confusion was bound to be a part of it. However, based on the bits and pieces of what he was overhearing, confusion was only one of the many problems.

"We don't have enough troops on shore!"

"Forty percent of the landing craft have been lost. No wonder we're shorthanded."

"Son of a gun! Unloading is going too slow. We got to get the shooting stopped so we can start unloading."

"How is it possible we still don't hardly have any supplies and limited vehicles on shore? Where is everything?[43]"

"Where is General Patton? Why isn't he here yet to direct these landing troops?"

Although General Patton planned to be on shore, seven French Destroyers intercepted the *USS Augusta* shortly before his staff and he got into his loaded landing craft a little after 0700 hours. A naval fight broke out, and his landing craft was cut loose[44] as the *USS Augusta* took off through the water with orange flames bursting from her 8-inch guns. Good choice words flew out of General Patton's mouth over losing what was already loaded, but he was relieved he hadn't placed his iconic ivory handled guns[45] into the craft yet. After his brutal words about the Navy at the shore conference, he ironically

---

[43] Less than 2% of the supplies and only 16% of the vehicles were unloaded that morning.

[44] This is one story of General Patton's landing craft, but there are others. One such story says that his landing craft was caught in the firing and exploded, instead of being cut off.

[45] It was said that General Patton's iconic guns were an ivory handled Colt .45 Peacemaker and an ivory handled Smith & Wesson .357 Magnum.

Chapter 5 – Pushing Forward

received a remarkable view of what the Navy went through to get his troops ashore as planned.

Even so, General Patton was stuck on the ship with limited communication to help oversee what was going on with his landings. The one source of communication that should have been available from the *USS Augusta's* Radio One was bogged down with too many machines run by too few men and communication was at a standstill. Therefore, the commanders on the beach had to come up with their own solutions.

Unbelievably, even with such challenges, objectives were still being met. It was announced the first landing troops had taken Fedala under American control around 0600 hours—shortly after the first Germans on land were captured[46]. Good news for sure, but he wondered why the shellfire and attacks from the batteries and French ships had not stopped. In fact, if anything, the Vichy French Navy was fighting harder than ever and had kept the American Navy in constant action all morning.

Without a jeep replacement, Carl waited for his new assignment. Busy and chaotic, there was a lot going on, but it wasn't long before he was called to take a liaison officer up to the front to find gunner placements. His assignment went right along with the 7th Infantry's mission of capturing the town and Cape of Fedala while neutralizing the guns on the Cape. The infantry liaison could relay quick and accurate command while establishing close communication.

Strategically driving through a light haze of smoke screens and gun smoke, the sun shone across the clear, vibrant, blue sky above as they located the offending targets. Surprisingly, a thrill of the challenge settled upon him as he sped across the front. It was like doing something with the full knowledge that the chance of getting caught was right around the next corner—literally. Being front and center with the ones who had killed so many good American men caused a wave of adrenaline to rush through his body and any fragment of fatigue or fear was pushed to the side for that moment.

---

[46] A group of the German Armistice Commission was captured as they tried to leave, but the head of commission, General von Wulish, managed to escape.

Finally, the morning changed to afternoon and the beautiful autumn air appeared unaware of the manmade calamity. About this time, most of the ground resistance in Fedala ended when up to 200 French troops (mostly Senegalese[47]) gladly surrendered. Then the objective was to get the rest of the shooting completely stopped—especially the French Navy. The sooner they could gain control of the Fedala ports, the sooner the Center Attack Group could finish unloading necessary supplies and vehicles.

It was hard for him to find a minute between runs to catch up with the guys in his company, but for a brief moment, he ran into Brian Bethem[48] and Ruben Rodriguez[49]. They were about as different as two friends could be. Bethem was tall and skinny with blond hair and blue eyes. The way his mouth turned made it look like he was always smiling even when he wasn't. It was hard to take him seriously sometimes, especially with his big ears, laidback personality, and light Southern accent.

On the other hand, Rodriguez was Hispanic American with black hair and brown eyes. Born and raised in California by parents who migrated to Los Angeles as children in the early 1900s, he spoke English as well as anyone. He was about an inch or two shorter than Carl, but maybe fifty pounds heavier. At first glance, a long scar running down his right arm made him look rough, but his quick wit and sarcasm quickly changed that perception.

The first thing out of Rodriguez's mouth when he saw Carl was, "Where've you been, Good? You haven't been at the casinos now, have you?"

Playing along, Carl answered, "It woulda been nice if that's what we came for. Beautiful place, but after what I seen, I'm not interested in hanging around."

---

[47] People from Senegal, West Africa. Senegal was a territory of France during WWII.
[48] Character created for information and dialogue
[49] Character created for information, dialogue, and represents the Hispanic Americans who fought in WWII (Unlike African Americans and Asian Americans, Hispanic Americans were integrated in regular military units)

Chapter 5 – Pushing Forward

Under any other circumstances, he could see why Fedala was considered a favorite fishing town and beach resort. The palm-lined streets and formal gardens would be refreshing with the light ocean wind blowing inward. But after witnessing the murder of so many, this town was not a beautiful resort full of hotels, casinos, racetracks, beaches, and gardens—it was a slaughterhouse.

Rodriguez said, "Me and Bethem here landed late. There was still some shooting, but not too bad."

Carl couldn't tell if Rodriguez was putting on a tough face, or it hadn't been that bad. It didn't help to look at Bethem because he couldn't tell from his facial expressions unless something was really wrong and his eyes gave it away. Otherwise, he always looked happy.

"I'll tell you about my landing later," Carl told them. "You won't believe what happened. I lost the jeep and Lt. Ralphston got injured on his way in."

"Then who ya drivin' for?" Bethem asked.

"Whoever needs a driver. I'm supposed to be a personnel driver, so I guess I'll keep driving for the Cannon Company, but I don't know at this point. You guys know how it is with the supply shortage and all. I drove for the liaison officer earlier this morning and I'm waiting for my next run. I'm sure there are enough assignments to keep me going day and night. The need for drivers is kinda scary—where they all going?"

Rodriguez nodded his head, "Yeah, I heard there's also a shortage[50] of men. They'll keep you hopping all right."

"I can bet y'all that we'll have complete control before too long by the number of prisoners we keep pickin' up," said Bethem.

Rodriguez looked over at Bethem, "You better save your betting for the casinos. There's no betting in war unless you're betting for something we can eat. Man, I'm starving here."

Carl laughed. "Rodriguez, food hasn't even crossed my mind... until now. I don't imagine the food is even unloaded. Looks like we'll be sleeping hungry tonight—if we get any sleep that is. We may have

---

[50] Only 7,750 men and officers had made it in by 1700 hours

accomplished the objectives outlined in the attack plan for Fedala, but you know there's no rest until Casablanca is secured."

Rodriguez patted Carl's arm before turning to walk away, "What is this... No food? No sleep? We must be in the Army now."

"Welcome to the war, Rodriguez. This is only the beginning."

Darkness fell on that first night and the shellfire stopped. Despite the many difficulties, the 3rd Division had gained control over the harbor, the river bridges at each end of town, and the high ridges that commanded Fedala and its beaches. However, having driven through the area, he knew the price that accomplishment had cost. He had seen the darkened bodies quickly decomposing in the open, warm weather before getting covered in a quickly dug trench. That was the real price paid to get control over Fedala, a small town of 16,000.

What would the price be to secure the main American objective of Casablanca, a sprawling city of 250,000 only fifteen miles away? It wouldn't take long to find out. They needed Casablanca to be a supply base and railhead for the Army in North Africa.

Figure 14: The sprawling city of Casablanca (Public domain)

Orders were immediately issued to keep things moving and by 0730 hours the next morning[51], he was already advancing toward Casablanca with the right flank of the 7th Infantry. There was little resistance from the ground forces, but the naval elements continued to bother them with shellfire. To add to the problem, the operational coast batteries were preventing the necessary supplies and vehicles from getting ashore.

General Patton got lucky when he was able to set up a much-needed command post with the mimeograph machines, paper, ink,

---

[51] November 9, 1942

and other office supplies the German Armistice Commission had left behind when they hastily evacuated their headquarters in the Hotel Miramar the day before. Although that helped, communication remained a major issue. Much of the equipment was ruined by salt water and the natives were stealing the telephone wire as quickly as it was put down.

They needed the vehicles for unloading, further advancement, and relaying messages. Therefore, it wasn't a surprise when the 7th Infantry was halted in their advancement toward Casablanca that afternoon around 1400 hours because of the critical supply situation and lack of transportation. Carl was talking with Rodriguez and Bethem when he heard his name being called out, "Good, your company CO[52] is calling you to drive."

Fully aware there were still coastal batteries firing, he also knew enemy snipers kept the area alive and well. Patrols were sent in hopes of clearing them out, but he knew the risk. One wrong turn could end their lives. In fact, all he knew was the commander needed him because he had lost his driver. He wasn't sure what had happened, but he hoped he didn't make the same mistake. Here, you didn't get a second chance—one mistake and you're out.

As he drove, the commander sat to his right and a lieutenant was in back. Suddenly, the sound of enemy fire broke through the air. It didn't take a brain surgeon to know the shots were meant for them. Speeding up, he heard the commander yell, "Get off this road into that field."

The sticky, reddish clay-like mud flew off his wheels as his jeep slid and he tried to regain traction. The saying among jeep drivers of *either drive it, or park it* remained true. There was no time to think.

"Zig zag," was all he could hear through the wind as the commander tightly held onto the jeep.

Experience of driving through the Kansas snow and mud covered fields had taught him what to do, but the blood pumped through his head as the direness of the situation increased. He knew he couldn't leave a straight shot for the enemy as they flew through the field, but

---

[52] Commanding officer

he also had to keep the jeep upright and everyone in it. The sharpness of the turns pulled at his body and bounced him in his seat as he fought to keep control in the rugged fields.

He veered to the right. Out of the corner of his eye, he saw the lieutenant lose his hold and fly out of the jeep, landing hard into the muddy field[53]. Shots were still ringing through the air, but he couldn't go off and leave the lieutenant behind. Tightly clenching his teeth, he sharply turned the steering wheel hand over hand and skidded across the mud to a stop near the bewildered lieutenant.

Carl waited for the commander to berate him for his driving, but was surprised when the commander yelled at the lieutenant, "You had better get your ass in this jeep and hold on. You fall out again, and we're not coming back to get you!"

"Yes, sir," the lieutenant yelled back as he jumped in and held on tight as the jeep veered on the mud when Carl pressed the gas to get out of there.

Making it back onto a quiet road, the mud clunked and spit out behind their wheels as they sped on toward their destination. Wind blew through the open jeep and he processed the near miss as the adrenaline began to subside. He tried not to laugh aloud as he remembered how the lieutenant looked flying out of the jeep and landing in the mud. He couldn't wait to tell this story to his buddies— one more spill and thrill to add to his North African experiences.

Later that evening, Carl yawned in the chilly air as he thought, *Looks like another sleepless night.* General Patton had warned them about that and so far, he hadn't been kidding. By midnight they were ready to start out again as they continued toward their attack positions on Casablanca once again.

A bone chilling wind joined a light rain that had already started. Still waiting for his own jeep replacement, he walked with a few others from his company. A shiver ran through him as his wet uniform slapped against his body. Tired, drenched, and cold, he stumbled in a muddy, plowed field.

---

[53] Event as told by Carl

It was quiet and nobody was saying much. Rodriguez caught up to him and said in a hushed voice, "Man, this is worse than being hungry."

In his misery, he wasn't expecting to hear that and it made him smile. "You're telling me. Of all nights."

"I heard you had an adventure today," Rodriguez continued in a whisper.

He couldn't talk loud and he wasn't in the mood, so he said, "Did I ever. But I'll tell you one thing… driving may come with its risks, but it sure beats walking."

They stopped at a fence. He forced the energy to climb over it and sank into the mud on the other side. Bethem fell and Rodriguez and he helped him back up. He knew Bethem had to be cussing up a storm inside, but you couldn't tell by looking at him and it was too dark to see his eyes. After that, they moved forward through the night in silence. When they made it to an asphalt road, Carl took a deep breath and marched in the rain along with the others.

Shortly after daylight, the march was halted. "Why are we stopped," he asked.

"Sounds like there's lots of hostile shellfire, the commanding officers of Company E and F were injured or killed, and we got to clear out the offending attackers," answered a lieutenant who was standing nearby.

"Is everyone in our company okay?" he asked as they waited.

"I heard someone sayin' Stevenson, Meloviews, and Lunderquist[54] are all missin' from our company," Bethem said.

Men were moved and transferred from time to time, and Carl didn't know Stevenson or Meloviews very well. Lunderquist was a tall, reserved boy with Swedish blood who'd give you the shirt off his back if he saw you needed it. He sent up a silent prayer it was only a rumor and the three of them were not KIA[55].

---

[54] Names are not actual, but three soldiers did go missing from his company that night
[55] Killed in Action

Early the next morning, November 11, fighting positions surrounded Casablanca so it could be taken over once and for all. Prisoner reports throughout the night said Casablanca was calling an armistice. Although some companies claimed to have seen the verifying white flag, General Patton had no proof of that yet. Until there was solid proof, the attack would continue as planned.

Prepared troops were already in position and air and naval support were only waiting for the orders to attack. Five minutes before 0700 hours, word quickly spread through the companies of a definite truce. However, that left General Patton with just under twenty minutes to call off the final attack orders. Feverishly working, he had difficulty communicating with air support as bomber planes readily flew through the sky above their targets. If they let loose, there would be unneeded fighting, and it could ruin further cooperation and support.

At the last minute, General Patton succeeded in getting air support stopped, and they entered the city without a shot being fired. While the port area, power plant, and other objective areas were occupied, a peace conference in Fedala was immediately scheduled for 1000 hours between the Vichy French and American commanders of the region. It was decided that besides gaining the Vichy French cooperation, little else would change with the takeover. The French would still proudly fly their flag and retain their arms. As prisoners were returned, there was no intention in making the Vichy French look inferior or to humiliate them in any way.

In fact, the Vichy French's help was greatly needed for the next steps of the plan in going against the Axis and keeping the natives under control, especially the fighting Berbers. Morocco was known for having the highest population of Berbers, and they were of great concern. Being of Arabic decent, the Berbers were excellent swordsmen, horseback riders, and snipers. They were already showing an unsettling habit of sniping at soldiers and ever so quietly knifing them in the dark. After all, they had been there first—they were the natives of the area. Even Germany had left that part under French control with the condition the Vichy French would fight if they were attacked—which they obviously had.

Chapter 5 – Pushing Forward

The United States and their Allies were taking steps to meet the ultimate goal, and that was to stop Germany. There was no time to deal with more challenges, which the Berbers definitely presented. The French had already proved successful in keeping things flowing peacefully between all the groups in the area, and this was the easiest way to continue moving forward. Therefore, for the overall success of the plan, it was said that the Vichy French had not surrendered, but simply quit fighting and joined the Allies.

For now, objectives were met, and Carl moved back with the 7th Infantry to a camp made at the racetracks on the outskirts of Fedala. They would stay there in a defensive position while things got organized and unloaded. Rodriguez hadn't forgotten his words from earlier and said, "So we got Casablanca, Good. Does that mean we get to rest?"

"Maybe you'll get to rest. I doubt it means much for me as a driver," Carl said.

They walked through the racetrack gates with Blake Michaels[56] not far behind them. Michaels had light brown hair and hazel eyes, but his mouth frequently got him in trouble. Everyone could tell Michaels had grown up getting what he wanted.

He heard as Michaels called out, "This looks like a pleasurable place to stay. I love a good horse race."

Funny, Carl was thinking of being on the other side of the race with the horses. "You guys do any work with horses?" he asked.

"Not me. I was raised in the city," Rodriguez said, "but I think Bethem might be from a farm somewhere in the South." Looking around, he added, "Where'd he go anyway?"

"I haven't seen Bethem," Michaels answered, "but I can certainly say I don't have any experience with horses… unless you count betting on them. I was studying at the university before getting my call, but I didn't mind going. Life was pretty ordinary and this was the change I was looking for. Father said he could get me out of it, but I looked at it as an adventure." Then with a nod toward a rocket launcher that had been taken from an enemy antiaircraft battalion that was stationed

---

[56] Character added for information and dialogue

there earlier and was now being used to get any leftover shooting stopped as they moved in, Michaels continued, "I think it would be safe to say there haven't been any horses here for a while."

"Yeah," Carl agreed, "but being here reminds me of when I use to rodeo with my friends." As he spoke, everything smoothly and effortlessly blended together to form a picture of distant memories—the sound of people, the smell of animals, the feel of the rope tightly wrapped around his hand, the familiar scene of paddocks and stables, and sometimes the taste of blood running down his nose or lip. "Man, I sure miss riding. If I had to pick one passion in life, it'd be living a country life—the animals, the outside, everything about it calls to me. Guess it's in my blood."

Figure 15: Rodeo Buddies (Carl, third from the left in the white shirt) before a rodeo in KS (1936/1937)

"I've had my share of working in the sun and I don't care for it," said Rodriguez. "Art's my passion. I'll show you some of my sketches sometime."

Carl wouldn't have guessed Rodriguez to be an artist. Then again, it was hard to know. The draft had called men from all over the United States from all occupations and walks of life. For now, they all dressed the same, had short hair, and had one occupation—a soldier. Only their unique characters and memories of the past separated them.

Suddenly, a loud explosion made them jump. There had been some resistance when they moved in to take the racetrack and it had to be cleaned out. However, that wasn't the only resistance. Later that evening (November 11), black smoke and deafening explosions filled the evening air. "What was that?" Carl asked, looking toward the Fedala Harbor.

Nobody had an answer, but before long, bits and pieces about the details of the explosions started floating around camp. It was said torpedoes had flown through the Fedala Harbor and hit three[57] out of the fifteen transports and cargo ships that were still anchored there. Even though German U-boats had become a growing threat, the decision not to move the ships to the safer Casablanca Harbor had been made not even an hour earlier. The Casablanca Harbor was being reserved for the approaching D plus 5 follow-up convoy[58].

In under an hour, the *USS J. Hewes* had sunk with the captain and 90% of the cargo still onboard. Fortunately, the troops and most of the vehicles were already unloaded and deaths were kept to a minimum as the surviving passengers were quickly plucked from the water for a second chance. The *Winooski* and *Hambleton* did not sink and could be repaired.

By the next day, November 12, it was almost 1800 hours when Carl heard another massive explosion from the harbor while he was driving. Thick, black billows of smoke blew inland with the gentle, evening breeze. He wasn't sure what had exploded, but from the color and amount of smoke, it was something big as it burned through the night.

He didn't know the details, but the transports in Fedala Harbor hadn't been moved after the first attack. Instead, security was increased as the U-boats thickened in the water. However, it wasn't enough when one U-boat—the *U-130*—managed to get through a small opening of the protected area undetected. It moved so close to shore it scraped across the bottom before quietly taking position and aiming at the transports still floating in the water. In rapid succession, the first four torpedoes tore out of its front bow tubes. Then it flipped around and one more torpedo tore from its stern tube.

Before anything could be done about it, all five torpedoes hit. Consequently, three transports[59] burst into floating infernos—their flimsy construction as ex-passenger lines rapidly burning. Those who were not be in the area of explosion or trapped by the heated fires

---

[57] The transport *USS Joseph Hewes*, the tanker *Winooski*, and the destroyer *Hambleton* were all three hit
[58] Convoys arriving five days after the main attack
[59] *USS Edward Rutledge* (AP 52), *USS Hugh L. Scott* (AP 43), and *USS Tasker H. Bliss* (AP 42)

were quickly taken to shore where they eagerly awaited placement on another ship. Others were not so lucky and their screams broke through the air as they floated in the water amidst burning oil, begging for a quick rescue.

The next morning was still smoky as Carl passed by a casino that had been converted into a much needed first aid station. An unforgettable, pungent odor made his stomach turn. He was familiar with the stink of burning animal skin and feathers, but this was a hundred times worse. It was the smell of burnt human flesh and hair as countless soldiers with burns and injuries waited to get help.

He saw a few with their skin gruesomely hanging off their bones—burns so deep the nerve endings had been burnt. Yet others screamed out in agonizing pain. He tried not to internalize the pain he could feel just by seeing them out his open window.

He found out the first two transports quickly had sunk, but the *USS Tasker H. Bliss* was the one causing the continuous smoke as it burned into the early morning before going under with thirty-four lives. He was shocked. How was it possible that a ship he had perceived as being so sturdy and strong could completely burn and sink within nine hours? He had stood on the deck overlooking the ocean and felt its strength as it plowed through the water, and now it rested on the bottom of the ocean floor—a 12,568-ton, steel-hulled victim of the ruthless *U-130*.

Lesson learned. In a matter of days, the remaining transports were moved to Casablanca, unloaded, and escorted home. However, the memories of those left behind would remain a silent reminder of why this war was being fought. Carl knew why he was there, and he was ready to continue the fight against the Axis.

Chapter 6

CORK OAK FOREST

WITH THE VICHY French fully committed as Allies now, their earlier fighting was classified as a brief and bloody misunderstanding. Their cooperation considerably lessened the unrest, but didn't completely stop all the fighting—there were still pockets of other fighter groups in the area. It wasn't safe to feel safe, but the first mission of the Western Attack Force was successfully completed. The Axis no longer had access to supplies and submarine bases in Northwest Africa, and an Atlantic port was secured where American forces could enter and help the British squeeze the Axis out of North Africa.

In a few days, the time had come to move from the racetrack. More troops were coming in and the move across North Africa was on. Carl was dispatched a new jeep and moved a few miles to the C.O.C field with his company. Usual field duties resumed, but boy did it feel good to sit in the driver's seat of a jeep with his name assigned to it again. Instantly, he felt comfortable with the feel of the seats, the large steering wheel positioned against his body, and the grip of the tires as he drove and maneuvered across the dirt roads—something he did every day.

By mid-November, things were settled down enough that the troops were allowed to visit downtown Casablanca to buy from the street vendors and check out the strange sights, smells, and sounds of a new country. There was plenty to do. After all, Casablanca was the commercial capital of Morocco. Carl had picked up a few shiny rocks along the way, but he wanted something small from the market—a simple memento.

A windy, wet day got Rodriguez, Bethem, and him a pass to go out to the street market. They loaded up in the jeep and were about to leave when Michaels came over and asked, "Where are you boys headed?"

"We're going to the commercial part of town where they hold the market," Carl answered.

"Let's go!" Michaels said, showing Carl a pass and getting in the jeep.

Carl was in awe Michaels hadn't even asked, but just assumed he was welcomed to go along. Turning in his seat, he looked at him and said, "Okay, but be on your best behavior because we don't want no problems out there."

Michaels sounded offended at the thought that he would cause a problem. "Ah, come on, Good. You know me."

"I'm only saying—"

Rodriguez interrupted, "Exactly. We do know you, Michaels. Remember how to act around these people. You give one wrong look to a woman and you could get us all killed. There's no funny business out there. It doesn't matter who you are."

Surprisingly, Michaels didn't say anything as they drove into town. After finding a place to park by the market, a small group of French soldiers[60] walked up to the jeep. They spoke in French as they walked around it. Carl looked at Rodriguez beside him, "What do you think they're doing?"

"By the look on their faces and the excitement in their voices, I'd say they're impressed with the jeep," Rodriguez answered back.

They got out to talk to them the best they could. The French soldiers were young, maybe nineteen or twenty. Since they were interested in the jeep, Carl swept his hand over the jeep with his hand. "What do you think? You like?"

It was better than anything the Frenchmen had and years ahead of their equipment. The French soldiers looked at each other. One of

---

[60] Carl did visit the Casablanca market, but the details of meeting the French troops was taken from a young French soldier, Raymond Lescastreyres, who described meeting Americans in downtown Casablanca and what it was like (Lescastreyres, 2001). Conversation has been added.

them stepped forward as he tried to speak through broken English as he pointed at the jeep, "Yes, we like. Much gooder." Pausing for a second, he made a face and smiled as he nodded and pointed to his outfit that was quite different from the American uniform and said in half French half English, "Yes, you...*tenue militaire*...," he waved his hand up and down his uniform, "much gooder too."

Carl smiled as he looked down at his own neatly tucked uniform. The French uniforms were different, at least with this group of French soldiers. They wore a tall, red chechia (hat) with three black bands. Their dark jackets were tucked in their trousers, and they rolled a broad, red, flannel belt around their waist with a leather belt buckled over it. Not to mention they were wearing puttees—a long strip of cloth, like a long bandage that tightly spiraled around the lower part of the leg from the ankle to the knee—that made some of the Americans laugh.

New leggings, as those Carl and his buddies wore on duty, had been around for years. Maybe certain American soldiers still wore puttees in other locations, but they were more commonplace during WWI. The puttees worn by the French this day covered the bottom of their trousers to the top of their boots and tied off at the top with a tightly wrapped piece of cotton tied with a hitch knot.

Michaels pointed at the puttees one of the French soldiers was wearing and said, "How much?"

The Frenchman looked at Michaels. His eyes squinted as he tried to figure out what he was saying.

Michaels tried again, "What do you want?" He pulled out a pack of cigarettes, pointed to it, and then back to the puttees. "Trade?"

With a strange look, the Frenchman looked down. He pointed at his puttees and back at Michaels. Obviously perplexed, the Frenchman looked at his comrades and said something in French.

Carl was sure the Frenchman was saying something like, "Why does this crazy American want my puttees. They are used and worn, but if he wants them for cigarettes, I'll trade him."

The French soldiers laughed and Carl looked over at Michaels and asked out of curiosity, "What do you want those for anyway? You ain't ever going to wear them."

Michaels laughed, "They're my souvenir. What? For some cigarettes? I'm getting the better deal here, and I want a pair for memory's sake."

Rodriguez smiled and said, "What are you talking about? I want this war over with so I can go home and forget it ever happened. I don't want no sweaty, stretched out, old bands of cloth to remind me."

Before making the trade, one of the French soldiers pointed to the cigarettes still in Michaels's hand and asked, "What mark?"

"What do you mean, what mark?" Michaels asked in confusion.

The Frenchman repeated it in French, "*Quelle marquee?*" Then, with a heavy accent, he tried again in English, "What mark? Looky Strikee, Mo…rris?"

Even with the heavy accent, Michaels figured it out, "Oh, you mean what brand? Like Lucky Strike or Phillip Morris?"

Michaels held out the pack and showed him, "These are some Old Gold."

The Frenchman put his foot on the nearby curb with a laugh and took them off one at a time. The tops of the Frenchman's pants were tied just below his calves and the tops of his worn, black boots were now exposed. They made the exchange each laughing at the oddness of the situation.

A strange, but quick friendship formed between the two groups. The Americans didn't have a problem with the French, and the French were impressed by the sophistication of the equipment, the landing, the uniform, and the way the Americans were adapting to campaign life. One of the young French soldiers was particularly interested in the jeep.

Carl waved him over and showed him some of the features as Michaels and Rodriguez leaned against it and lit a cigarette. They knew how the French liked their American cigarettes and held out some saying, "Good smokes."

The Frenchmen didn't hesitate to grab one. Carl thought of the ones he had given away or used for trade since he didn't smoke—didn't care for it. Come to think of it, he hadn't seen Bethem smoke either, but it appeared like most everybody else did. Cigarettes were part of their Army rationing and they were plenty available.

Chapter 6 – Cork Oak Forest

It was obvious the French soldiers were basking in the glory of a quality, tobacco-filled cigarette. It had been months since they tasted a quality one and even the smoke filled air brought them simple delight. For them, it was a pleasant change to the cigarettes they called "troop" to which they had become accustomed in the last several months.

Today, they were pleased it was cigarettes the American shared with them. However, friendly Americans were known to share other presents, such as gum, chocolate bars, and sometimes cans of pork and jam, or meat and beans. The French were satisfied in every sense of the word as they all walked toward the busy section of the market before splitting off.

A darkened sky threatened rain, but withheld. The wetness from the day before hung in the air as they walked along the narrow, brick-lined street. Tall, white buildings welcomed them with their shop doors opened and displays of bright, colorful goods.

Arab children came out of nowhere and crowded around them holding out their dirty, little hands. Their soiled robes hung loosely on their thin bodies, and the smell testified washday was few and far between. Carl had been told this would happen, and he was prepared as the children excitedly yelled out the only two English words they knew, "Candy? Gum?"

Reaching into his pocket, he found the gum he had brought. "Gum," he declared with a smile as he randomly handed it out. Rodriguez, Bethem, and Michaels did the same as the kids happily jumped up and down around them.

He wondered how these children could have so little, yet still smile, laugh, and genuinely be happy. More kids gathered around him and he wished he had more to give. When he felt his empty pocket, he pulled it inside out to show there wasn't any more. The kids smiled before skipping on down the crowded streets.

Once the kids were gone, he looked to his right and noticed a shop with an old bicycle parked along the curb. Two white signs with the word *Bata* written in dark, black letters stood out, but he wasn't sure what *Bata* meant as they walked on by. Some shops had brightly colored clothes hanging along the outside wall to lure customers inside. Others had tables with stuff setup on them. People were everywhere and there was a lot of everyday noise as buyers negotiated, bells clanged, and sellers called out. It was clear the market was a social occasion for the local people.

Unsure of what he wanted to buy, he kept walking. He didn't have a whole lot of money, so he wanted to get something small and practical. He stopped to look at some odds and ends at a little corner setup and his buddies walked on ahead. On one of the tables, he saw a unique writing utensil. He picked up the small, one of a kind tool to get a better look.

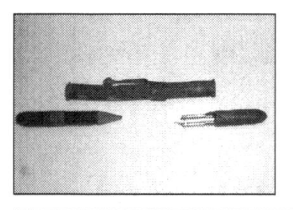

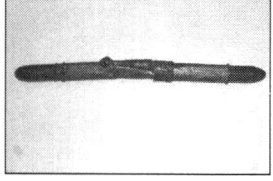

Figure 16: Pen/pencil Carl bought at the market in Casablanca

It was created to hold a small pencil on one end and had an ink nib on the other. The brass tube in the middle was aged and showed signs of wear and the old carrying clip stood out, but it was still fully functional as a writing utensil. All the parts were there, including the two caps on both ends. Not only was the pencil commonly known as every soldiers writing instrument, but it would serve as a memento as well. He wanted it and figured he could get it for a good deal.

Bargaining with the Arabs at the market was an art, and he would have to negotiate. The listed price simply was a starting point. Carl figured he probably wouldn't get the best bargain based on the newness of the tradition. However, if both ends of the bargaining ended up happy, it was a success. If he did it right, he would also get some foreign coins in return—those being his biggest memento of all.

Although the currency varied throughout the areas, two could be used in French Morocco, Algeria, and Tunisia. He had a little of both and wondered if he should use the paper francs and metal pieces, or the money issued by the bank of Algeria. Unsure, he opted for the paper francs in hope for a variety of coins in return. He thought it would be neat to collect the coins from the different countries as they fought their way through.

Most of the street vendors did their best to communicate and this one held up his fingers upon seeing the francs in Carl's hand. With room to negotiate, Carl countered the offer by putting up half the number of fingers in return. They went back and forth until they both agreed on a number. The bargaining process reminded him of an auction and there was a certain thrill about trying to get the best deal.

Happy with his purchase, he walked by a small coffee shop. The smell of coffee called to him and he took a few steps back. He wasn't sure where Rodriguez, Bethem, and Michaels had gone, but he figured he'd buy a nice, hot cup of coffee while he waited. He said coffee and the man working nodded his head as he handed him back a cup in exchange for a few coins.

Back outside, he took a sip and gulped hard, forcing himself to swallow. He looked down at his cup. He wasn't sure what it was, but it was not normal coffee. Slowly, he lifted the cup to his lips and took another sip. It had a woody, bitter taste. He wondered what he had been given as he watched the scene around him.

Another group of soldiers was walking through, and he instantly recognized one of them. He called out, but nobody from the group stopped. Before they got too far, he yelled out again, "Eli Lewis."

Lewis looked around this time. He saw Carl and went back to where he stood, "Hey, Good. What you been up to?"

"Just driving day and night. Gosh, it's good to see you. Have you seen any of the others—Bellis, Schondermier, Garretts? I've been wondering how everyone fared at landing?"

"I saw Bellis," Lewis said, taking a deep breath before adding, "He told me... he told me that Schondermier didn't make it."

Lewis's words froze in the air.

After a brief moment, Carl shook his head and said, "That ain't right. That kid had so much potential." They both stared ahead and then he added, "Remember Billy—the young kid I talked to on deck that day? He didn't make it either. I saw his body all shot up on the beach that first day. Those things don't leave ya, ya know?"

Lewis slowly nodded his head.

Darn it, Schondermier and Billy were both good guys, and he wished he could have been there for them. Lewis changed the subject, "What are you drinking?"

"Heck if I know. I ordered a coffee and this was what I got."

Lewis looked at it and said, "I heard there's a common French coffee that's served along here... some kind of chicory coffee or something."

"That's probably what happened, but it's no good," Carl said as he debated whether he should dump it out or not.

Lewis smiled, "I'll keep that in mind. Who'd you come here with?"

"I brought some buddies from my company, but I finished up and thought I'd stand here and wait. Ya know, as I've waited, it really made me see how different the cultures are around here."

Lewis looked around, "You're not kidding. I've counted five different languages so far, and I'm certainly no master in language. Those were only the ones I could tell were different."

Out of the corner of his eye, Carl noticed three Arab women walking in their direction. "Don't stare at those women coming."

"Oh yeah, I read about that, but it's hard not to look at them with the strange clothing," Lewis said, looking straight at Carl as they passed.

The women were completely covered in white—a white robe covered by a long piece of white material that completely covered their heads and hung half way down their bodies. Only their eyes could be seen through a slit barely wide enough for them to look out. The women quietly talked amongst themselves, but otherwise completely ignored their surroundings.

Once the women were in the distance, Carl asked, "Did you see their shoes? The only thing that made them look different was each of them was wearing a different style and color of shoe."

Lewis laughed, "No, I didn't look at them."

"Well, I wasn't looking at them either, but their shoes stood out against the white as they walked by," Carl said as he took another sip of coffee. He made a face. He didn't want to waste it, but it was too bitter for him.

"Well, I got to catch up with my group," Lewis said as he gave him a brotherly hug. "You take care and we'll see when we bump into each other again."

Not long after Lewis left, Carl heard Michaels's voice headed his way. Their day at the market was a success. Nobody had accidentally offended anyone and everyone was happy with their purchases as they walked back to the jeep.

It was interesting to be around all the different cultures, and it was quite evident North Africa was full of them. However, it was hard to miss the fact the native Arabs ruled in this area—and that was part of the challenge. Being on good terms and gaining their trust was a crucial part of moving through the area. The natives would either help, or help kill… depending if they liked you or not.

When they got back to camp, Carl pulled out the *Pocket Guide to North Africa* he had received before landing. He read it earlier to have an idea of what to expect, but the women he had seen at the market made him want to reread what was written about them. The purpose of the book was to help soldiers know how to deal and work with the people of the country and to know how to gain their friendship and cooperation.

Several things were still fresh in his mind from the market as he flipped through the pages. This book didn't refer to the natives as Arabs, but as "Moslems." He saw a section labeled "Details of Native Dress," and he skimmed through it. In regards to the women he read:

> When seen in public, a Moslem woman is usually covered from head to foot in a plain white wrapper, with a white veil stretched across her face just beneath the eyes. But under this unattractive costume, the women wear garments of very bright colors which are revealed only in the privacy of their homes, the idea being that a Moslem woman is not supposed to look attractive in public…These

few rules are to be strictly observed with relation to the Moslem women:

Never stare at one.

Never jostle her in a crowd.

Never speak to her in public.

Never try to remove the veil.

This is most important. Serious injury if not death at the hands of Moslem men may result if these few rules are not followed.

That confirmed what he already knew—it was hard being in another country. It was way too easy to offend someone and not even know it. It was nice to get out and see something different once in a while, but he preferred to stay where he understood the language and the culture.

Soon after his day out, he was dispatched to the 7th Division Regional Headquarters to drive on a special assignment for Lieutenant Colonel John O. Williams[61]. He liked driving for Lt. Colonel Williams, and his assignment was to take him about 60 miles northeast of Casablanca to Rabat—the political capital of Morocco.

It was a clear, cloudy day on November 21, so he uncovered the folded down windshield and put it into place as he prepared to maneuver the clear coastal road. While the roads were safer, he still had to be cautious of the constant sniper attacks or booby traps placed by determined enemies. Some clearly did not want them there, obviously the Germans, but also some of the Vichy commanders and their Colonial troops.

Evidence of the cold, wet downpour from three days earlier remained, and a cool wind blew through the jeep even with the windshield up. Usually he drove with the windshield folded down and covered with a piece of canvas—especially if it was muddy. Unfortunately, the wipers were only good enough to spread the mud, and there was nothing good about trying to see out of a dirty window.

---

[61] Real name

Chapter 6 – Cork Oak Forest

However, the sun was the biggest reason he usually kept his windshield down. He couldn't risk a shiny flash reflecting off the window to give away his position when on an important mission. With him running back and forth between companies and the front lines, this was imperative for his safety. Today was cloudy, and he was staying on the main road so he could use the windshield with less worry. But he knew better than to ever completely relax. The enemy was always looking for ways to stop communication and supplies. Of course, tanks were a higher risk target, but ways to stop jeeps were continually developed as well.

Although he hadn't seen it himself, he heard other drivers talk about a booby trap made for jeeps and their drivers. It consisted of a thin wire tightly pulled from one side of the road to the other at the height of the windshield. Its purpose was to decapitate the people in the jeep when the windshield was down. For that reason, a wire-cutting bar was added onto the bumper and extended to the top of where the windshield would be. He was glad they were one step ahead in that aspect.

It was easier to hold a conversation with the windshield up, but they didn't talk about home. Instead, they talked about everyday things. Based on Lt. Colonel William's age, Carl guessed he had a family at home, but didn't dare ask. The scenery began to look familiar, and so he said, "I don't know if this looks familiar because it all looks the same, or if I've gotten used to the landscape in the last two weeks."

Lt. Colonel Williams laughed, "Oh, the landscape will change. You wait and see. Most people think Africa is only desert, but they're in for a surprise."

"Yes, sir. I realized that driving across muddy fields after landing," he said as the specified location came into view.

In Rabat, Lt. Colonel Williams got out of the jeep. There were French and Americans gathered for a combined memorial service for all those who had died on both sides. Solemn notes of the taps drifted through the jeep window as it was played over and over again.

He thought of his Army buddies being honored at that exact moment—Billy, Schondermier, Lunderquist, and God knew who else.

As the familiar 24 notes continued... dum dum dummm, he knew *if* he made it home, he wouldn't consider himself as doing anything special to get there. The real heroes were the ones in an unmarked grave in a country they didn't even know.

A deep and lasting memory was formed with each note of that bugle call—notes that would forever transport him to that dreary time of war and death. So far, he was one of the lucky ones, but he knew as well as anyone that every day was like a game of Russian roulette—the cold muzzle of a revolver placed squarely against his head and the cylinder clicking as it rapidly spun. Eventually, the bullet would appear, shiny and ready to kill. Only he didn't know when the trigger would be pulled. He didn't know when the taps would be played for him.

Figure 17: North African graves (Library of Congress)

The ride back to camp was quiet. There were no words to say after that, but the thoughts stayed active in his mind as the daily rumble of Army life continued. Although his thoughts didn't make him fear death, they made him choose to live for those who could not.

When the time came a couple days later to move to another C.O.C field about three miles out, he was ready. Even with a light sprinkle, the move was an easy one. Rodriguez stopped by his jeep before they headed out, "You got your stuff nice and dry in your jeep. Don't be surprised if your bag goes missing tonight, Good."

"There are advantages to my hectic job. I probably won't get to use it anyway if I get called on a run. As far as the rain, this is only the beginning," Carl said with a laugh.

"I know, I know... the rainy season has just started," Rodriguez said as he dramatically rolled his eyes, "but if I have to deal with this cool wetness until at least February... and maybe even into early March like they're saying, I think I might go crazier than I already am."

Chapter 6 – Cork Oak Forest

"Then I'm going to start calling you Crazy Cal. You're from California, right?" Carl asked. "Anyway, the rain itself ain't so bad. It just makes for bad roads."

Rodriguez turned to leave and said, "Oh, I know about that. We've got to walk them."

A couple days later, on November 26, it was Thanksgiving—the first of many holidays to be spent away from home. Carl sat next to Bethem and asked, "You think we'll get something special to eat for Thanksgiving?"

"Bethem shook his head, "Nah, we're in a transition area. The food kitchens don't set up unless we'll be stayin' for a while. Until then, I bet it'll be ration packs."

"I keep ration packs in the jeep to make up for missed meals when I'm driving. There's nothing special about them," Carl said with disappointment.

When they sat down to eat, he looked at the can of stew from a regular "C" Ration and said, "Darn it, Bethem. I was hoping you was wrong. I heard some companies talking of turkey and I was hoping we might be one of them."

Bethem looked up, "This ain't so bad. Back home, we lived a ways from the city and if we didn't hunt it—we didn't eat. This food here is easy to come by."

"You're right. We should be grateful to have something to eat..." Then with a smile, he added, "Even if it's a cold can of stew the size of a coffee cup on Thanksgiving."

Carl knew the struggle of not having enough to eat. It was ten years to the month since his dad lie dying of a gangrene infection from a ruptured appendix. He had picked up a lot of the family responsibility since then, but it hadn't been easy. Somehow, food always made it to the table in one way or another, but they were poor.

Bethem's question interrupted his thoughts, "So what was Thanksgivin' like for y'all?"

From duck, to turkey, to ham, everyone did something a little different. It was a strange realization that the "traditional" Thanksgiving meal was different for everyone. He heard something mentioned about hunting, but he was lost in thought as he slowly chewed his cold stew.

In his mind, he thought back to what it was like for him. It was as if he could almost smell the freshly plucked chicken cooking in the oven at home. He imagined the chunky mashed potatoes, green beans home canned from the garden, chicken gravy, sliced tomatoes, and pumpkin pie sitting on the old, white tablecloth that was used for special occasions to hide the scratched table. Mmmm, that was a traditional Thanksgiving meal to him[62].

Usually he tried not to think of home, but some days were harder than others as a small pang of homesickness settled low. He wasn't sure if it was from missing family and food, or the fact that Thanksgiving was when his older sister, Edith, caught a cold at the age of five that turned into pneumonia and took her life two days before Christmas. Her death made the holidays a tender celebration of life for the other children.

In fact, he knew his family would be sitting down to be thankful for another year and the unseen power of prayer would ascend to the heavens for him. Far away, but never forgotten, he waited for that subtle reminder in the form of a letter or a little package from home. He hadn't received anything since landing, but he had heard the first mail arrived two days earlier. Processing times were slow, but they would eventually get to him, even if they were a month or two late.

Once a week, his mother wrote him the current news from home —good or bad. He heard about the wellbeing of relatives and friends, what his brothers and sisters were doing, what had been planted in the garden, and any other news his mother deemed important at the time. As long as it was regular everyday information, then nothing would get blackened out by the censors.

Not knowing if his letters would even make it home, he was careful with what he wrote. It was common knowledge nothing should be said about location or anything that would be of value to the enemy. The letters needed to camouflage how strong the troops were—nothing to make them look weak. Ultimately, his unit censor

---

[62] Carl's family's traditional food as remembered by Bert (Carl's brother)

would decide what was appropriate or not and if the unit morale was getting low. If a letter did not make it through the censor, it could be confiscated, but the writer wouldn't know.

Sometimes it was easier to state at the beginning of the letter that he couldn't say much. The point was to let them know he was okay. His family was fine with that. Every letter they received from him meant he was still alive. If the letters stopped, something was wrong. Although the letters from home brought normality and hope, the dreadfulness of war made him feel as if he was living a separate life that couldn't be interconnected again.

Figure 18: Actual censored letter sent to Carl from his mother in 1943

But interconnected or not, time forged forward like a soldier pushing through thick mud with the hopes it would not turn into quicksand and swallow him up. They had made it to December and it was time to roll forward again. For added protection, the company tanks rumbled close to the ones who had to hike. They made it twelve miles before stopping for the night at an unknown place along the road.

It was unsettling to stop in an area where they knew the fighting Berbers were ruthless, but they had the protection of being together in a group—or so they thought, as the darkness enveloped the landscape around them. There was a cold, brisk breeze, but fortunately no rain. It was a quick rest and there was no time to get comfortable.

They were tired from the long day, and Carl quietly rested in his jeep, as did the new driver behind him. A couple guards kept eye on the convoy and the night was unusually calm. They didn't know there was one lone enemy lurking in the hidden shadows of night—a stealthy Berber who had no intention of getting them all at once, but slowly and steadily... one... at... a... time. The Berber's head was neatly wrapped in dark cloth and his eyes were all that penetrated through the darkness. Like a snake, the Berber patiently waited for just the right time and then silently slipped away after the deadly strike.

The next morning, at the break of dawn, it was discovered—a quick slit to the throat and death had yet again claimed another life.[63]

When Rodriguez and Bethem heard, they stopped by to check on him before they started out again. "Man, you okay?" Rodriguez asked. "We heard a driver had been killed in the night."

"It was the driver behind me," Carl said still a little shaken. "A straight slit to the throat. One more... and it would've been me."

Figure 19: Troops and tank of the 7th Infantry, 3rd Division, inland of Fedala (National Archives)

That particular thought had been running through his head since it happened. That was when he understood firsthand why the Berbers were taken into consideration when fighting in the area. He had to expect the unexpected and never relax—not even when he was sleeping.

More alert and ready to make their destination, they pushed harder. After going for sixteen hours, it was midnight. The guys walking needed a break. Still four miles away from their resting point, their company commander angrily announced, "We're not going to be able to make it tonight. Don't let your guards down. Unfortunately, as we learned yesterday, you don't know who's out there."

---

[63] Carl told the true story of awakening to find the guy behind him had gotten his throat slit during the night

Thankfully, December 3 turned into a new day without incident. Had anyone been able to get any sleep? Carl knew he hadn't as he watched the darkness around him.

The sun shone bright in the sky when they arrived at the racetrack in Rabat around noon. Hungry and tired, they had until tomorrow to get rested up. The hustle and bustle of Casablanca was left behind. Rabat was much quieter, even though it was the actual political capital since the French moved it there thirty years ago.

There was little fighting action in this area, but the 200,000 soldiers in the Spanish Morocco territory, a couple hours northeast, caused some concern. So far, Spain's dictator, Franco, had not joined in the fight, but was carefully watching from a distance. If Spain did decide to join the Axis, they would make it extremely difficult by taking control of the Straits and cutting communication between Allied forces.

Figure 20: Map of Morocco (PAT public domain maps)

Through extensive purchases of oil by the Allies, the situation was pacified and Franco was kept happy—so far. He also knew of the landings a couple hours in advance and was guaranteed they would not affect Spanish Morocco or Spain. Officially, Franco remained a nonbelligerent[64] ally of the Axis, but he stayed quiet with the negotiations. Troops were positioned close by just in case that changed.

---

[64] Spain was not engaged in the war, but sided with the Axis

Besides that concern, things in the area were fairly quiet. Tomorrow they would travel to their new camp area by motor trucks—not hiking. With no need to hurry, they stayed at the racetrack in Rabat until 1100 hours and then loaded up the trucks.

After traveling northeast about ten miles, they arrived and stopped at a beautiful area where they began to set up camp. They had stopped in the Mamora Forest—nearly 520 square miles of forest. Quite the change, this massive forest of trees was a couple miles inland in the middle of the cactus-filled desert and rich coastal landscape.

He noticed most of the trees had a thick, knobby, dark gray bark. The trees were maybe forty to sixty feet tall and were still covered with dark green, weakly lobed leaves about 2" long. As Carl stood looking at one, Rodriguez and Bethem walked over to him, "What ya lookin' at?" Bethem asked.

Figure 21: Cork oak tree bark (Public domain)

"These trees. I ain't ever seen anything like them," Carl answered as he picked up a fallen odd-looking, one-inch, green acorn half covered by a long, prickly, fringed top. "Have you guys?"

"Not in California," Rodriguez answered."

"I've never saw the such," Bethem said. "And I've saw lots of trees."

"In order for it not to drop its leaves, it has to be some kind of evergreen. But it ain't like no evergreen I've ever saw in the States[65]," Carl said, looking over the acorn in his hands.

"I don't know. It's just a dumb tree. Come on," Rodriguez said as he moved on.

---

[65] These trees are mostly found in Portugal, Spain, France, Italy, Algeria, Morocco, and Tunisia.

Chapter 6 – Cork Oak Forest

Carl threw the acorn he was looking at and hit Rodriguez in the back, "It's an interesting tree," he said with a laugh.

When Rodriguez turned around, Bethem was the one who took off running for some reason. Carl just stood there and laughed as Rodriguez ran past him and after Bethem. Shaking his head and laughing, he headed back to camp.

From the name they called their camping grounds in the Morning Report—Cork Grove or Cork Forest—Carl quickly discovered they were cork oak trees. This is where cork was harvested, right from the outside trunk area. Rodriguez wasn't interested, but Bethem agreed with him that it was impressive. It was a tree with the unique ability to regenerate its outer bark after harvesting, and it could be harvested every nine to twelve years without causing harm.

This forest of cork oak, eucalyptus, and other trees, was an oasis of peace in the middle of chaos. Hidden from enemy planes, it felt like a safe place to have camp. Of course, the regular field days of firing practice and training served as a constant reminder of why they were there, and he stayed busy making runs to different batteries within the 7th Infantry that sometimes took him over a hundred miles in blackout conditions.

One such night, Carl looked into the starless sky as he loaded up with an officer and guard to deliver an urgent message to the main headquarters. It was too dangerous to drive through the dark with his jeep lights on and driving blackout was usually enforced. He pushed the switch that only allowed use of the attached blackout lights and locked the normal lights.

The front blackout lenses were hooded and prevented the diffused light from escaping up. Through the use of angles, the light was directed in a horizontal pattern. It helped others to see him straight on, but it wasn't bright enough to help him see much of where he was going. The other lights on the jeep were equally protected and allowed distance and speed to be measured when traveling in a convoy.

Although it was a good system to prevent accidents and detection by the enemy, he still depended on the brightness of the moon and stars to help him see the roads. Tonight was cloudy and he leaned forward as he squinted through the darkness. When he stopped at their destination, the officer said, "Wait here. Won't take but a minute."

The dim light from inside the large tent shone through the opening where the officer entered, but it could not be seen from the outside once it was closed. As Carl waited, he could hear a gruff voice yelling out and cursing. He could tell there were several people in there as they conversed, but he couldn't exactly hear what was being said. In a moment's time, the officer came back out, got in the jeep, and said, "Let's go."

Trying to release some of the tightened tension that returned with the officer, Carl looked over at him and said, "Boy, sounded like that guy got hold of some sour grapes."

Even in the darkness, he knew the officer was choosing his words carefully. "You know who that was?"

"No, sir."

"That was General Patton."

"Don't surprise me none by the way he was talking," Carl said as a cold, lost breeze blew through the jeep and unexpectedly made him shiver. "I ain't met the man face to face yet, but I've heard him."

"Oh, his bark is worse than his bite. You get used to the man somewhat, but he sure makes it hard to be the deliverer sometimes," the officer quietly said with a smile.

The early morning haze still hung low when they arrived near camp. The flip side to driving through the night was being up at the break of dawn when some of the most brilliant colors illuminated the sky. The sun never stopped rising even on the dullest days.

Still too early for breakfast when he got back, he figured he'd get a few hours of sleep and see if he got up in time to eat. The camp kitchen was set up now, and he could usually grab a bite between late night and early morning runs. If not, he had the ration packets in his jeep. Sometimes it tasted like the same stuff anyway. The only difference was the kitchen heated it up and served it with a good cup of coffee.

Since he was a driver, he could sleep in later than the rest if he didn't have an assignment waiting for him. It was hard to sleep in too late with the noise coming from where the company tanks were practicing maneuvers in coordination with live artillery outside of the

Chapter 6 – Cork Oak Forest

forest area. Plus, they had some time to train the French troops on the use of American weapons. They were fighting against the Germans now and they had to be prepared.

Although General Patton despised inaction, he made sure his troops were prepared while they waited. If they couldn't be part of the main action headed toward Tunisia, then he wouldn't let them forget why they were there with his coarsely ordered weekly trainings and maneuvers that lasted a rough and sleepless twenty-four hours. It was General Patton's responsibility to prepare and organize them for future combat, but boy, did everyone know he hated that part—he wanted to be out fighting.

As the cool, rainy days continued, December was quickly approaching its end. Carl wasn't at all excited for Christmas that year, and the days were mundane with driving and keeping up with his company buddies when time allowed. Most of them felt that way.

"At least the kitchen will be set up on Christmas and we'll get a better meal than we had for Thanksgiving," he said while talking to Bethem.

"Maybe… if we get lucky," Bethem said without much hope. Carl changed the subject. "In better news, did you hear about the parade in Rabat to celebrate the armistice between us and the Vichy forces?"

"I'm going to be in it," said a guy named David Nyleve who was sitting nearby.

Nyleve hadn't been in their company long, but he appeared to be a hard worker from what Carl could tell. Stocky with a long, pointed nose, and bright, piercing, green eyes, Nyleve was a tank driver—which was a job Carl respected, but didn't want. He had talked to him a few times between runs.

"Yeah, I heard there were going to be some of our tanks in it. I'll be driving the jeep through." Carl looked at Bethem and said, "I can't believe you hadn't heard. Where you been? It's December 20… this Sunday."

"Yeah, if you're not in it, you're invited to watch. The different companies will be getting together and showing off their units. This is a big deal," Nyleve added before dropping it.

Bethem shrugged his shoulders, "I reckon I ain't in it then."

Something out of the ordinary like this *was* a big deal. When the day arrived, the French and American troops got ready. Carl double checked his uniform and welcomed the change of pace.

Gray clouds covered the sun and a cool breeze blew through. He wondered if it would rain. The streets already looked glossy and wet from a previous sprinkle, but Rabat's mild, temperate climate caused the temperature to stay around the average[66] of fifty degrees. Decked out in full Officer's Dress (OD), the coolness was refreshing.

Tall, white buildings and open archways provided a great background for the parade. The white buildings glistened, even though the day was cloudy. Slowly, the procession began with four of his company's 75mm tanks and three of their 105mm tanks carefully driving through the tightly laid brick streets. The turnout for this parade of friendship was surprising. The streets were lined with bystanders and other troops. Even the balconies of the buildings had people waving and cheering them on.

Noise filled the air, but it was a pleasant noise. It was the sound of people—happy people—talking, laughing, and waving. The stars and stripes of the American flags proudly flew, as did the bands of blue, white, and red of the French flags. It felt good to have a normal activity—something that didn't remind him of war. General Patton and French General Nogues watched together from a viewing stand, both proud of what they were seeing—good men fighting for their countries as one. As the day died down, Carl felt good. It almost felt like an ordinary day in an ordinary place for a brief moment.

But it was far from ordinary as Christmas Eve silently arrived and echoes boomed through the crisp air as four 75mm and two 105mm tanks made their weekly practice. He tried to remember why Christmas was his favorite holiday. They didn't have much. There were no fancy gifts wrapped in glistening paper… no new bicycles waiting outside. Sometimes, there wasn't even a Christmas tree with its sparkling lights. Yet something about it made it special enough to celebrate with what little they could.

---

[66] Average temperature from December to April

Chapter 6 – Cork Oak Forest

It was a time for the family to gather and open a few small handmade presents. His mother worked hard to make sure all of her children got a small bag of Christmas candy and nuts to eat as fast or as slow as they wanted. As they got older, his older brother, George, made the trip home from Wichita where he worked at a grocery store and brought a store bought gift—a small bag of marbles, or maybe even a little toy[67].

The next day, there wasn't any of that as Christmas day brought mild temperatures and no Christmas joy. The Army did little to bring the real Christmas spirit into the camp, and if it did, he completely missed it as everyone passed through the day in a daze. It wasn't the same living in tents with a bunch of men thinking about past Christmases and too gloomy to talk about it.

As Carl reminisced on his own Christmas memories, he thought about the special dinner that replaced the everyday food of bean soup made with the Golden Wax beans picked from the garden[68]. The normal garden staples tasted better than usual that day, and there were a few extras like homemade pies. Even though there wasn't much, it was a time of joy, fun, celebrating with family, and ice-skating on the river if the ice were thick enough. That was all that was needed to make it special.

Christmas came and went. It was cool and rainy a couple days later when he was called out to drive for a 3rd Division chaplain[69] who had tirelessly conducted multiple religious services for the different companies within the division. These Sunday services were offered to anyone who cared to join, as long as the company wasn't on assignment elsewhere. Those who usually didn't care much for religion hungered for the comforting words offered. To the chaplain's joy, the attendance had been great that night.

Although the chaplain was still smiling when he got out to the jeep, Carl instantly noticed the worry line that permanently crossed his tired and worn face. Army life was rough, and the chaplain was

---

[67] Christmas memories from his brother, Bert
[68] Foods as remembered by his brother, Bert
[69] Some of this 3rd Division chaplain is based on experiences from the diary of Chappie (Carpenter & Eiland, 2010)

obviously older than the typical soldier. As they drove, the chaplain looked over at him and asked, "Do you believe there is a God in this world filled with war and pain?"

Although Carl believed there was a God, he wasn't sure why things like war happened. He guessed it was due to choices made by man. He finally answered, "Yes, sir, I sure do."

"You're a good Christian man then?" the chaplain went on to ask.

Carl respectfully looked over at him, "I certainly try to be, sir."

The chaplain grinned at him. "That's where you're wrong, son. There's no try about it. Either you are… or you're not."

"Well, I guess I am then."

They talked, and he learned the chaplain had given up a lot to share the message of hope, peace, and comfort in a war full of hardship and pain. Even with the fear and frustration of leaving his young family behind, the chaplain hoped to be the light in the darkness the Army had begged for. After all, the soldiers knew a chaplain was one of the few men they could trust as he patiently listened to their stories, shared their pain, and prayed with them in their deepest moments of fear and despair. Talking with the chaplain was a breath of fresh air in a dark, drunken world that sometimes felt like it was off balance and spinning out of control in an unknown direction.

Upon reaching their destination, the chaplain opened the door and started to get out, but stopped. He sat back down and gave Carl a small, dark book saying, "My assistant and I handed out thousands of these mini *New Testaments* before we left the States. Did you get one?"

"No, sir," Carl said, looking at the small book.

Figure 22: The original New Testament given to Carl by the chaplain in 1942

When the chaplain stood back up, he said in a serious and sure tone, "Young man, you take that book and keep it with you, and you'll be sure to go home."

"Thank you, sir!" Carl said, safely placing it in his front shirt pocket. "I'll keep it with me from now on."

He didn't really know if what the chaplain said was true, but at that point anything sounded good if it helped him make it home alive. Either way, he wasn't going to take a chance—he planned to do exactly what the chaplain had suggested. He had nothing to lose.

A few days later, New Year's was the same as Christmas—it came and went without too much recognition. However, it did leave one gift behind—the gift of a new year to continue in this lethal game of chance. He didn't know if the bullet would come for him or from where, but he did know there was a chance of it coming.

Chapter 7

1943

THE INVARIABLE PING of rain bounced off Carl's little pup tent as he lay and listened to it. January had started much like December ended—cool and rainy. There was no fighting in their area. Yet the days steadily ticked by with training and guarding along with his daily runs and tasks of delivering reports and driving officers. Night guard duty was also required by everyone to keep the camp safe.

On a cold, wet night, he got ready for his shift on guard duty. He had just returned from a run, but he had a few hours before his scheduled time of 0300-0530 hours. Shift times varied, but they were usually about two hours at various times during the day or night.

When he got there, he stood ready and alert in the coldness of the early outside air. His warm breath left the mark of life as he exhaled. The moon hid its shining face in the starless sky, leaving a black night. Breaking through the normal noises of the grove, he blew warm air into his hands and rubbed them together as his rifle drummed lightly against his back.

He hadn't had to use his rifle much here, but he had been shooting since he was old enough to hold a gun. He had a good shot. In fact, if he had fifty bullets for hunting, he'd come back with forty-nine rabbits. Food and money were scarce in their home, and the rabbit meat had been given to his mother to be canned or ground in with some pork meat from the hog kept in the smoke house. There was only one hog a year, so it had to last.

That was why it hadn't taken him long to get his expert in machine gun medal. He had become an expert in shooting a long time before

Chapter 7 - 1943

the war broke out. Although he always carried a gun with him, it was a comfort to know he was prepared and able to use it if necessary. Every sound was important and every movement was imperative, especially at this early hour while most of the men were sleeping.

Through the blustery darkness, he heard a vehicle moving in his direction. Although there had been some light rain, right now it was quiet and calm. Even on safer ground, the drivers had to drive in blackout conditions much of the time. This was an effort to keep the camp area safe from detection and prevent night attacks.

He waited for the approaching vehicle. From experience, he knew getting too comfortable in any situation spelled danger. *The moment one quits expecting the unexpected is the moment one can expect to die* ran through his mind. He didn't know if he had heard that somewhere, or if it had randomly popped into his head, but by keeping it in mind, he managed to maintain the number one post as he thoroughly reviewed anyone coming through.

In fact, only once had he gone light on a guy. It was one night when Michaels came in too drunk to remember his own name. He smiled as he thought back to that night[70].

Most of the guys had already come back for the night as curfew was set at 2100 hours unless given a special day pass. Out of nowhere, an unearthly sound broke through the silence. It sounded like someone was singing, or trying to sing. However, the song being yelled out was unrecognizable as the person moved toward where he was standing guard. Unable to recognize the song, he recognized Michaels's voice. Still, he proceeded as he normally would by calling out, "Advance and be recognized."

Michaels staggered toward him and he heard, "D...d...don't shoot... ddon't shoot me nowwww! Yy...you know meeee."

"What on earth you been drinking?" he asked.

Michaels's head rolled back and jerked forward again as he answered, "I don't knooow, but it waaas goooood."

He shook his head in disbelief, "You better be careful out there. Now go on and give me the password so you can go on in and get to bed. You're going to get us all in trouble."

---

[70] Event told by Carl, conversation added

Drunks coming in making noise like this had already gotten everyone in trouble once. There were two parts to the password, and everybody was made aware of what the words were for the day. Today was an easy one. As always, the guard started it out with the first part.

He waited for Michaels to say the second part, but instead Michaels looked at him with a blank stare, stumbling over his words before finally sputtering out, "Nooow, wha that passssword? D...id they... do yooou thiiiink... did they ggive that to meee?"

"Everybody got it," he replied.

Michaels squinted his droopy eyes and Carl wondered how he even made it back to the camp and why in the world he was alone. Motioning to the ground, he had looked at Carl and said, "I'ma... I'ma gonna sit dooooown a minute? Pass...wooord?"

He watched as Michaels sat down and wondered if he would pass out. A minute later, Michaels opened his eyes wide and said, "I gotta... pee."

Surprised at how fast Michaels got up and stumbled to the side of a cork oak tree, Carl wondered if the urine soaked into the cork that would be harvested later. After all, the trees were used as urinals often, especially on cold nights when no one wanted to walk down to the latrines. It would sure make him think twice before opening a corked bottle with his teeth.

Michaels stumbled back. "Got that password now?" Carl hopefully asked him so he could move him through.

"I juuust think I miiight...," Michaels ventured, but then said nothing.

He looked at Michaels with his shirt untucked and it looked as if he might have fallen a time or two.

Michaels reached his hand out and put it on his shoulder. The smell of booze on Michaels's breath was strong as he pleaded, "Now, ddon't shooooot mee. I...I don't know the pppassword."

"Hell...only this one time, Michaels. You know I take my guard duty serious. Go on in before you hurt yourself and get everyone in trouble."

The next morning Michaels didn't remember much. After he told him the story, Michaels thanked him for not turning him in—or shooting him for that matter.

His thoughts returned to the approaching vehicle as it was in viewing distance now. Situations like Michaels certainly didn't happen often, and his main concern was keeping the camp safe from the enemy. He didn't care where he was, he was going to make sure the enemy did not slip in the camp unseen while he was on duty. With the threat of snipers always on his mind, he was ultra-careful. In fact, snipers had gotten two night guards at another camp, and they made it plenty clear they weren't playing around—they liked to peel guys off whenever they got a chance.

The jeep came to a complete stop in front of him. He placed his hand on his rifle as he told the driver, "Go."

He could tell the driver was running a list of words through his tired mind and an awkward silence ensued. He knew the feeling and although it was usually only seconds, time would stand still as if it were minutes. The driver briefly closed his eyes and then opened them as he mumbled the second part, "Stop."

With the appropriate password, he asked them to get out of the vehicle so he could do a quick, but complete inspection. The lieutenant beside the driver loudly huffed and said while cursing, "You know who we are. Why do we need to get out?"

"I'm only doing my job. Now get out of the vehicle please, sir."

It didn't bother him any that he could hear the lieutenant loudly complaining and cursing under his breath as they all got out. This wasn't the first time he had made people mad when he thoroughly checked their vehicles, especially the lieutenants. They thought it was a pain to get out of the vehicle and get checked, especially if he knew who they were. To be honest, he didn't care if they got mad.

He knew these vehicles inside and out, and he searched for anything out of place or missing. On his knees, he shone a flashlight under the vehicle. It would be easy for an enemy to get under there and get a "free" ride into camp. With nothing out of place and clear identities, he let them pass into the camp.

He settled back into guard position. If the sun chose to rise that day, it wouldn't be long before the dawn sent beautiful pink, orange, and yellow colored light glistening and streaking through the gray sky—graciously ushering in another morning. He was used to getting up early for work and seeing the break of dawn, but it was always refreshing to watch as a new day propelled through the circle of life no matter where in the world he was.

He thought he might skip early morning breakfast so he could fit in a couple hours of sleep. Almost to his tent, he ran into Nyleve. "Hey, how'd you sleep?" he asked.

"Ahhhh... since getting a board and straw to put our bedrolls on, I've been able to sleep so much better," Nyleve said with a stretch.

"I hear you. It's still not a bed, but with all this rain that falls around here, sure helps to keep from waking up in a puddle," Carl agreed. "One less thing to get soaked. I've got stuff I've been trying to dry for two days and then it rains again."

"And it's an earth-cleansing, pond-filling kind of rain too," Nyleve complained.

"I guess that's what makes every day an adventure. There's always another chance for excitement, challenges, and disappointment with a new day," Carl said as he turned with a yawn.

He didn't know actual excitement was brewing when he said that. However, a few days later—January 21 to be exact, word circulated that President Roosevelt, along with his secretary, Stephan Early, would pass through on the main road near Rabat. Although the president's arrival was kept a secret until shortly before he was to drive through the tree-lined road, a few from each company in the 3rd Division would be chosen to go stand in a one mile stretch with bayonets fixed to see the president as he checked over the companies. He'd be traveling through with General Patton, General Anderson, and some other civic and military leaders.

Carl hoped he could go. He had great respect and admiration for the programs Roosevelt put in place to help those struggling with the Great Depression. After all, it was Roosevelt who started the Drought Relief Service—a program that bought starving cattle from desperate farmers. He remembered the day when they had come to their house.

It had been an unseasonably hot, early summer day that year in 1935. The dark Kansas dirt with clumps of dying brown grass was cracked and jagged every which way from the lack of rain. Wilted flowers hung their droopy heads as they struggled to live, and the same

Chapter 7 – 1943

feeling of despair hung low in the air as the depression dragged along with the drought. He stood outside with his mother and talked to the men under the shade of a tree for a few minutes while they looked the boney cattle over.

"We'll give you $18.00 for the one cow and $6.00[71] for the baby calf," they finally said.

It would leave them with only one cow, but they needed the money. Besides, that was enough to pay their farm rent for almost five months. His mother nodded her head and the deal was closed.

Carl looked up at the taller man and asked, "You need some help loading them up, sir?"

The man clenched a cigarette in his teeth as he looked down at him and said, "I reckon we do. Let us get the truck ready first."

The three cattle stood in the pasture and as Carl waited, he looked over at their thin, but strong bodies. It was hard to get rid of them, but he knew they couldn't afford all three of them. The weather was so dry the cattle didn't even have fresh, green grass to eat, and they couldn't afford to feed them. Yet they needed to keep at least one of them for milk, cream, and cheese.

The man came back and asked, "You ready, boy?"

"Yes, sir," he said as he walked toward the calf.

"No, leave that there one for now," the man said through a puff of smoke.

He wondered why they weren't loading the baby calf, but went on to help load the bigger one. Upon finishing, Carl walked toward the calf again.

This time, the shorter man spoke up. "Leave that one there," then he quickly added, "and stand back outta the way."

In one quick movement, the man pulled out his gun and shot it—leaving it as meat for their family. His mother looked at Carl through the brightness of the sun as he walked back to where she was standing. She used the dollar bills in her hand to fan herself from the heat and said, "Well, God is good. This'll give us some living money for a few months and it'll be good to have some beef on hand. Now, go get your brothers and get that calf cleaned and ready so it don't spoil out here in the sun."

---

[71] Prices as remembered by Carl

Man, the times had been hard. *Heck,* he thought, *times are still hard!* That's why he still sent most of his Army check home as he did back when he had worked with the Civilian Conservation Corps[72] (CCC)—another relief program started by Roosevelt as part of the New Deal plan. The purpose of it was to relieve the unemployed and poor, recover the economy, and reform the financial system to prevent a repeat depression. Yes, many people loved Roosevelt as a president for what he did to help the people, and he was going to be a few miles from him today.

Each separate unit in the 3rd Division was to be represented and those chosen from his company were to represent the 7th Infantry, Cannon Company. Patiently waiting, he listened as the colonel hastily called a group of names to get in full field uniform and go. Disappointed when his name wasn't called, he knew only a few men could go to represent them. He was sure to hear plenty about it later, especially since Bethem was going.

As he expected, Bethem's permanent smile matched his excitement when he came back and told them everything, "Ya know, there was a strong, bone-chillin' wind that started blowin' about the time the president was to arrive, but we didn't even feel it. Then, Roosevelt himself came ridin' through in the front seat of a jeep wearin' a gray business suit, gray felt hat, and a black band around his left arm."

"What did the black band represent?" Nyleve interrupted.

"I heard it's a mournin' band he wears for his mother who passed away over a year ago," Bethem quickly answered before continuing. "We stood and saluted them as they passed, and Roosevelt saluted us back and called out greetings to those who was close enough to hear him. Above us in the air, there was P-40 pursuit planes watchin' after him. It was really swell."

Bethem's excitement carried over for everyone, but that day passed and the excitement died down. Time rapidly encompassed January and threw February to the forefront. A grim rumor of what

---

[72] These programs were available due to the difficulty of finding work during the depression. Carl worked on different projects in soil erosion control, soil conservation, road construction, and a variety of other jobs that needed to be done throughout Council Grove and in the state of Washington.

was happening in Tunisia—a dry, rocky desert country the size of the U.S. state Georgia—came with it. The African campaign couldn't be completed until things in Tunisia were finished up, and it was taking a lot to get it finished up. Geographically speaking, it was a stepping-stone into the back door of Europe—known to some as Hitler's backyard.

Carl thought of Schondermier. He still couldn't believe he was gone. If he were there, he would have given them the history about why the fighting in Tunisia was so bloody and long. However, he wasn't, and many of them didn't realize the complicated history involved.

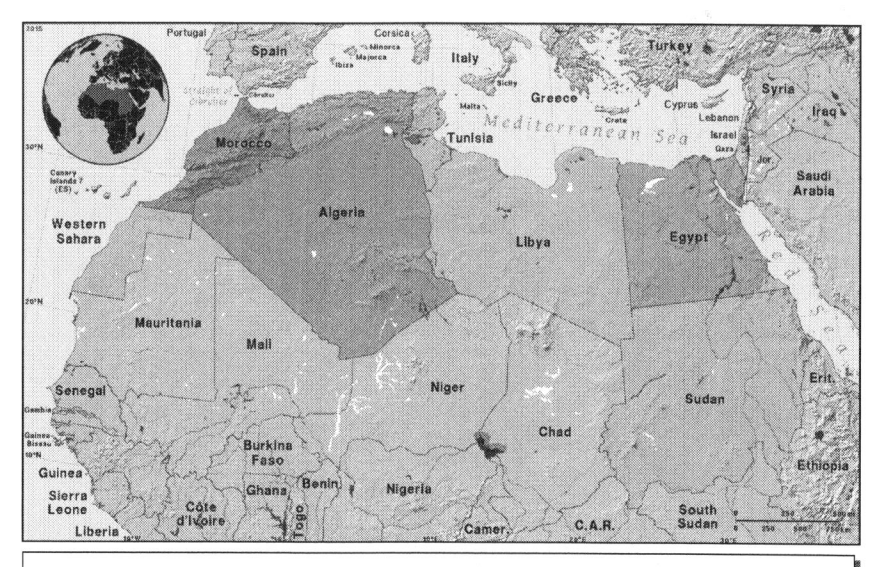

Figure 23: Map of North Africa (PAT public domain maps)

Libya had been an Italian colony for several decades, and the British had troops in its eastern neighbor of Egypt since the late 1800s. When Italy joined the fight with the Axis and declared war on the Allied Nations in 1940, they immediately began to push each other back and forth across the desert until a British counterattack in Egypt caused the capture of 130,000 Italians in December of that year. Hitler's response was to send General Field Marshal Rommel, a highly skilled German commander, to fight in Libya and Egypt with the newly formed and well-trained Afrika Korps.

Since then, the war continued to rage in those areas and the British had finally managed to push the Axis up into Tunisia where they would have Allied support from the November landings. Hardly feeling threatened by the Allied troops at first, the Germans remained confident in their skills and tactics. At that time, they were better organized, had better communication with their chains of command, and better equipment, including the superior Mark and Tiger Panzer tanks, and they knew it.

When the Eastern Task Force (British and Americans) landed in Algeria back in November, the intentions were to move ahead and gain the Bizerte and Tunis ports of Tunisia—only forty miles from one port to the other. However, they weren't expecting Kesselring, another one of Germany's most skillful commanders, rapidly to send enough forces and supplies over from Sicily to provide fierce competition to make sure Tunisia stayed under Axis control.

As things intensified in Tunisia, Rommel moved his forces to help with the fighting there and to be closer to his supply lines coming in from Sicily. By this point, the U.S. also had moved American and French units through Algeria to join with the British in fighting for control of Tunisia. This meant two main Axis armies were fighting two main Allied armies in the smallest country of North Africa.

On top of the severe resistance from the Axis, the wet, rainy weather had caused numerous problems, especially the length of time fighting—now already into February. Yet they still needed to meet their last objective to get all Axis control out of North Africa. The Allies needed the crucial ports being used as a major supply route for the Germans—which the Allies needed to cut as much as the Axis needed them open. The fierceness of the battles showed the desperateness of gaining Tunisia as the battle with the Axis continued to grow with Rommel being put in charge of command.

By mid-February major battles developed, one through the Pass of the Atlas Mountains—the gateway to Algeria. The fight there was devastatingly hard and many Allied supplies and complete units were lost by late February—many due to the inexperience and confusion of the new American fighters. In a crucial turning point, the Axis decided to back down from that area due to a growing lack of supplies,

Chapter 7 – 1943

the inability to make a break in the Allied line, and a shift in priorities. However, that didn't mean the fighting was over, but instead the Allies were gaining a much-needed foothold in the area.

With parts of Tunisia under Allied control and the fighting slowing down, there was an immediate reexamination of Allied plans and organization. General Anderson was re-assigned to the U.S. in late February and General Patton was strategically moved to Tunisia in early March. General Patton's goal was to let the Axis know the Americans were now a Panzer-killing force and would not fail as they moved forward with new determination and leadership.

Under General Patton's command, every man played his part and was dressed to match the outcome he was there to achieve. No more sloppiness—they were to act as top soldiers. This attitude immediately changed the way the troops worked and success followed, but there was still the need for replacement units, vehicles, and tanks.

And that led up to March where Carl and his company were still camped in the Cork Grove in Morocco. How long before being called in for support? He didn't know for sure, but he did know his company had the needed supplies. He could feel they would be leaving soon.

He wasn't surprised when Major General Truscott took General Anderson's place of command on March 7 and things immediately began to move forward. So much so, they instantly received orders to pack up and be ready to leave early the next morning. With a wink of sleep, he was ready by the expected time of 0100 hours. It was an old trick to leave under the cover of night and helpful in preventing unnecessary detection.

He saw Rodriguez walk by and said, "You better make sure you didn't leave nothing behind. The natives will take anything to use as supplies. Why, they'll even take the wooden latrines if they're left."

"They can have that crap," Rodriguez said, laughing into the early morning darkness at his own pun.

He nodded his head and smiled at Rodriguez's pun as he put the jeep in gear and rolled out of the area where they had spent the last several months. Headed in a northeast direction with the convoy of motor trucks, he watched the blackout lights ahead of him so he knew how close he was driving. The cork oaks stood solid in the moonlight

115

of the Mamora Forest and stretched along the side of them. They weren't going far; it was a little under an hour to arrive at the new camp—eight miles from Port Lyautey, Morocco. However, there was a sense of excitement to be moving on.

Shortly upon arriving to the new area a little after 0200 hours, he watched as the rest of the men grabbed their supplies and looked around for a place to put their bedrolls on the damp ground. He stayed in his jeep to sleep. In a few hours, they would be ready to get up early and finish setting up their tents and the rest of camp.

The starry heaven glowed bright, and he stared at it through the trees as he thought about the conversation he had with the chaplain earlier. Why did things like war happen? Greed? Money? Power? As he thought, he was glad they hadn't moved out of the protection from the Mamora forest. It provided a familiar tinge of comfort from the unanswerable questions that lingered in his mind.

The light of day came and he could clearly see the new area didn't look much different from what they had left. He remembered what Lt. Colonel Williams had told him about how the African landscape quickly varied from place to place, and he knew the change would come before long. For now, the protective forest had a familiar look and feel to it.

The Northern Attack Group from the Western Task Force had landed near here. They had met their objective, but it was not without a fight. The Vichy French were more determined in their resistance, and the numbers of American casualties were greater. Now, it was their bivouac[73] area while they prepared for their next assignment.

There were no guarantees as to what would come next, but it was no secret that many men had been sent to replenish lost troops in Tunisia. Therefore, nobody was surprised when the order was issued four weeks later[74] to pack up and move forward. After a two-hour march into town, they had to wait until the next evening to catch a dark, dusty train headed for Oran, Algeria.

---

[73] A bivouac is a military encampment made with tents or improvised shelters. These are usually without shelter or protection from the enemy, but Carl's group still had the protection of the Mamora Forest here.

[74] April 9, 1943

Chapter 7 – 1943

It wasn't an ideal situation to travel with a trainload of hot, thirsty, hungry, and tired men in a confined space, but he supposed it could be worse—until he saw their train. Not sure what to think, he didn't say anything, but he looked over at Rodriguez and Bethem and raised his eyebrows. Rodriguez mumbled in return, "So, this is what we get to travel in, huh? Hope those Krautheads[75] don't need target practice today."

It wasn't like the modern day boxcar. It was an old one like they used in WWI. They were called 40&8s—meaning big enough to carry forty horses and eight men. Once those train doors closed, there was no fresh air, food, or extra water for the long, overnight ride.

He had no room to stretch his legs as he hunkered down for the night with Rodriguez, Bethem, and Nyleve not too far away. It was assumed the safest way to travel through the night, but it definitely was not comfortable. When someone accidentally stepped on Bethem's foot, Bethem snapped, "Watch where ya goin', won't ya!"

Carl looked over at him, "You okay? I don't think I've ever saw you mad before."

Rodriguez said with a smile, "Aww, he's fine. Look, he's still smiling."

Already cranky from the miserable situation, Bethem didn't find Rodriguez's joke funny and responded by punching Rodriguez in the shoulder. By the look on his face, it was a little harder than he planned. When Rodriguez scowled back at him, Carl wondered if Bethem had overstepped his boundaries in the hot train car that was only going to get hotter. Luckily, they both sat back and let it go. They should try to rest before the next morning came, but it was hard to sleep in those conditions.

The next morning, within hours of the 0800 hours arrival time, he had his jeep. The company loaded on trucks and headed to their new bivouac area. Headed out on the roads of Algeria for the first time, they left the palm-lined sprawling city of Oran behind. It felt strange being out of the protection of the tall cork oak trees to which he had grown accustomed. Instead, there were rock-studded hills with oak

---

[75] Derogatory term used for the Germans

scrub trees and small sagebrush dotting the landscape—the hardened ground barren from much else[76].

It wasn't wet enough now to fill the empty irrigation ditches or small canals along the bottom of the hills. He wondered what this area was used for in a typical year. It was much too rocky to grow food. Perhaps the canals filled with water during heavy rains, or maybe the area had been used for grazing animals at different times. For now, it looked useless. He was certainly glad the farmland in Kansas looked nothing like this, and it made the years farming in drought conditions not seem so bad.

Twenty-four miles away from Oran, they arrived at their new bivouac area, only six miles from Arzew. From the looks of things, he was sure he wouldn't get more than a rocky night's sleep in the time spent there. They didn't have straw to put under their bedrolls as they had in Morocco. Although most of the rain was replaced with heat, it still occasionally came to get everything wet.

He could tell getting camp set up would be a challenge and felt sorry for the ones in charge of digging latrines and water detail that time around. The ground was solid and rocky. However, out of all the hardships they had to deal with out in the open, the Army took great care in making sure the water detail always found a good source of water to provide for them. Once a good source such as a well, spring, or river was found, they used their gas pumps to bring it up to purify it into five-gallon containers. Clean water was a necessity. One bad batch and a whole unit could be out sick.

Most of it ended up in the kitchen for cooking and things such as coffee, but not all of it. Although there wasn't a lot extra, they had enough to use some for cleaning off the obnoxious dirt and sand every so often by using their helmets like a bowl. It was enough water for a quick shave and sponge bath when permanent camps weren't available. In the more permanent camps, he could actually take a quick shower once in a while—but there were no guarantees there'd be

---

[76] Some of the description from this area with the help from Bud Wagner's book, *And There Shall be Wars*

hot water. After a night in a hot train and the drive to the new area, he would have liked to wash off, but he'd have to wait for now.

Instead, he looked around the new area. Shortly after their arrival, he had seen Arabs dressed in dirty, ragged clothing along the road selling oranges—a typical Mediterranean crop along with olives, figs, dates, and other citrus fruits. There was little civilization in this area, and he wondered where they came from. He imagined they were from a small outskirt town hidden somewhere around them, but he didn't know.

Bethem came back with a few oranges in his hand, and Carl was surprised. "You better be careful buying that fresh fruit off the road."

Without a word, Bethem easily peeled the sweet fruit. "Wow! Look at that color!" he said, holding up the deep, purplish-red flesh for Carl to see. "Do ya want to try a piece?"

Curious, Carl ate a small section even after his warning. He wasn't expecting the sweet and juicy flavor that leaked into his mouth as he chewed it. "Interesting. Are those the Blood Oranges people are talking about?"

"Ya know... I'm not sure. Ya goin' to buy some?" Bethem asked.

Carl shrugged his shoulders and said, "I don't think I want to deal with the sticky mess when I'm traveling and training in the heat. I done had my share of that when I worked in the fields. Sticky don't combine well with dirt, and there is plenty of sand around here. Not to mention the flies that showed up with the heat."

With that, he had successfully convinced himself for sure that he didn't want to buy any of the juicy oranges. The annoying, buzzing flies were bad, especially at mealtime. He didn't want to be attracting them more with the sweetness of an orange. Anyway, he was sure there would be more opportunities to buy some oranges later if he changed his mind and caved in to the taste of the sweet citrus.

Now, if those were apples on the other hand, he would have bought as many as he could and stuck them in his jeep for later. He loved a good apple. He was rarely sick and he attributed it to his apple a day when he was at home. Out here, they were harder to come by, but so far, he didn't have a sick day to his name.

Now was a good time to remain healthy. Arzew was the place to start intensive training while meeting up with the rest of the 3rd Division, and they were only six miles away from Arzew. How intensive, he had yet to find out, but he was sure the name would live up to its reputation. After all, they only had a few weeks before moving out again. A limited time schedule could only mean one thing —they were going to wear them to the point of exhaustion.

Sure enough, the trainings under the large, hot, African sun began hard and potent for everyone, not only the infantry, but everyone— Army, Navy, and Air Force. They were preparing for the next combined operation, and they needed to be able to work together. A successful landing was contingent on meeting the objectives and being prepared as a team physically and mentally.

Since the 7th Infantry had been out of direct combat for the last several months, General Truscott felt they were not up to standards. Even though he had thought for years that the standards for marching and fighting in the infantry were too low, he used their current inactivity to his advantage. To do that, he put a plan in place that included his main component of speed marching—that more than doubled the traditional pace and distance of a moving army.

Suddenly, the six-mile hike to Arzew sounded like nothing compared to the newly introduced speed march called the Truscott Trot—a vigorous thirty-mile march meant to increase endurance, strength, and most importantly, quickness in battle. It wasn't required all at once as they began to train, but building up to it in the next months was a requirement to move on to the next operation. Only the fittest were used for the next landing. If they didn't pass the Truscott Trot, they weren't going to move on with the rest of the company.

That first day they were up early and Carl stood in a neatly formed line as they began to march. With the new pace set at five miles in one hour, he watched as some of the troops struggled to keep pace for the whole five miles. His tall, black Army boots felt hard and uncomfortable on his aching feet as the march neared its end, and every pound of the fifty-pound pack he carried on his back could be felt. Sweaty, dirty, thirsty, and tired, he finished the hike only to get a small break long enough to refresh for the next exercises. He knew he would get used to it as every man and officer was required to do this twice a week until leaving.

The following morning, he rolled over to get up and felt the soreness of yesterday when he moved. His whole body ached from the trainings, but felt good at the same time as he recognized the pain to be a sense of accomplishment. Today would be the same, or maybe even worse, he thought as he rubbed his sore muscles and prepared to get ready for the introduction of the second part of the Truscott Trot.

This part was to be practiced once a week from now on and included completing a grueling eight miles in two hours. He could feel his beige-dyed undershirt soaking in sweat as the yellow ball of sun shone through the clouds and heated up the day. It was going to be a scorcher and unbelievably, he was starting to miss the coolness of the rain.

Ignoring the initial burn of his legs, he knew it would get easier the longer he marched. It was like running; eventually he wouldn't feel the pain as long as he kept going. It wasn't so much the distance that was difficult; it was keeping the same pace of four miles an hour for two hours. Not about to give in, he pushed as he completed the eight-mile stretch. This was only a glimpse of what was to come.

After those first two goals were met, they put them together to make thirteen miles. Yet the completed trot included the last seventeen miles marched at three and a half miles an hour—totaling thirty miles in less than eight hours. This was a feat of champions—the overall total distance was more than the distance of a marathon. Not all of them made it at the beginning, but they would have to build up to it or be humiliated by being left behind and assigned elsewhere.

As if the Truscott Trot wasn't enough, there was plenty more training to fit in as they prepared to meet the enemy. Physical condition and preparation was obviously a top priority with a mock village setup with live ammunition, close range grenades, flying debris, and street fighting. The list of physical activities went on to include logrolling, obstacle course running, bayonet training, and even hand-to-hand combat. The stakes were high, but he knew he was in better physical condition than most due to his days on the farm. Still, that

121

didn't mean his body was resilient to the sudden on pour of muscle-tearing activities.

A change in pace was welcomed with a day of amphibious tactics and simulation of the enemy maneuvers. It was still demanding, but less physical. As they prepared, Rodriguez looked over at Carl and said, "I heard they use live ammo on us to simulate battle."

"I heard the same the other day. I suppose we should be used to it by now," Michaels loudly interrupted.

Rodriguez sarcastically continued as if Carl had been the one to answer, "Don't get much better than getting coffined by your own country."

Even though he thought it was ironic that they would fire at their own troops in preparation for meeting the enemy, Carl said, "Guess they look at it as a few casualties now will save more later."

"Yes, you are presumably correct, but I'd rather get hit by them bastards than by my own country," Michaels said.

Carl nodded his head in agreement and said, "Well, nothing we can do about it... just don't get hit."

Laughing, Rodriguez agreed, "That's danged right, Good. Danged right."

They didn't know where they were going for their next operation yet, but it was clearly going to be a fight to get in. The most obvious guess was that they were going to cross the Mediterranean Sea and go straight into Sicily. The problem with that was it was so obvious the Germans surely would be expecting them. If they were going to land there, they would have to trick the Germans into thinking they were going to land elsewhere. That wouldn't be easy, but they had learned from their mistakes in Tunisia.

More troops from the 3rd Division were still rolling in for training in the area when his company received word they were cutting it short and moving forward. On April 26, after a little over two weeks of blood draining training, he was called to get his jeep and head to headquarters. Not sure why, he followed orders and found a group of four officers, thirty-one E-Ms (enlisted men), fifteen jeeps, and three 75mm tanks gathered. Nyleve was already there in one of the tanks, along with Rodriguez.

Quickly briefed, they were to travel over 700 miles to Kasserine Pass—an American catastrophe where full units were completely wiped out. Reinforcements were hurried over—including more than 3,500 of the best 3rd Division soldiers already. With only one day in Allied possession, the Kasserine Pass area was a grave to some 10,000 American soldiers—and that's where he was headed now.

Figure 24: Map showing distance from Arzew to Kasserine Pass
(PAT public domain maps)

Chapter 8

CALL OF TUNISIA

UPON HEARING HIS destination and knowing what happened there, Carl's heart raced with anticipation of what was to come. They were sending him up front, and he wasn't sure what position he would hold upon arrival. He remembered officers passing on the detailed stories they heard about what General Truscott had witnessed at the fight for Kasserine Pass. As he thought about that, he heard little else.

The wind blew through the gray, cloudy sky as they prepared to leave. It was a little unnerving as they traveled the long unknown terrain through the dry, hilly countryside. Snipers were always a threat, and he knew they had to travel quickly and remain alert at all times. A large convoy averaged less than 15 miles per hour, but he hoped the smaller convoy could move at the top speed of the three 75mm tanks—around 28mph. It was a high expectation, but he knew the trip would take them several days, depending on how hard they pushed it and how the weather held up.

Along the way, they stopped at a small village. Although the sky still threatened rain, it stayed in check. They were moving at a good pace. Meeting up with Rodriguez and Nyleve, he said, "They're lucky enough to have the water trough here at its center. Saves them a nice walk down to the river."

As Rodriguez was filling up his canteen, Nyleve whispered to them, "Careful where you look. There's a group of women headed our way."

They were Arab women in the same long, white robes that covered everything but their eyes. The women seemed interested they were there, but didn't directly look at them and kept their distance. A square piece of wood balanced on top of their heads that held their laundry, food, or giant, ceramic jugs of water as they walked to and from their typical plaster covered homes and barns.

Carl made sure not to stare and quietly said, "I've seen them carry stuff like that before, but it never ceases to amaze me how they can balance all that weight on their heads."

"Why is it that only the Arab people grab our attention? I mean, we see many cultures and people living in these areas, especially other Europeans," Nyleve asked.

"The other cultures blend in with what we're used to seeing. There's nothing that makes them really stand out as being different besides the language," Carl said.

The Arabs were a strong, traditional people who had been in the area for hundreds of years and had been overrun by other governments more than once. Yet they didn't bend to the new cultures brought in with those changes. It was their traditional status that stood out to the Americans—unusual clothing, selling fruits along the roads, or doing other things that were odd to the American culture—like the oddity that the women, children, and men weren't seen out together as a family unit. They lived a completely different lifestyle.

Ready to leave again, he sat in the jeep. While he waited for the convoy to get ready, he pulled out his *Pocket Guide to North Africa*. He thought maybe there was a reason why the Arab men were like that. There... right under the heading "North African Social Life":

> The social life of North Africa is very different from our own, not only because of its leisurely character, but because Moslem men do not make companions of their women. A man's wife attends to the home, bears children, and may work in the fields, but she is in the position of a chattel[77]. If her husband cannot afford to support more than one wife, he still can divorce her with ease and be free to marry again.

---

[77] A personal possession

Interesting, he thought as he skimmed the rest of the information. That explained why he didn't see them walking together. Even when they went out as a family, it said the woman had to keep several paces behind so others would not notice they were together. Everything about it was strange to him—so different from what he was used to.

He respected women and felt like Arab women were lost in the culture. Of course, for the Arab women, it was a normal part of life and generally accepted. In fact, maybe they felt sorry for him for living a different life than them. Either way, he decided the next time he wrote a letter home, he would be sure to mention to his fiancé how glad he was to be American—for lots of different reasons. Not being able to say much more than that without it getting censored, he would fill her in on the rest when she was safe in his arms.

They made it to Kasserine Pass right as the heavens broke loose and blew in a heavy rain. Under the protection of a large meal tent, the rain bounced off the tent and pounded into the ground around them. Carl looked over at Nyleve and said, "Looks like we made it in the nick of time. Can you imagine getting stuck in this along the dirt roads?"

Rodriguez butted in, "Better yet, we made it in time to eat the evening meal."

"Rodriguez, do you ever think about anything besides food?" Carl asked.

Nyleve was still watching the rain, "Look at it pour. I wonder if it will last several days like it usually does."

"Well, at least the wind's not blowing sand around. I think it finds particular joy in blowing it in my face... and in my food. Ain't that right, Rodriguez. Nothing quite like feeling the crunch of sand in your teeth when you're eating," Carl said with a quiet laugh.

"Don't you know? That's what the coffee's for—to wash it down," Rodriguez said as they stood in the chow line.

They got their food and found a place to sit, but the rain still blew into the tent. He looked down at his rain-splattered food and had to smile. It sure didn't look too appetizing, but it had to be better than the ration packs he'd been eating on the way over there. The kitchen tried to serve hot meals protected from the elements, but they were outside—it was impossible.

As they ate, a soldier next to them told the story of a soldier[78] who had bought fresh dates from the Arabs in a nearby town. He started with a laugh, "Going against the Army's advice of not buying fruit from street vendors, he couldn't resist the temptation to have something fresh. In his eyes, it was well worth the risk. Anyway, he cut off the ends and hungrily popped them into his mouth until he was full... saving only a few for later. The next morning, he broke the last ones into smaller bites to savor the taste. By chance, he happened to look down and noticed they were full of little white worms."

"Gross," laughed Rodriguez.

"Lesson learned... you darn well better check your food when buying it fresh," Carl added with a laugh.

As they finished eating, a few men came in and got their food. From behind, he felt a hand on his shoulder and heard a heavy Southern accent, "Well, butter my butt and call me a biscuit. We meet again."

Carl recognized that Southern drawl without even having to turn around and look up. "Gosh, it's good to see you!" he said as Bellis sat down at the same table. "You come down here with the 3rd Division replacement troops?"

"I tell ya, they got us busier than a moth in a mitten down here," Bellis said as they talked a little about how things were looking so much better in Kasserine Pass. Carl smiled. He missed hearing all of Bellis's unpredictable Southern expressions.

Suddenly, Bellis's face dropped. "Did ya hear about Big Red?"

He felt a sense of dread. Those kinds of questions didn't usually end well. "No, the only one I've run into is Lewis and that was back in November. What happened to Big Red?"

"Can't say for sure, but I reckon he went crazier than a bess bug when a buddy got shot up in front of him. They a-sayin' he shot himself," Bellis said.

"What?" Carl asked in unbelief. "Big Red Garretts?"

Bellis nodded his head.

---

[78] Based on a true story from the book of Bud Wagner: *And There Shall be Wars* (Wagner, 2000)

"I can't believe that! Darn it, my goal is to make it through the war without letting things get to me. But when bad things happen, I can feel my heart harden. I know that can't be good either. I hope I have a heart left after this thing is over," Carl said with a shake of his head.

Hardening himself was the only way he knew how to deal with it. Otherwise, the dreariness would pull him down into the depths of despair and ultimately win him over. He had already learned firsthand from the hardened strands he had gained from the landing, and he knew there were plenty more to come.

Unfortunately, it wasn't uncommon for the ones who couldn't bear it to get a one-way ticket to the crazy house, or like Garretts, end up shooting themselves. General Patton had no patience for that and let them know he expected fighters, not a bunch a pansy cowards. Obviously, Patton didn't understand the despair that stress and trauma could cause the human mind—another complicated and unpredictable outcome of war.

He would have liked to stay and talk to Bellis, but he had to meet with the accompanying company officer who had gone to meet with the commanding officers in the area. Nervously, he waited to be told his new position. He hoped he would at least keep his jeep.

The area around them was wet and war torn and it was obvious the Germans had done a number on them. The Germans were brutal—showing a whole new view to what this war was all about and how to fight it. If they saw a foxhole or trench, they'd take their advanced German tanks and crush the men below with a half turn. They were also sure to blow up any bridges and to set booby traps and mines throughout the area they were vacating. Earlier defeat in this area had been good for one thing—giving a better knowledge and understanding of what to expect from them. Nonetheless, the scene before him was intimidating. When the officers returned, one of them stepped forward as he said, "Well men, we won't be here long."

Not the news they were expecting, Carl asked, "Excuse me, sir, but what will we be doing?"

"We will be helping with cleanup. They don't really need us—only our vehicles. They have the troops they need for reinforcements. Get your stuff out of your jeeps and tanks and prepare to leave them here."

"Yes sir," they responded in unison.

"Upon leaving here, we'll meet up with the rest of the 3rd Division. If those useless Krauts[79] won't give up on their own, we'll be moving forward to make sure they don't have a choice."

That was not what they were expecting, but they realized the magnitude of what had happened here. It had become death on wheels for many unfortunate drivers. He already knew his job was precarious, but this doubly affirmed it. He hated to part with his jeep, but he pulled his belongings and turned it over.

After helping with cleanup for several days, they got up early one morning and ate a quick breakfast. For once, he'd be riding, not driving, along the bumpy, muddy roads as they bounced their way back north to meet with their moving company. This time the trip would be much faster and closer as they headed toward the 3rd Division meeting place in Ghardimaou.

They'd find their company somewhere along the way. They had heard units not too far ahead of them had plowed forward and gained occupation of Bizerte and Tunis on May 7. However, there were still pockets of the enemy lurking around Tunisia, and the goal was to clean them out and finish with the final campaign for North Africa. Now, it wasn't a matter of *if* the Axis would fall, but when.

Only days behind the main fighting action, they joined their company and he was issued a different jeep. The days were getting hotter, and as he sat in his jeep waiting to move on to Beja, the heat penetrated through his clothes and radiated through his body. Sweat formed on his brow and he thought about those juicy, fresh oranges back near Arzew.

Why did he pass those up? He craved the sweet wetness in his dry mouth. Maybe his body craved the Vitamin C, or maybe it was the hot sun shining down on him, but whatever the reason, his mouth watered at the thought. Instead, he opened the canteen he always carried with him. The warm water wasn't the sweetness he craved, but it was wet as it went down his dry throat. It was a small drink since he needed to

---

[79] An offensive term for Germans

save some for the trip—little else compared to running out of water on a hot day.

Upon arriving at Beja, the bivouac area was already set up for a quick one-night stop. With so many units on the move, it was always ready for the next group. It was nice not to have to worry about setting up, taking down, or even cooked meals for that matter. When traveling, a ration packet was the meal—it was better than nothing, but certainly not brag worthy.

Through the darkness, he could see the outline of the mountains dotted with cork oak trees. Being one of the more beautiful and greener regions of Tunisia, Beja was blessed with dark, fertile soil. At this hour, it was too late and dark to see much else. There was enough time to catch some shuteye before moving out with his company in the morning.

In what felt like only minutes, the sun began to rise. The colors brightened the sky like fresh paint covering a blank canvas. Morning calls were performed, and the convoy prepared to leave. Today, he looked forward to a short trip as a nice wind provided some relief from the heat.

Beja's natural beauty that was hidden last night boldly tried to stand out above the war torn roads and bombed out equipment sporadically littered about. Unfortunately, this serene city had involuntarily become the place of fighting between the Germans and Allies from November-February and it showed. Desperately trying to destroy its use to the Allies, the Germans freely bombed it as the Allies stood to defend it.

Looking beyond the destruction, there were many components of nature in one small area. Mountains, broken hills covered in green trees, farm fields of grain, and an occasional vineyard here and there, graced them as they drove. When they passed by a majestic field of wheat blowing in the wind, he caught the sweet scent of home for a brief moment.

It was odd how the comparison crept into his mind when he was so far away, but there was something familiar about Beja. What it was, he wasn't exactly sure, but after passing forests, fields of cactus, soil too rocky to farm, and sandy desert, Beja was different. It had a hometown kind of feeling with open and beautiful scenery, nice people, and an extremely important geographic location. Not only was it a doorway to the mountains, but also a crossroad to many important places—including their next stop twenty miles over.

It took two hours to drive the twenty miles with the convoy, but by 1000 hours, they entered into the green lowlands of Mateur. Recent evidence of fighting still lingered in the air, and it was as if the smoke hadn't even had a chance to settle yet. Death and destruction were deeply etched into every aspect of living, along with the ever-widening graveyard in the area.

He gazed upon the open area where the shelled out vehicles and crumbled buildings made it blatantly obvious the Germans had given it their all before fleeing into Bizerte. However, from there, the Germans had nowhere else to run as the Mediterranean Sea capped the area. This meant only one thing—the Allies were getting closer to meeting their final objective.

They had part of the afternoon free as they prepared to bivouac for the night. He met with a few others who were going out. Michaels and Bethem were in the group, but Rodriguez was sick and stayed back to rest.

Vendors were already set up along the narrow streets to chance a sale to the passing soldiers. There was a lot to look at as they walked. "I heard this is a common selling spot in Tunisia, but it's downright crazy so soon after such a bloody fight," Carl said.

Bethem agreed, but added, "I reckon since the bombin' stopped and new troops are movin' in, they feel as safe as they can at a time like this. Most surely they need the money."

Carl stopped at a small setup and Bethem and Michaels waited. A leather billfold was on a table and he picked it up to get a better look at it. Not usually spending a whole lot of money on himself, he debated whether to get it or not. He was impressed with the fine stitching and simple design as he held it up and looked at it—fantastic. Yes, he would spend a little money on himself, but he wouldn't use the wallet until he made it home from this war. If what the chaplain had said earlier was true… he would be going home.

The selling Arab walked over in his dusty, white robe and stood in front of him. Noticing the handcrafted, special leather created with the utmost care, he looked at the seller and slowly pronounced each word of his question, "What is this made of?"

The seller squinted his eyes as he tried to process what Carl said and repeated, "Whut et izz?"

With the different climates within Tunisia, Carl knew there were a wide variety of animals. He had seen a lot of camels, goats, wild sheep, gazelles, and of course, he had heard the coyotes. He pointed back at the special leather and answered, "Yes, what material? What animal?"

The seller nodded his head as if he understood and pointed to his skin saying, "Yanni… Go…tt."

Yanni was a word commonly said when thinking. Otherwise, the seller distinctly stressed each syllable. Putting it together, "Goat skin?" he guessed.

"Yes, go...tt zkeen," the seller repeated.

Carl smiled as he pointed to the seller, "You make?"

The seller pointed to himself as he nodded and pointed back to the billfold.

"Nice. I like. How much," he asked showing a few French francs and beginning the negotiation process.

That evening as he was putting it in his bag, he pulled out some of the rocks he had picked up along the way. North Africa had provided such an unexpected array of scenery and landscapes. In fact, not far from where they were camped that night, along the borders of the Mediterranean Sea, was the Ichkuel Lake.

Figure 25: Goat skinned billfold Carl bought while in North Africa
*Note – Carl lost one billfold to the Germans, but this one was in his bag and returned to him many years later.

Fed by rivers, it was the biggest natural lake in North Africa. Together with the wetlands, it created a haven to migrating birds—scenery he didn't imagine he'd see in North Africa. He'd been told Tunisia

Chapter 8 – CALL OF TUNISIA

was a dry, rocky desert, but that wasn't true along the coast. He could honestly say he'd seen a little bit of everything. Now it made sense why there were so many divisions and cultures in the area. Everyone wanted a part of the natural beauty and of course, any monetary value that came with it. After all, that is one of the reasons why they had landed in North Africa under French resistance and not that of the natives. Even their next destination, Ferryville[80], had been colonized by the French since 1881 and was thus named after a French minister, Jules Ferry.

That afternoon, as he drove to Ferryville with the motor convoy, the 15-mile trip took a little under an hour and a half. They arrived in the heat of the early afternoon and although it was hot, they still had a few hours to work. The fighting in the front was going so well that his company was currently at a hold. Therefore, along with their normal camp duties, they were to be on salvage duty for a few days.

Small teams were chosen, and they had to go out and salvage anything they could find that was left from the fighting. Together with Bethem and two others, they slowly drove along the twisted dirt road. Since the fighting was recent, there were all kinds of things to be found. "Stop. I see somethin'," Bethem called out.

If the sun hit right, there was a dim sparkle in the dirt. What was it? Carl could see what looked like a piece of metal or something, but it was mostly covered under the loose dirt. How Bethem had seen that hidden item, he didn't know.

Bethem returned with the object and held it out for them to see. "Just an ole pair of pliers," he said as he tossed them in the back.

"They're salvage worthy. Tools like them can always be used," Carl said as Bethem jumped back in.

"Well, at least they be American and not a total waste of time," said Bethem.

"Most likely they were used on a damaged vehicle and accidentally got left behind—it happens," Carl said.

When they rounded a large curve in the road, he saw something barely visible in the tall, green grass off in the distance. He couldn't tell

---

[80] After Ferryville went back to Arab control in 1956, the name was changed to its current name—Menzel Bourguiba.

what it was. They all got out and cautiously walked into the tall grass—keeping in mind how the Germans and Italians loved to booby-trap and set out mines anytime they could. It could be a trap.

Through hand signals, they silently communicated and kept watch on one another. He positioned his gun to fire. Enemy equipment could mean finding live soldiers who could still kill even if they were injured. Part of having a gun was being able to use it first. As they got closer, it looked like a small piece of a plane[81] that hadn't been down long. Oddly enough, the rest of the plane was nowhere to be found. After a search, no enemy soldiers or bodies appeared to be left in the area either.

They were supposed to bring back any enemy equipment, but planes especially provided wanted information about the opposition's technology and plans. It gave valued perspective to know what exactly they were fighting against. If they were lucky, maybe they'd stumble upon some documents or orders. Although Carl knew that was highly unlikely considering the rest of the plane was missing.

They had to move it quickly—before the evening hour settled in. Evening brought mosquitoes... and mosquitoes carried and spread malaria. With so much water around, there were plenty of them as they laid eggs and multiplied.

He remembered the little Atabrine[82] pill he had been given daily by the unit medic at the end of the chow line for a short time before leaving Arzew. It was a nasty little devil that was supposed to prevent malaria. It was so bad the medic stood and watched each soldier to make sure it got swallowed.

However, Carl wasn't the only one who got stomach cramps from it, and many troops even got sicker than that. Poor Rodriguez was camped on the latrine for days. Lucky for him, the Army couldn't afford sick troops, so they stopped enforcing it. Although they could wear long sleeves and pants for added protection, they also had mosquito creams and mosquito nets. But even then, it was hot and those dang mosquitoes were everywhere.

---

[81] Although Carl was on salvage duty, the stories of items they found were added to show the importance of what they were looking for and why it was important.

[82] Same as Mepacrine

Other than that, he didn't think salvage duty was so bad. In fact, it was somewhat exciting as they explored the new area with hopes of finding something great. Ichkuel Lake on the west and Bizerte Lake on the east helped provide a cool breeze for relief from the heat during the day, and it was almost cold at night. He knew it wouldn't be too much longer before the Germans had nowhere to go.

Sure enough, the next day, May 13, brought the good news—the North African Campaign officially was over. A bloody six-month fight had ended, and with it came some 275,000 enemy prisoners. The war was far from over and occasional bombs still dropped, but North Africa was finally under Allied control.

As a group of prisoners passed by him, he couldn't help but notice the difference between the captured Italians and Germans. Viewed as an obvious sign of weakness, the Germans walked with their heads down and defeat on their face. In stark contrast, the Italians carried on and didn't appear to be much offended over the capture. A thought ran through his mind, *Don't get captured, and if you do, don't let it be the Germans who capture you.* He could tell what the difference would be. With a shudder, he dispelled the thought as his company awaited orders to move.

Operation complete, they helped with cleanup for two days and prepared to drive for more training outside Philippeville—150 miles back in Algeria. In his jeep, he could already feel the air warming up, and it was only 0800 hours. By noon, the suffocating heat was relentless and made driving with the windshield down miserable as thick, hot air made it hard to breathe. On a short rest, he mentioned to Bethem, "Has the thought of colder times crossed your mind?"

Bethem's smile deepened, "Sure... at least 'til evenin'."

"Don't you boys be complaining," Rodriguez's voice broke in, "You know we're headed to Philippeville to do some intense training for mountain warfare. Then you'll be wishing for the heat again."

"I reckon that's right," Bethem said, "but why's it gotta be so difficult—hot, cold, wind, rain, sand, and now there's goin' to be snow throwed in there too."

"Let's hope we make it through before winter. That gives us a few months," Carl said as they prepared to leave again.

They drove into the night and made it to their training point. From the late hour of arrival, it looked like it was going to be a night to sleep under the stars. In the light of the moon, the area was checked. Rodriguez walked by his jeep and said, "Good news. We didn't see fresh animal droppings in the area and that's always a good sign for us sleeping out in the open with only a light blanket."

He could hear the jealousy in Rodriguez's voice, but he didn't feel bad. He gave up a lot of meals and sleep as a driver, and he didn't feel guilty to enjoy the benefits that came with it. "Well, Rodriguez, just be glad it's not raining," he said as he rested back in his jeep.

The dark night sky was clear, and there were a million tiny stars shining above them. Even with the six-hour time difference, a connection was created as the same stars shone through the distance over what he missed most—home. It was okay to think about home, but he had to be careful. It was way too easy to get slowly caught in the sticky web of depression if he let his thoughts go too far. Sleep was the best way to clear the mind and remain strong, and he was grateful his mind and body hadn't given in.

Setup began early in the morning as a training schedule was implemented. However, only a week into getting a routine solidified, there came an order to move fifteen miles over near Lannoy. Bethem had his things ready to load and passed by him saying, "Have ya heard why we leavin' so soon?"

"Just that General Truscott decided it wasn't meeting the training objectives for mountainous terrain here," Carl answered.

If General Truscott wasn't satisfied, they could leave as quickly as they had arrived. The time was passing by fast and training was kicked into high gear for everyone. Even as a driver, he had to be prepared for everything.

Removing his sweat-drenched socks after a hard, hot day of training, Carl said, "Can't believe it's already June."

"This training is honestly insane," Michaels said, rubbing his arm. "Every day I don't think I'll make it through it in the boiling heat, only to start over again the next day."

He noticed how Michaels winced in pain as he spoke. "What happened to you?" he asked with a nod of the head.

Michaels looked up. "Nothing major. Only a bruised up arm."

After the password incident, Michaels appeared to calm down a bit. Maybe the excitement had worn off, or maybe he had seen one too many tragedies to remain spoiled and carefree. Whatever it was, he was different.

One thing for sure was that the trainings were so intense they were wearing on everyone. After three exhausting weeks near Lannoy, the awaited announcement arrived for intense landing drills. This meant packing up and traveling back to Ferryville for practice in the bay. Nobody complained much, even with the long, all day trip back. A change of training schedule was a welcomed thought for most.

However, the amphibious trainings were equally as intense and direct as he drove his jeep onto a flat-bottomed LCT (Landing craft, tank) that looked a lot like a small floating flatcar. A few tanks from his company were with him and Nyleve was in one of them. Within hours, they had their vehicles secured and were cutting through the waters of the Mediterranean to unknown locations to practice beaching exercises and skills that had plagued them on the first landing. They had to stay one-step ahead—and this time they had some time and experience to do it.

Several nights, as the sun set behind the wall of sea, they slept onboard out in the bay. Never knowing what to expect, the sound of enemy aircraft always made his heart jump. Like hungry vultures, he could see the enemy as they circled above watching for gatherings—trying to find the right time to let their bombs loose and get the most out of it. Nevertheless, the Allies were also watching, and night after night, a couple more enemy planes were knocked out of the sky.

By the end of June, there were fewer bombings, but something bigger was brewing. If he and the others could tell, he was sure the enemy could too. One night, Nyleve told him, "I swear, this is it—we'll be landing on enemy territory soon."

"We woulda been briefed by now," Carl argued, "I know a first-class soldier don't find out first, but surely they woulda told us something."

Later that night, on June 26, they were told they would be getting in landing positions. Nyleve looked at him, "I told you."

137

He couldn't believe it. Maybe they weren't going to get briefed this time. The moving craft cut through the sea and then came to a stop. Silence followed—perfect silence that only happens on a dark night right before an attack. Was this the beginning of the next operation?

It certainly appeared to be as they were told the landing time was set for 0300 hours. In the darkness, they removed the chains that held the vehicles in place and anxiously awaited the call to move forward. The time ticked by... an hour had passed and still they waited. What was taking so long? Then it was 0415 hours and nothing was happening. If there was one thing he hated, it was standing around waiting with nothing to do.

Fifteen minutes later, when his impatience was getting to the boiling point, they were told to go to shore. The ramp door to the LCT dropped down and they drove into the shallow water. They started moving inland and looked for higher ground. The landscape had a familiarity to it and he was pretty sure they were still in Africa. It had only been a dry run.

"How'd you like that dress rehearsal?" he asked Nyleve when he saw him next.

"So you were right, Good. But that only means the real deal is almost here," Nyleve said as they met up with the rest of the company.

That was obvious, but now they needed to make it the ten miles back to Ferryville. After a few minor problems, they made it to camp that evening. Exhausted, he sat down and got ready for a couple hours of sleep. His body slightly jumped as he relaxed enough to enter the silence of his dreams. Moments later, the sound of planes broke through the night.

Startled and dazed, his heart heavily pounded in his chest as he jumped up and ran to a prepared foxhole nearby. Heat still penetrated through the ground from the afternoon sun and added to the discomfort he felt from the sudden rush. He closed his eyes and took a deep breath to stop his spinning head. He thought he should be used to this by now—it had been happening for weeks. When would they stop?

Annoyed, he waited for them to pass. The addition of 1,000 soldiers in the area made the enemy especially interested in making their presence known. Luckily, they didn't usually cause much damage before being spotted and fired upon, and soon it was safe to go back to bed.

Lying back down, he took comfort in knowing large groups of Allied bombers flew over daily on their way to bomb the Axis (in and around Italy) and had been since May. That thought made the night annoyance manageable. In fact, any thought that put the Axis in an uncomfortable or dangerous situation was a good thought... then maybe this war would finally end.

For the next few days, they continued with usual camp duties. Besides physical conditioning and the Truscott Trot, the intense training was starting to die down—another sign the time was approaching. On the upside to that, there were fewer hours in the blistery heat and more down time. They knew it wouldn't last long, but it was too hot to enjoy the break much. Rodriguez put it best when he said, "It's too hot to even talk or move if you don't have to."

Everyone silently agreed.

About that time, word came that General Patton was going around visiting units. Nobody ever knew what to expect as Patton fiercely laced his speeches with profanities and obscenities to preach the call of duty along with a campaign of hate for the Axis. It was what made him who he was—bright and colorful. It also landed him and his temper of fire in trouble at times. Yet he rarely apologized—strongly believing if he chewed them out, they'd remember it. As a professional in the art of war, he could get away with it—most of the time... and he knew it. In his mind, he was toughening them up with his language.

In fact, certain things Carl had heard from General Patton still resounded boldly through his mind. After reminding them they were trained and picked for the 3rd Division, Patton said something he would never forget. "This time we're playing for keeps. If you want to go home, you damn sure be first!"

It ran through his mind like a hot blade searing a scar across his flesh. The time to be first was quickly approaching, and he was well on his way to take the test—again. General Patton had the name of "Ole Blood and Guts" for a reason and everybody knew how he worked— he would send as many men as it took as long as the job got done and he was first in doing it.

He didn't deny that General Patton sure knew how to get things going and he admired him for that, but somehow he hated him just as much. Although he didn't personally end up hearing Patton as he went through, he heard the most colorful parts from others. Based on what he heard, Ole Blood and Guts continued to live up to his reputation.

The hot sun set behind the olive trees as a few more days passed, and then they moved eleven miles from Bizerte. Bizerte was a port and that meant they were closer to loading. Along with the anticipation, a countdown began with the month of July.

July 4th was celebrated with unit reviews and a speech to the whole 3rd Division. As General Truscott's voice boomed through a loudspeaker system, Carl felt a wave of American pride as General Truscott reminded them who they were and why they were there. When General Truscott ended his speech, he said, "You are going to meet the 'Boche'[83]! Carve your name in his face!"

A temporary high filled the area and an aggressive spirit of combat took root. Carl knew he was there fighting for the continued freedom of his family, friends, and future, and it felt good. He could have stayed home, but he had chosen to fight. Not only that, but the day before he had made it to his 24th birthday.

Birthdays usually were just another day, but he was glad he had made it another year in these conditions. Michaels had asked him if he was going out on a pass to the closest town. In other words, he wanted to know if he was going to celebrate with a drink or find a woman for a few hours. He told Michaels he wasn't interested in that. He wasn't a drinker by choice, and he had made a promise to his fiancé he planned to keep. Apparently, Michaels didn't understand that and had shaken his head saying, "You're the one missing out."

The way he saw it, Michaels was the one missing out. He may not have lots of money or a polished last name, but he had integrity—that's what made him stand out. He was sure it didn't matter to most, but it was what he depended on to make it through the war.

General Truscott's words were still fresh in his head when the next morning, July 5, he moved into Porto Farina with his company.

---

[83] Derogatory slang for a German soldier

Chapter 8 – CALL OF TUNISIA

Anxious and ready, he still didn't know exactly where they were headed. Sicily was still high on the rumor list, but there were other likely possibilities such as Sardinia[84]. Either place would be fought with the hope of knocking Italy out of the war once and for all. Anywhere under Axis control in the Mediterranean Sea was worth considering and not only included Sicily and Sardinia, but also Greece, Italy, Corsica, and all of France.

It wouldn't be long before they found out. From the information they were given so far, there would be a trip on the Mediterranean Sea for sure. Other than that, all he knew from the sand table model they were shown was that they were landing on a beach that had guns, German pillboxes[85], mines, and lots of booby traps.

Figure 26: Map that shows Tunisia, Sicily, Sardinia, Greece, Italy, Corsica, and France (PAT public domain maps)

With that information, *Operation Husky* was about to begin. The time had come to split up and load as part of General Patton's Seventh Army—handling the left flank of the operation. Although Patton wasn't happy being put to protect and move behind General

---

[84] The second largest island in the Mediterranean Sea
[85] A small cement dug-in guard post with openings to fire weapons that usually camouflage with the surroundings

Montgomery's British 8th Army during this operation, it was true the 8th Army had more experience.

Placed in the Western Attack Forces for another complicated three-pronged attack, Carl was in General Truscott's JOSS Force. On the Navy's side, Admiral Conolly was the one responsible for making sure the 25,000 troops in the JOSS Force got to their designated landings. However, there was a serious lack of transport ships for their force.

Unfazed, Admiral Conolly was confident he could get the JOSS Force landed by combining infantry and vehicle travel with what they had available—shore-to-shore landing crafts[86]. The landing craft hadn't been tested on a large-scale landing before, but he had forty 158-foot LCIs[87] (capable of carrying 200 troops), thirty-six 328-foot converted LSTs[88] (capable of carrying 500 troops), and the LCTs[89] for more vehicles and their drivers—enough to get everyone to shore. LCTs could also be used to carry cargo, missiles, and other supplies. If Admiral Conolly could pull it off using the landing craft, it would be the first shore-to-shore operation for the U.S. in real war conditions. Overall, with the other vessels[90] in his force, he had 276 vessels with the *Biscayne* as his flagship.

As the infantry from his company got into a LCI, Carl drove his jeep onto a LCT. It was designed to hold 150 tons—enough to carry four 75mm tanks (about thirty-five tons each) along with his jeep chained to its open, flat surface. Once again, Nyleve was in his group with his tank and crew.

Once they had secured everything in place with chains crisscrossing under the vehicles from on side to the other, Carl looked over at Nyleve. "Here's to a successful landing."

"Well, the dry run went well on these things, so let's hope we'll make it to wherever it is we're going," Nyleve answered back with a nervous shrug.

---

[86] Meaning the same craft would be used from the departing shore to the arriving shore
[87] LCI – landing craft, infantry
[88] LST – landing ship, tank
[89] LCT – landing craft, tank
[90] This includes submarine chasers, minesweepers, and screening destroyers

Even with the LCT crew of thirteen (one officer and twelve enlisted men), they were a small group under forty. The crew stayed in the small quarters along the side of the craft, but he and his group stayed with their vehicles on the topside of the craft. It sounded better than fighting for a hot, crowded place to sleep in one of the swinging, stacked hammocks in one of the overcrowded carriers for this trip.

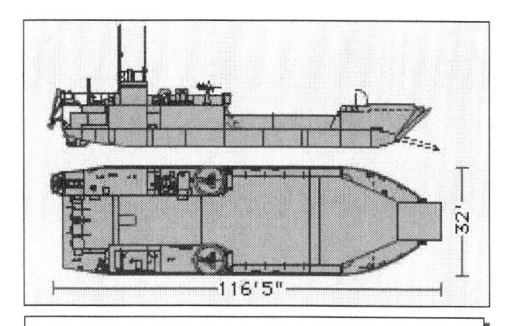

Figure 27: LCT(Fox, 2014)

The craft was designed so it could be used as a connecting ramp on the bigger and deeper LSTs, and it was a little unnerving being out on the open sea since the bombing hadn't completely stopped. He certainly didn't expect it to stop now, especially as all the crafts gathered on the water. It wouldn't take long before the enemy noticed them and took advantage of getting them all in one place.

Startled, but not surprised, it actually wasn't long before he heard the sound of planes roar overhead in the still darkness. They had only been onboard one night, but in seconds, every ship, transport, and any type of gun support jumped into action as prepared spotlights around the water's edge brightened the night sky into day. German targets were illuminated and shot down with ease.

Onboard, he saw the firepower and glowing tracer bullets as they buzzed upward. It looked like the Fourth of July all over again. It was a relief when the Germans were caught off guard by the sudden and unexpected display of firepower and hurried on. The enemy left with the loss of quite a few planes, but hadn't caused any major damage.

The night returned to normal, but an electrifying energy was left to buzz through the units. This was the beginning of what was about to come. Wherever they were headed, there would be enemies calmly waiting for them… waiting to kill them if they got the chance. There was no doubt about that!

143

Chapter 9

EX AFRICA SEMPER ALIQUID NOVI

THE ANCIENT MOTTO of *Ex Africa semper aliquid novi*—"Something new is always coming out of Africa" could not be truer as the sky lit up with the colors of daybreak on July 7, and the new joint operation code-named *Operation Husky* was under way. In staggered layers and separate routes, they moved out of Bizerte with the purpose of deceiving the enemy. "Here we go," Carl said as they sat out on the deck of the LCT and watched the craft move around them.

"Can't wait to see where we're going," Nyleve added.

"I'm not betting, but if I was, I'd bet on Sicily," Carl said as a few of the men started a bet between Sicily and Sardinia.

Sure enough, as soon as land was out of sight that morning, the officer began sharing information and maps with them. When the booklets were handed out, he looked down at the front title—*A Soldier's Guide to Sicily*. The few who had bet for Sicily widely smiled and patted the losers on the back. He looked over at Nyleve, I would've won some money on that one.

"Sicily? Are you kidding me? Isn't that kinda obvious. They're gonna sit on the beach and shoot us as we come in!" someone muttered.

Although he hadn't said it aloud, those were some of the same thoughts running through his head. How in the living Earth could they pull it off? How would they

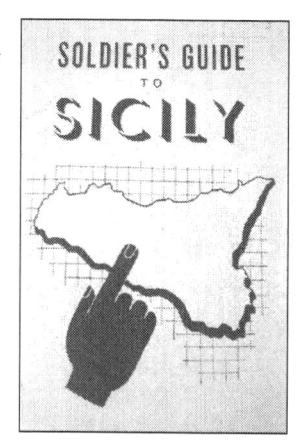

Chapter 9 – Ex Africa Semper Aliquid Novi

convince Hitler not to have thousands of German troops ready and waiting for them by the water's edge?

The officer's next words caught his attention, "He who controls Sicily, controls the Mediterranean…"

If that were true, then the rest would follow. The Axis had played havoc on Allied supplies passing through the Mediterranean long enough, and it was time to show them a thing or two—again. The Allies were tired of going 12,000 miles around the Cape of Good Hope to get supplies to the troops. It would also allow access to new fleet bases in the Mediterranean and allow bombers closer to Italy.

Along with the advantages on gaining control of the Mediterranean, the control of Sicily would isolate it from the rest of Europe and keep German troops from crossing into Italy from Messina. General Patton had made it a personal goal to do whatever it took to capture important airfields and reach Messina first—before the British 8th Army. In a three-mile stretch, Messina dominated the Strait to Italy and provided a quick and easy getaway for enemy troops. If they got there fast enough, they would capture enemy troops and equipment before they had time to escape. The hope was all of that together would deliver a second punch to the throat and prevent Italy from being an Axis player.

Of course, there was no real way of knowing what to expect until they landed, but he knew that as a soldier he had to trust in the planning and go forward. No matter what it took, he was ready to help knock the enemy out of position. He was sure there were plenty more reasons why Sicily was chosen. Even if he didn't know all the details, he'd do his job. There was no room for fear—for fear was the exact opposite of faith, and he knew he was going to need all of his faith.

The briefing ended for the morning and the warm air blew across the deck. Left to flip through the booklet on their own, Carl looked at the back page where some common phrases were found. Since the pronunciation of words in Sicily varied from words in standard Italian, the list included words and phrases that could be understood by either place. He could hear Nyleve trying to read a few phrases from the written words, "Good Evening… Boo-on-ah say-rah… *Buona Sera*, Please… Pray-go… *Prego*, I do not understand… non ka-pis-koh… *non capisco*."

It sounded funny to Carl as he looked at how the pronunciation was broken out into English. They were simple phrases, but he was sure they were being completely butchered by heavy American accents. It was all new and foreign to him, and he hoped he wouldn't find himself in a position where he needed it for survival.

Who would have guessed he would be here on the edge of Europe trying to remember words in another language—it hadn't occurred to him as an American cowboy that he would ever need it. He decided it wouldn't hurt to try to remember a few words as he looked down at the strangeness in front of him. *Bread might be a good one to know*, he thought as he looked at the words, "Bread... Pah-nay... Páne."

He sat with a few other guys in the shadow of a tank that provided shade from the glaring sun. Even then, he felt the sweat rolling down his back. "It's too danged hot out here!" he said as he used his booklet as a fan.

Nyleve was still reading the booklet and randomly made comments, "Did you read the note on the first page?" he asked the group. "Interesting information there."

These little handbooks were helpful in explaining what they were getting into and how to react with the people. He flipped back to the front and read the message:

> We are about to engage in the second phase of the operations which began with the invasion of North Africa.
>
> We have defeated the enemies' forces on the South shore of the Mediterranean and captured his army intact.
>
> The French in North Africa, for whom the yoke of Axis domination has been lifted, are now our loyal allies.
>
> However, this is NOT enough. Our untiring pressure on the enemy must be maintained, and as this book falls into your hands we are about to pursue the invasion and occupation of enemy territory.
>
> The successful conclusion of these operations will NOT only strike closer to the heart of the Axis, but also will remove the last threat to the free sea lanes of the Mediterranean.

Chapter 9 – Ex Africa Semper Aliquid Novi

> Remember that this time it is indeed enemy territory which we are attacking, and as such we must expect extremely difficult fighting.
>
> But we have learned to work smoothly alongside one another as a team, and many of you who will be the first ranks of this force know full well the power of our Allied air and naval forces and the real meaning of air and naval superiority.
>
> The task is difficult but your skill, courage, and devotion to duty will be successful in driving our enemies closer to disaster and leading us towards victory and the liberation of Europe and Asia.
>
> –Dwight D. Eisenhower, General, U.S. Army, C.-in-C.

"You're right, Nyleve. That does explain a lot of unanswered questions," Carl agreed.

"Did you see the section under *Hygiene and Health*?" one of the others named Seth Dugley asked.

"Which part?" Nyleve asked. "The part that said the insanitary condition of the Island is one of its best defenses against an invader and casualties from disease could well be higher than those caused in the field, or the part that listed the preventive measures for catching the top diseases?"

Dugley laughed, "Either, I guess. Doesn't sound too attractive."

"That's what I thought. It looks like Sicily is going be hot, dirty, and disease-filled," Carl added.

"I'm sure it depends where we're at, but that's how it sounds. They make it sound like nobody would *want* to live there. I wonder what keeps them in those parts," Dugley said.

"Imagine they're too darn poor to leave, or they don't know better places exist in the world," Nyleve said.

Looking back at the booklet, Carl said, "I don't know, but it won't be long before we find out."

Based on what they had read, they wouldn't have guessed Sicily was actually full of strong and resistant fighters who had been defending their country from conquer for centuries. The Sicilians were the best Italian fighters by reputation. Only a history buff would have known the Greeks, Carthaginians, Romans, Byzantines, Saracens, Normans, Angevins, and Spaniards had each taken their turn in ruling this island off of Italy and had taken years in gaining control.

Great Britain's Prime Minister, Winston Churchill, knew that, but not many others. Churchill knew Sicily would not be the "soft underbelly" of the Axis as some thought. Add twelve airfields and difficult mountainous terrain into the mix, and Sicily was definitely defensible.

However, there was hope that all the Allied bombings that had been plaguing Sicily since May had taken its toll on the general public morale. If German support in the area was low and the people were already feeling tired and defeated from the bombings, the Allies could have a much-needed advantage. It also helped that although the Sicilians were excellent fighters, they were not good Fascists. Most of them had a strong dislike for the war and hated the Germans—feeling like they were a sacrifice to an alien power. What this meant for the Allies would soon be discovered. Would the Sicilians fight under German power?

It remained an unanswered question as the afternoon wore on. The bright sun sparkled and reflected on the water as their thoughts and conversations were interrupted by a relayed message from the Royal Navy's Admiral Cunningham[91]. They stopped talking and listened:

> We are about to embark on the most momentous enterprise of the war—striking for the first time at the enemy in his own land.
>
> Success means the opening of the "Second Front" with all that it implies, and the first move toward the rapid and decisive defeat of our enemies.
>
> Our object is clear and our primary duty is to place this vast expedition ashore in the minimum time and subsequently to maintain our military and air forces as they drive relentlessly forward into enemy territory.

---

[91] British supreme naval commander

In the light of this duty, great risks must be and are to be accepted. The safety of our own ships and all distracting considerations are to be relegated to second place, or disregarded as the accomplishment of our primary duty may require.

On every commanding officer, officer and rating rests the individual and personal duty of ensuring that no flinching in determination or failure of effort on his own part will hamper this great enterprise.

I rest confident in the resolution, skill and endurance of you all to whom this momentous enterprise is entrusted[92].

All was quiet for a few minutes afterward as everyone processed Cunningham's inspirational words. The reality of what was happening soaked in. Although this trip was nothing compared to the voyage to North Africa, the mounting tension was the same. They were on their way to go ashore and fight the enemy. It was their duty!

The evening sun faded along with the hour and Carl noticed the odd color of the sky. "What the..." he muttered as he stood up and walked to the side of the craft where Dugley was already standing. Nyleve joined them. "Have you ever saw such a bright sky like that before?" he asked them

"Never in my life!" Nyleve said in awe.

"My gosh, it's the deepest blood red!" Carl said without looking away.

"Sure hope it's not a sign," Dugley replied as a passing crewmember joined them in looking.

The crewmember looked at the sky and then looked over at them, "You know what the *Sailors' Guide for the Mediterranean* says about that?"

"No idea," Carl answered. "I've never saw anything like it."

In monotone, the crewmember stared at the sky and continued, "Says if the western horizon is red at sunset or misty at dawn, strong

---

[92] (Morison, 1959)

winds are comin' our way." Then as he walked away, he looked back and added, "Looks like we're gonna feel the wrath of God soon."

That night Carl kicked up his boot-clad feet and tried to get comfortable in the seat of his jeep. Thoughts about what the crewmember had said filled his mind as he waited for the winds to start blowing. These LCTs had not been tested for a trip like this, let alone in a strong storm out in the middle of the open sea. *Would they even hold*, he wondered as he fell asleep.

Unconsciously waiting to be awakened by the storm, his dreams were rapid and dark as he was pulled in and out of a deep sleep throughout the rest of the night—but the storm didn't come. At the light of dawn, July 9, it was dark and murky—the second sign the storm was still brewing in the heavens above. So far, the wind wasn't too bad. If they could get through the day, they would be in landing positions in less than 24 hours. Would the storm hold off that long?

A sudden rush of cool air blew over the deck where he was sitting with the other members of his company. He unexpectedly shivered and rubbed his arms saying, "That felt good, but can't help but think a sudden cold front can't be a good sign right now."

His words were pushed away by the onset of heavy winds and the sudden chill brought with them. The afternoon crewmembers quickly traded duties with the morning crew as the wind picked up to nearly a gale. He didn't know much about being on the Mediterranean, but he knew going from a 3-force wind to a 7-force wind so quickly could not be a good thing as a fury of wind swept across the open deck.

Hunkered down in his jeep with a life jacket in case he was swept out to sea, he dreaded the rough ride he knew was coming. Vaguely, he thought he heard a voice yelling into the blowing wind. He looked out and saw a crewmember haphazardly waving his arms by the crew's quarters. It sounded like the crewmember was yelling something about getting to their quarters.

He quickly got out of his jeep. The heavy wind pushed at him with long, invisible hands as he fought to stand upright. Head down, he moved toward the door. Out of the corner of his eye, he saw a wave grow over 15 feet high. He was a tiny speck in an angry, unforgiving mass of blue swirls, like paint thrown on a canvas with an insignificant

Chapter 9 – Ex Africa Semper Aliquid Novi

spot randomly lost in the middle. He was an ant ready to be put out of his earthly misery in the depths of the sea.

If he wanted to survive the storm, he had to get to the crew's protected quarters now. It wasn't far, but he struggled to jog against the wind and blowing water as the LCT dropped through the waves. Hunched down, he grabbed whatever was closest so he could keep moving forward.

This craft did not cut through the waves, but instead, chugged its way up and over each one and speedily dropped down the other side like a timed roller coaster. If he didn't know better, he would have thought the heavens were angry about the attack plan. The timing was too precise.

In the small, protected quarters, he was glad to see the others were already there. Scattered shards of hope that the storm would settle down before dusk remained, but after being out in it, he wasn't so sure. He didn't bother voicing his opinion to the experienced seamen though. They knew this weather better than he did.

Instead, he tried to relax in the small quarters, but it was like working with prickly hay while wearing short sleeves, shorts, and no gloves—uncomfortable. Although there wasn't the threat of finding a rattlesnake hidden in the hay, the threat of being blown through the sea was far scarier than any ole rattlesnake, or even a rattlesnake pit for that matter. He knew how to deal with those kinds of problems. Here… it didn't matter what he did or wore—he was completely at the mercy of the sea.

Sitting on the wet floor, he wrung the water out of his shirt and asked Nyleve, "Is this going to happen before every single landing?"

"Oh, there will be more I'm sure. Guess it's the new trend," Nyleve answered.

Oddly enough, even with everything going on, a low rumble in his stomach made him aware of the evening hour. The quarters had a small place to cook a meal, but it was Army rations for them. He missed eating good, home-cooked meals.

The night wore on and the storm only intensified. Tossed through the waves like a toy boat, it felt like the LCT was standing on both ends at the same time as it dipped over the wave's crest and slapped into the

151

trough below. He wasn't surprised when he heard two crewmembers discussing the chance of delay.

"There's no news of delaying the assault, but then again, it would be hard to get the message if there were," one of them said.

The other shrugged. "That means we will be moving forward as planned."

"It worked the first time, but can we be that lucky twice?"

"Let's hope. I guess we keep pushing through the stormy waters with a hope of calm seas by the time we reach the landing beaches."

"It's more the challenge of staying on track and steering through the storm in this LCT."

"Yeah, I wonder if the admirals are taking these small craft into consideration since they're on a ship. We're by far the smallest[93] craft out here."

"Moving at less than two and a half knots[94] isn't helping any in this storm. I mean, in good weather we can any go a max of eight knots[95]. We're just crawling."

They both agreed, and the conversation died down as the darkened sky continued to drop rain through the wind. Suddenly, a loud noise sounded from outside the quarters. "What the devil was that?" Carl asked.

Obviously, by the following stir he wasn't the only one who heard it. It wasn't but a few minutes later when a rain soaked crewmember came back to the quarters cussing as he yelled out, "We need help! A chain broke loose!"

Carl stood up to help. "What chain?" he asked, but his words vanished into the commotion as they went toward the open deck.

"We got to get out there and secure that tank before it shifts everything off balance and we all drown!" he heard someone yell back at them.

A few choice words flew through the area as the situation was assessed. Of course, the chain needing fixed was on the other side

---

[93]   112-feet
[94]   2.9 mph
[95]   9.2 mph

Chapter 9 - Ex Africa Semper Aliquid Novi

toward the end. This was the last thing they needed as the storm continued to drop them through the water. Time was of the essence.

"Create a human chain and get 'er fixed!" someone yelled out.

One Army officer had already been swept off the deck of another ship, but fortunately for him, he was picked up four ships later. However, the chances of that happening again were bleak—whoever got swept off deck this time was sure to drown.

"How?" someone asked. "The person in front will need both hands to reconnect the chain."

"Crawl," came the reply. "Hold onto the legs of the man in front of you and no matter what happens, don't let go!"

They tightly held on to one another as they slid forward on the rain soaked deck. Heavy rain pelted his face and ran into his eyes, but he could only blink away the wetness. Dugley's large hands tightly pressed around his ankles. At that moment, he was glad Dugley was a big guy and could hold on tight—especially when a high wind blew the carrier down a crested wave and slapped it into the water. As they dropped, they flattened out and held on tightly as the force shifted them onto their sides. Thankfully, nobody lost grip and the carrier didn't shift the tank enough to cause more of a problem.

He knew what would happen if the wind blew just right. Finally, they began to inch back to the door that led to the protected quarters. Once inside, he took a deep breath as the adrenaline rush subsided. There was still no news about a delay, and he sure hoped the storm would subside by early morning like expected. Only time would tell.

It was hard to guess the evening hour with the darkened sky, but he knew it had to be getting late. Not expecting much sleep for the night, he wished he could be in his jeep where he could have some space for himself. *Oh well*, he thought, *it was only a matter of hours before landing anyway.*

Fury spewed from the sea like a heaving monster as they divided into three separate forces west of the Mediterranean island, Gozo. His force was headed toward the Gulf of Gela where areas of rocky cliffs coarsely contrasted the sandy beaches. Located near the center of the south coast at the mouth of the Salso River, their landing beach was in Licata, Sicily.

The tick of the clock transformed the moments after midnight into July 10, 1943—the date picked for attack because of the particular phase of the waxing moon. It provided a shining moon for the midnight airdrops, yet a darkened sky a few hours later for ground forces to secure beachheads before daybreak. Although the seas were still rough, the storm was dying down. Recovering from lost time in the storm, the LCTs took a shorter route than planned. It worked, and with only seconds to spare, they made it to their beaches along with twenty other LCTs from their convoy.

Echoes boomed across the early morning, and he could hear the sounds of war on the beach. Memories of his first landing flooded his mind. Suddenly, they were stopped by the commander of the Red Beach naval force and told to wait.

Wait for what, he wondered. He didn't know they were trying to get the fire on the beach silenced so they didn't risk losing the Regimental Combat Team's (RCT) supporting armor and artillery carried on some of the LCTs. However, four LCTs ignored or completely missed the command as they moved in. His group stayed put and waited as instructed.

Still wet from last night's rain, he waited in his jeep as the dark skies lightened. Water slapped at the short-sided craft, but only one sound penetrated through the passing minutes—the sound of his heart pounding loudly in his chest. It was nerve-racking to enter a war zone, and General Patton would go on to say, "Every man is scared in his first battle. If he says he's not, he's a liar... The real hero is the man who fights even though he is scared."

This wasn't his first battle, but few things in life compared to the feeling of getting ready for an invasion and having no idea of what to expect. It felt unreal knowing the landing beaches were ahead. Like all amphibious landings, it was all or nothing and that was a scary thought. One of two things was about to happen... a triumphant win... or a miserable loss.

Coastal plains led to the hilly, scalloped mountain wall in the distance, and they would be trapped in an unforgiving position if the enemy was prepared and waiting. However, to their advantage,

Allied ships[96] covered nearly a third of the shores of Sicily. It was sure to appear even more daunting to the Sicilians as the first threads of golden light illuminated exactly how many of them there were.

As the time passed, there was nothing to do but wait and find out. Anxious and wet from the night's activities, he prepared to get off the LCT and drive into the water as soon as the hinged ramp lowered. False beaches[97] were a concern, but he hoped for a smooth exit from the craft precisely designed to give him that. There was no way he was going to lose another jeep in landing.

With the help of the destroyer, *Buck*, and the cruiser, *Brooklyn*, the firing on the beach slackened enough to start moving in. By 0722 hours, the sun burnt off the morning haze, and Admiral Conolly ordered them to beach no matter the cost. The ramp dropped and he drove down it into a thick smoke screen created to help conceal the landing.

His tires hit the soft, sandy beach—so far, so good. Luckily, the rocky ridges and steep-walled ravines hadn't provided the excellent defense it could have as he quickly met up with his company. Ready to move forward by 0900 hours, they established a defensive line on the arc of the hills bordering the western side of the Licata plain, and assured the protection of the beachhead's left flank. An hour and a half later, the 7th RCT's assigned objectives were secured, and they had made it to the next phase a lot easier than he had expected.

However, preparing his jeep, he knew the lack of communication between batteries would keep him running day and night for the next several weeks. Things were rapidly moving along and by that evening, an eight-by-fifteen-mile beach was secured. Although the Sicilians hadn't handed it over to them, the lack of Germans in the area made it easier. Where were they? There had to be more to it than he knew.

And there was—like British *Operation Mincemeat*. Pulled off in amazing detail, the British used a corpse kept in cold storage to help divert enemy troops to other areas. The corpse[98], renamed Major

---

[96] *Operation Husky* involved over 3,000 vessels total
[97] Created from surf breaking on the beach with a tideless sea
[98] Also known as the 'Man Who Never Was'

William Martin of the Royal Marines, was placed off the coast of Spain[99] in what appeared to be an airplane accident. "Major Martin" had fake secret documents planted on him to make it look like the Allied attack would be at Peloponnesus[100] and Sardinia. When Hitler immediately received the information, he appeared to be completely deceived and sent troops and materials to Peloponnesus, a Panzer division to Sardinia, installed coastal batteries along the Greek coast, diverted German motor minesweepers and torpedo boats from Sicily to Greece, and instructed Kesselring that Sardinia and Peloponnesus were to be first priority.

Prime Minister Churchill had said, "Anyone but a bloody fool would know it was Sicily," and was surprised to receive a message stating, "Mincemeat swallowed, rod, line and sinker."

However, not everyone was tricked by the operation—Italian admirals and German generals, including Kesselring, still expected a possible attack on Sicily. Kesselring sent the Hermann Goering Panzer Division across the Strait of Messina in late June. Nevertheless, it wasn't enough and the Allies had moved in and plowed strong and hard through any resistance that remained on the island.

The next day, July 11, supplies and reinforcements were pouring in as Carl moved through the heat with his company. Joining with the 7th Infantry, they sent the enemy fleeing toward Agrigento as they captured Palma di Montechiaro. With a moment to rest, he looked around him at the brown, dusty hills.

Bethem came by and asked, "Did ya see when we passed them threshin' floors with the harvested summer wheat and barley?"

"Sure did. Looked like the loose sheaves were thrown on the threshing floor to have the grain trodden out by the horses and donkeys. But did you notice it was harvested by hand with sickles? It looks like their agriculture is a hundred years behind ours," Carl added in surprise.

"It sure is somethin' different," Bethem agreed.

---

[99] Although Spain played neutral for the most part, they still favored the Axis and had Axis agents there
[100] A large peninsula in southern Greece that is separated by the Gulf of Corinth

Chapter 9 – Ex Africa Semper Aliquid Novi

"You know what's interesting?" Rodriguez asked without waiting for an answer. "The whole lack of color in general. It sure is refreshing when a sudden vineyard of forming grapes, a gray-green olive grove, or a deep-green almond orchard helps break up the dullness."

"That's the artist in you speaking," Carl joked, although he had noticed it also. Even behind the thick, stonewalls that protected the cities along the coast, the closely built clusters of gray, stone houses sat colorless with their gray, tiled roofs.

"I don't know much about color, y'all, but it's hot as blazes out here!" Bethem exclaimed as Carl prepared to leave on a run.

There was no doubt that… it was hot—scorching hot! As he drove an officer along the narrow, cobblestone street of a recently captured town, sweat rolled down his face when he stopped to wait for a heavy-laden donkey as it walked with its oversized load. He wondered how anyone could work outside in such intense heat. The idea of stopping for a long afternoon break or nap suddenly began to make sense.

When he drove by a town fountain, the officer told him to stop. They got out of the jeep and Carl stood to the side to wait for a few Sicilian women as they filled their earthen water jars. For the most part, the general population was glad they were there to relieve them from the Germans. He knew they were mostly friendly, so he smiled, but couldn't remember anything to say. One of the women looked at him and said something, but he had no idea what. She slightly smiled before turning to walk away, and he was left to wonder.

Had she said something about the water? He had read two-fifths of Sicily did not have a drinking water supply and all water from natural sources had to be treated—even if the locals could drink it. This water was from a town fountain, but it still made him a little uncomfortable. Then again, it had to be better than not having any water at all.

Summer had dried up most of the rivers, and he wondered how there would be enough water for the huge amount of troops passing through to meet their objectives. Both General Patton and General Truscott were in command and the pace of movement was intense. It would be hard, if not impossible, on such a dry, hot island.

157

Interestingly enough, when he got back to his company that night, a 1st lieutenant called him[101]. "Good, there's a well at the top of one of those hills over there. We need to go get water so it can be treated for drinking water."

"I'm ready, sir," he said.

When they drove by an area referenced as Four Corners, the lieutenant stopped to talk to the MPs. After a few minutes, he looked at Carl and said, "Gosh Good, I'm just going to stay here with these boys while you run up there. That well's just up this road a ways. You can find it."

Outranked, he didn't ask any questions and took off down the road—alone. In the distance, he could see tracer bullets lighting the darkness in his path. He knew he wasn't supposed to be driving alone, and he could tell this assignment was not going to be a walk in the park. Since the lieutenant stayed behind, he had no source of protection while driving.

Before long, a jeep came toward him and slowed way down as they passed. When it completely stopped, he backed up a bit to see what they wanted. It was a captain with his personnel. The captain looked in his empty jeep and asked, "Soldier, where are you going?"

"Well sir, there's supposed to be a well up there, and I'm going to get some water," he responded.

"Don't you see those tracers up there?" the captain asked.

"Yes sir, I sure do, but I'm under orders," he answered even though he could tell the captain was irritated. He was doing what his job required him to do—even if it was dangerous. This wasn't the first time he was placed on the line, and he was sure it wouldn't be his last.

"You don't got no business up there. You turn that thing around, and follow me back to Four Corners. Where's your rider?" the captain suddenly questioned.

"Back with the MPs, sir."

Keyed off that the lieutenant had stayed behind, the captain demanded, "He had you leave him there with the MPs? What's his name?"

---

[101] Event as told by Carl

"Lieutenant Ganders,[102] sir."

"That's a pure coward. That's none of his business sending you up there. I'll settle that when we get back down there. You're supposed to have a rider!" yelled the captain.

"Yes, sir."

"I outrank him, so you turn around and do what I tell you to do. You go back to Four Corners, and I'll meet you down there," the captain finished yelling out before speeding on down the road.

Quickly turning, he followed the captain's jeep. He wondered how this was going to play out since he knew the lieutenant shouldn't have stayed behind. What was the captain going to do?

The lieutenant had sent him by himself because he was too scared to go with him—he was an officer who was chicken all the way through. The more he thought about it, the more it bothered him. The lieutenant knowingly sent him into a death trap and didn't go to help him. If that captain wouldn't have come along, he was certain he wouldn't have returned. All the fighting was going on right there in front of him at the well—for the water.

He didn't claim to be the bravest out there, but he knew what his purpose was and he planned to do it. Four Corners came into view, and the lieutenant was surprised to see the captain ahead of Carl.

"Lieutenant Ganders?" the captain yelled out.

"Yes, sir," came the weak reply.

"What the hell were you thinking?" was the first thing out of the captain's mouth. However, that was only the beginning as the captain berated the lieutenant—making sure he knew where he stood by telling him where he was supposed to be, what he was supposed to do, and what he wasn't supposed to do. The captain pointed back at Carl and ended with, "And you don't ever send your driver to an enemy zone under fire alone! Do you understand me, lieutenant?"

After being chewed up one side and down the other, the lieutenant had nothing to say but, "Yes, sir. I understand. It won't happen again."

"It damned sure better not happen again!" was the captain's reply.

---

[102] Name known, but changed and withheld for privacy reasons.

Awkward silence followed as Carl drove the unusually quiet lieutenant back to their area in the darkness. He had a long day, but there was some good news when they got back. That night, by midnight, the 7th Army had reached the western segment that was calculated to take at least five days to reach—in only two days. Tomorrow morning they would boldly move forward with their company.

Soon after they left that morning, they came to an area where they could stay on the main road or go through what looked like a deep, narrow irrigation ditch along the side of the road. A debate broke out as to which route would be the safest[103]. A few tanks impatiently took to the ditch and infantry went in behind them.

It was too hot and dry to worry about water coming down the ditch, but that was the least of Carl's fears. There was no room for extra movement. Once the convoy entered, they had to go until they could get out the other side. He stopped the jeep.

Once again, he was driving for Lieutenant Ganders and he looked at him and said, "If we get down in there, we could get trapped. If the enemy sees us down there, why, they could sit at the end with a couple eighty-eights[104] and wait for us."

With the convoy stopped at him, the captain came up and asked, "What's the holdup here?"

Lt. Ganders coldly replied, "Private Good doesn't want to take to the ditch."

"Sir, they want to take the convoy through this here ditch. Once we get down there, there's no getting out. If they discover we're there, they'll just wait and shoot us at the other end. I don't think we should go," he explained.

The captain took a minute to look at the situation and said, "No. We're not going there. Oh no. That's all of that. Pull everyone back."

In the midst of the frustration and eye rolling of being pulled back, a Sicilian man and his two mules came walking toward the stopped convoy in the ditch. It was too far for him to go back so he tried to pull them up the side, but the edges were too steep.

---

[103] Event as told by Carl
[104] An 88 mm gun was a German anti-tank, anti-aircraft, and artillery gun.

Hot, tired, and in the middle of heavy combat, patience was already at the bare minimum—this man and his mules were in the way. Through hand gestures and plenty of inappropriate language, the Sicilian man was told to get out of their way. Plenty scared, the man desperately tried to pull his mules up the steep side, but he couldn't.

Of course, hotheaded Lt. Ganders couldn't keep it together. Getting out of the jeep with his Tommy gun, he walked toward the Sicilian man yelling, "I'll get him out of the way! I'll get him out of the way!"

You don't go around shooting civilians, Carl thought as he pulled out his own gun. That's it! He had had enough. Blood boiling, he walked over to the lieutenant with his gun and said, "Lieutenant, if you shoot that man, then I'll shoot you!"

The lieutenant lowered the gun. Carl could tell the lieutenant was still fuming, but he really didn't care. He wasn't messing around. "I'll help him over the edge," he said as he put his gun away and took one of the mules from the man.

Literally shaking in fear, the man got to the top with the mule and Carl handed over the other one. White as a sheet, the man looked at him saying, "*Grazie*[105]! *Grazie! Grazie!*"

He assumed that meant thank you and nodded his head as the man walked down the road. When he got back to the jeep, the lieutenant was mad. He wondered what stupid thing would come out of the lieutenant's mouth next. However, before anything could be said, the captain came back over saying, "Good, you did the right thing... you did the right thing. Let's get this mess turned around."

After that, the lieutenant kept quiet as everyone got out of the ditch. No doubt, it was a hassle, but it was safer than giving the enemies free shooting practice at close range. He knew the lieutenant was sore with him by the tension in the air, but he really didn't care. That was strike two, and he hoped he'd get to drive for somebody else soon. There was too much unneeded drama from the lieutenant, and he didn't care to drive for him.

---

[105] Thank you in Italian.

That night, there was an officer's meeting. When the meeting ended near midnight, he heard the lieutenant call out his name. *Oh boy, I'm in trouble*, he thought as he walked over to him.

"My Gosh," the lieutenant started, "I'm glad I didn't shoot that man. I'm sure glad you didn't let me shoot him."

Somewhat surprised he said, "Lieutenant, you don't know how close you came to getting shot. I was dead serious."

"Oh, I know, and I apologize," the lieutenant said before walking away.

What just happened? He hadn't expected the lieutenant to apologize. Honestly, he thought he might get court martialed for pulling a gun on a higher-ranking officer. Apparently, the colonel must have told the lieutenant a word or two about shooting civilians.

The next morning, as the 7th Infantry Regiment planned to investigate an attack on Agrigento, he was called in by the commanding officer. He wondered if his name had come up at the meeting last night and if it was good or bad. He wasn't too worried, as he and the commander got along pretty well. He had driven for him a lot.

After he reported, the commander said, "Good, I got good recommendations for your guard work. According to General Truscott, he says I'm supposed to find an upper place for you—a higher rating."

"General Truscott, sir?" he repeated in unbelief.

Guard duty was important to him, and he usually had the number one post. However, for General Truscott to notice was unreal! It looked like even though his thorough checks annoyed the lieutenants, it paid off with one of the generals taking note.

The commander continued, "Yes. But the thing is… I don't know what to give you. The only thing I really have left is a half-track right now. I don't really want to lose you as a driver though."

"Sounds good to me. I'd rather keep my little jeep here anyway," he said with a smile.

He kept it to himself, but didn't want anything to do with a tank. He had seen the blackened, burnt out shells of tanks left in fighting zones. In his mind, those were pert near death—like a coffin with

Chapter 9 - Ex Africa Semper Aliquid Novi

wheels in battle. If the enemy fired back with a jelly gun, there was no getting out—that and getting set on fire. *No thanks*, he thought.

"I'm glad to hear you say that, but we're not going to forget you, Good," the commander said. "Oh, by the way, you're being called down to the 7th Regimental Headquarters. Lt. Colonel Williams lost his driver and wants you to drive for him for a while."

"Yes, sir," he said as he shook the commander's hand.

"Well, I hate to lose you right now, but he outranks me. There's not much I can do about that," the commander said as he patted him on the shoulder.

"It's all right. Don't make no difference to me who I drive for," he said as he left.

For the first time in a while, he felt good about his future. Things were starting to look up. His hard work and values were getting him noticed. Plus, as an added benefit, he wouldn't be driving Lieutenant Ganders for now.

Driving for Lt. Colonel Williams (a regimental executive officer in the 7th Army) was sure to be a risky move in open war, but he had driven for him on and off for the eight months they had been out. He liked and respected him. Although Williams was an old bind hard as nails in battle, he was quiet, serious, dedicated, and had a real heart for his men. He looked up to Williams as a father figure and they worked well together—both watching out for the other.

Communications between the 2nd and 3rd Battalions were sketchy and completely out much of the time, so his jeep tires would get plenty of time picking up the fine, dry dust of the Sicilian roads. As he drove out that evening, July 15, he called out to Rodriguez and Bethem, "I'll see you soon, brothers."

Rodriguez yelled something about not missing breakfast, but he couldn't hear him. He waved back at them and quietly laughed. That Rodriguez was always thinking about food at the strangest times, but always good for a laugh.

Headed out for an all-nighter, he knew there'd be no breakfast for him. More important things were on his mind though—like talk of taking Agrigento as the batteries assembled throughout the area. He picked up Lt. Colonel Williams and two guards, and the dust flew out

163

from behind his jeep as they drove along the bomb-cratered roads toward Vittoria. Everything appeared to be normal enough, but there was something that didn't feel right—almost like a dread that hung low and followed them down the road.

Chapter 10

CAPTURED BY THE ENEMY

CARL WASN'T SURE why he felt that way as they drove through the predawn hours of July 16—he just did. He tried to brush it off by thinking about how successful things were moving along. In under a week, the 7th Army[106] was well on its way to overrun the western half of the island. He had driven over to Vittoria with no incident and was headed back to headquarters now—everything was fine.

It was hard to see in blackout conditions, but the brightness of the Mediterranean stars helped him see the coastal roads. Three rivers emptied into the sea, and he had to be careful with the bombed out bridges. It would be far too easy not to realize the bridge was gone until it was too late. He knew there should be one coming up, but where was it?

In the darkness, he stopped and got out to check. He walked to the front of the jeep and quietly said under his breath, "Well, that was a close one!"

One of the guards got out and walked to where he stood. When the guard saw the deep drop in front of them, he said, "Whoa! That was darn lucky, Good."

They got back into the jeep. "The bridge is gone. About ten more feet… and we'd have been goners too."

"Well, good thing you stopped, Good. There should be another way across here before too long," Williams said as he nodded in a different direction.

---

[106] Total strength of the 7th Army was 203,204

They hadn't been on the small island[107] for even a week, and it was going to be twice as hard to find the way in the dark. Although German troops knew it was too late to push the American Divisions into the sea, they were quickly replacing the captured Italian troops and reinforcing the cities that hadn't been taken yet. If he drove too far over, it would be extremely easy to end up behind those reinforced enemy lines.

The light of dawn would help them before long, but there was a lot to accomplish with General Patton's eye on getting through Agrigento and into Palermo (Sicily's capital). First, they needed to capture the port of Empedocle, which was found beside Agrigento. If all went well there, Agrigento would fall next—and then Palermo.

Ultimately, it was up to General Truscott to decide their next move. Truscott knew they could only get involved in Agrigento if it was sure to be an easy take. Otherwise, it was too risky to get caught in a big battle and not be able to withdraw if needed elsewhere. He felt there was nothing to lose and advancement on Agrigento—"the eye of Sicily"—was about to begin.

Germany needed a delay in Sicily while stabilizing Italy—knowing Benito Mussolini[108] was on his way out of power soon. Adamant in the fight, large numbers of German troops were being sent to protect Agrigento—the new front lines. That meant communication had to be clear between the battalions before they began to advance—something Carl would be helping with as he drove Lt. Colonel Williams. One mistake could throw the advancement off and end in tragedy.

They made it back to headquarters. Only able to catch a little sleep in his jeep that morning, he waited for Williams and his guards so they could make the next run[109]. First, they headed to where the 3rd Battalion remained in assembly northwest of Palma di Montechiaro. Williams got out with one of his guards while Carl and the other guard waited.

---

[107] The whole island of Sicily was just bigger than the U.S. state of New Hampshire
[108] Benito Mussolini was the Fascist dictator of Italy from 1922 until he was overthrown on July 25, 1943
[109] Story of his capture and the events that followed as written by Carl in his memoir and told aloud—details and conversation added

Chapter 10 – Captured By The Enemy

When they got back, Williams took a minute to look at a map of the area. The 1st and 2nd Battalions were occupying high ground east of the Naro River and patrolling the front. Their next stop was to connect with the 2nd Battalion, and Williams directed him on how to get there. The early afternoon heat bore through the jeep as Williams looked over at him and said, "We're close. It shouldn't be hard to see them up here on the hill."

Carl looked to see if he could see them, but the sound of a German eighty-eight opened up. It was meant for them and he pushed the gas and sped into a field where he could see a wooded area in the direction of the hill. Staying covered in the woods, he drove until coming to a wheat field. Dry dirt filled the air as he cut across it.

"They should be right around here. Where are they?" asked Williams to no one in particular.

They made it to the hill, but there were no troops waiting there. A massive explosion sounded behind them, and they all four looked back. "Well, we're in trouble. I think a lot of trouble..." Williams said when he saw they had gone up too far and were sitting in enemy territory.

The 2nd Battalion was on the hill behind them, and they were giving the enemy plenty as an ammunition dump exploded. "Looks like they got held back! We have to get back there!" Williams shouted as they sped back down the hill.

The tires gained traction as Carl hit a hard surfaced road. In front of him, he saw a big truck—full of German ammunition. "Let's take that in first," Williams told him as they pulled up to the side of it.

Williams and his guards pulled out their guns, pointed them at the German driver, and yelled, "Stop! Pull over or we'll shoot!"

English or no English, the guns pointing at the driver as they sped along beside him relayed the message. The driver pulled over and slowly got out with his hands up. Once the driver was taken prisoner, Carl grabbed a gray and purple incendiary hand grenade and threw it into the truck. It was used for destroying equipment, immobilizing and destroying vehicles, and for starting a fire in any area containing flammable materials—exactly what he needed for this load.

When the vehicle started on fire, they noticed something crouched in the brush and weeds off to the side of the road. Williams turned the captured driver over to Carl and went closer with his guards to get a better look. Before they got to the other side of the road, a German stood up and took off running. Apparently, the driver had a guard of his own.

The two guards chased the runaway German and Williams turned around and ran back to Carl. Taking over the prisoner, Williams urgently said, "My gosh, Good! They're coming! I don't know what I'm thinking, I'll tell you, cause you got to get this vehicle undercover somewhere. Drive up around that bend in the road about 200 yards back and take cover."

If they could hide, maybe they could wait it out. Somehow, they were caught in the middle of a large group of German reinforcements who were headed toward Agrigento. It was 1340 hours, and since the American artillery observers wouldn't see and stop the German reinforcements for another thirty minutes, they were completely on their own.

His tires spun on the road as he turned the jeep around. He looked back at Williams trying to take cover in the weeds away from the burning truck before he rounded the bend. When he looked back to the front, his heart stopped. An enemy motorcycle patrol was directly in front of him. He was boxed in with nowhere to go, and he knew the enemy had seen him.

With nothing to lose, he jerked the steering wheel to the side and skidded on two wheels down the weeds into the ditch. Surprised he didn't flip it or get injured; he jumped out and placed an incendiary grenade on the transmission to disable it as he had learned in training. He didn't imagine ever having to use all that stuff, but here he was.

His mind raced a million miles a minute as he grabbed his gun. But before he could even get his single shot 03 Rifle up, a mix of ten Germans and Italians surrounded him like flies. With their rifles and pistols directly aimed at him, they jabbered something in their language and he waited for the sting of death. Then surprisingly, one of them spoke to him in English—near as well as any American, "Answer our questions… or we'll kill you!"

It was obvious that this guy and his bloodthirsty helpers intended for this to be his end. Their pointed guns looked like cannons to him and equally as powerful, but he remained silent and refused to answer anything—they would kill him anyway. He jumped when a fury of shots fiercely rang through the air from where he had just come from.

If those shots weren't for him, it could only mean one thing. He knew without looking over that Williams and his two guards didn't stand a chance against so many—those two prisoners they had captured had turned into a colossal two. He said a quick prayer and waited, but no bullet came for him.

The last shot echoed through the air and they grabbed his arm and pulled him up the ditch. Defeated and empty, there was nothing he could do as they turned and riddled his jeep before leaving. So, this was the dread he had felt all day.

His leg banged into the side of the motorcycle as he was violently pushed onto it. He wondered why they hadn't killed him and were taking him further behind enemy lines. Why had they killed Lt. Colonel Williams and his guards, but not him? Did they think because he was a jeep driver he would tell them the Allied locations? He had a good idea of where things were, but he had a surprise for them because he wasn't talking.

Dark and putrid hate began to fill him as they arrived to an area where the roads divided like a four corners. Hundreds of Germans appeared to be getting reorganized in the area. He thought back to when he had seen the captured prisoners in North Africa and had hoped not to get captured—especially by the Germans.

Now, Carl was being pushed over to a German captain and his officer. Without wasting time, the captain pulled out a pistol and stuck it to Carl's head as he spewed a language he couldn't understand. At that moment, he felt completely void. Suddenly, he didn't even care what the captain was saying. At that point, it no longer mattered. They had a gun to his head and had already killed Williams and his guards—he knew he was next.

He said nothing—he would not talk for them. The captain angrily waved his gun at a car across the road and yelled something out in disgust. They shoved him like a dog across the dusty road toward the car. He figured they were taking him to their German headquarters in Agrigento, but he didn't know for sure.

Agrigento was an ancient city and old buildings lined the street. They pulled up to one that looked like an old courthouse and forced him out of the car. Pushing him toward it, he thought, *Unbelievable—this can't be happening.* Not even an hour ago, life was as normal as it gets while fighting in a war and now, he had stepped through the doors of a nightmare.

Once inside, a large staircase led to the second floor. He could feel their guns pushing into his back as they climbed the stairs and walked down a long, dark hall. They went through a door and a little afternoon light came in through an old window. A tall, thin German officer sat smoking at a desk.

Words between the officer and his guards were exchanged as he stood there. The officer pulled out a revolver and set it on the desk and the grilling began. "Tell us what we want to know, or he no problem killing you," an interpreter said in broken English.

He didn't doubt the officer would have a problem killing him. In fact, he was sure he was going to kill him no matter what. They could go ahead and kill him—he wasn't going to tell them anything. Inside he was shaking, but he tried to remain calm as death's hot breath blew on his neck from behind. "My name is Carl Good, serial number 37158596," he started.

"What you rank in the Army?" came the next question.

"Private First Class," he answered.

The next question burned his insides, "Who you driving for?"

"They should know. They killed him," he said in controlled anger.

The questioning and grilling grew more intense, and he knew he couldn't and wouldn't say anything more.

"Tell us what going on? What the plans are?" they demanded.

"I don't got that information," he said flatly.

"You a liar! We know you know because of who you driving," was the comeback.

"I know nothing. I am only a Private. I don't know that information," he insisted.

Not about to share more than what was allowed by the Army—name, serial number, and rank, he clammed up as they continued asking the same questions.

Chapter 10 – Captured By The Enemy

Suddenly, the officer picked up the gun on the desk. The officer pressed the smooth barrel tightly against Carl's temple and yelled out in German. His German words meant nothing to him. The interpreter quickly repeated, "What the plans are?"

"I already told you. I don't know," he said.

"You don't know? We know you know! You are a liar!" the officer yelled out in German for the interpreter to repeat.

"I don't know," he repeated.

After what felt like an hour of this, the officer shouted out something as he threw his gun back on the desk. What that meant—he had no idea, but it probably wasn't good. Four other soldiers came in the room with guns and bayonets. Holding up a long, black scarf, the interpreter asked, "You see this?"

He wanted to say, *Of course, I see it! I'm not blind!* but only answered with, "Yes."

"If you no answer questions, I put this over you eyes." The interpreter pointed to the guards with their guns and fixed bayonets before continuing, "And then, I put you against wall, and one man shoot you."

He felt his insides knot, but looked into the officer's blue eyes and directly said to him, "I have no information."

The interpreter walked to where he stood and pushed him against the wall. This was it. Finally, the barrel for Russian roulette had slowly stopped spinning and the bullet was one hundred percent in place. It was his turn to face the bullet at the hands of the Germans; his turn to get the taps played for him.

He blinked his eyes and struggled to see clearly. It felt like the world was closing in around him, as if he was being sucked in by a vacuum and thrown into endless darkness. Yet somehow, the blades on a small, metal fan on the officer's desk kept rotating at their normal speed and sound. The long, black scarf was lifted, and lightheaded he froze in place. Loudly he uttered his last chosen words, "My God, help me."

At that moment, a loud explosion shook the building. Bombers were flying over—the 7th Army was preparing to move in. The open window rattled from the blast, and he could see part of the city stretched before him. *Our boys are coming in*, he thought as the bombers roared over the city. Another bomb and the shrieking of sirens rang through the air. In panic and chaos, the officer grabbed at papers from around the room and yelled at the others.

Several ran out of the room as the interpreter grabbed him by the arm and pushed him into a cell within the courthouse. There were no lights, but he knew it wasn't a place he wanted to be as bugs and mice crawled through the filth and stench of old trash. Not even Army life had prepared him for a place so dirty.

Not wanting to sit down, he stood in the darkness—tired, alone, and unsure if he would live to see tomorrow, but somehow grateful he had lived to finish today… so far. Finally, exhaustion caught up with him, and he sat on the dirty floor to rest. He didn't want to lean against the bug-covered wall, so he sat by the front of the cell with his arms tightened around his knees and rested his head on top of them. An unexpected noise made him look up and he saw the interpreter looking down at him. "You talk now?" the interpreter asked.

"I already told you. I know nothing about what you want," he said, wondering how long it was going to take them to understand that he wasn't going to talk.

The interpreter waved his finger at him, "You a liar! You know more. They coming now."

"I don't have information," he said, looking up at him.

"Fine. It be your way." The interpreter said as he walked away with two others.

He wondered when they would finish the deed. They almost had him dead that time, and he knew they would eventually realize he wasn't talking and shoot him—it was just a matter of when. His hope was completely extinguished as he thought about not seeing any of the boys again and never returning home to America.

He remembered the *New Testament* he carried in his pocket. He still had it. In the dark, he held onto it and said a prayer—that was the only talking he was going to do.

Again, the interpreter came back with the same men as before. This time they brought wine. Holding it out to him, the interpreter said, "Here… you drink."

Chapter 10 – Captured By The Enemy

"I don't drink," Carl said flatly.

"Okay, but you get thirsty," the interpreter said as they walked away again.

Get thirsty? he repeated in his head. *What do you mean? I am thirsty, hungry, and tired now, but get me drunk and then pump me... I don't think so...* and he lowered his head back to his knees.

Over and over again it was the same thing as they came back to see if he had changed his mind—"Wine? Give us information."

Then, they came back with a small bowl of macaroni and held it out to him, "Eat."

"I am not hungry," he lied as his stomach loudly growled in disapproval.

It was hard to turn away the food, but he was afraid it might be doped. There was no way he was going to fall for their tricks. They wouldn't be getting any information from him. It wouldn't be long before the 7th Army moved in anyway, and then they would find out what was going on for themselves.

He thought of Rodriguez and his food jokes. He wondered what his company was doing. Did they know he was captured?

He didn't know his company commander cried as he had the company get together and say a prayer for him[110], and he certainly didn't know if he would live to see tomorrow. Between the Germans threatening to kill him and the bombs falling around Agrigento, it looked bleak. Only this one time he hoped the bombers didn't find and bomb the German Headquarters.

Although the city hadn't been taken yet, it would be soon enough—he was sure about that. In fact, it had already begun. By 1900 hours, the 7th Army took the needed port of Empedocle and was indeed prepared to take Agrigento by early morning. The troops were getting closer and he could hear shooting in the distance.

Night fell and he slapped off bugs that crawled twice as fast and bit twice as hard as he drifted in and out of sleep. The next morning, July 17, he could feel the cell start to heat up with the rising sun. He opened his eyes and saw a bit of light streaming down a hall outside

---

[110] Carl was contacted by Sergeant Edwards in 2010 and he told him that

his cell. *Odd nobody has come to get me*, he thought as he wiped the sweat of his head with his sleeve and scratched at newly acquired bug bites. Ugh… what he would do for a shower—even a cold one.

Finally, a couple soldiers came in together without the interpreter. They brought another small bowl of macaroni. "Eat. Eat," they said as they pushed the bowl at him.

He hadn't eaten since early yesterday. He was plenty hungry, but he did not trust them. Afraid the grumble of his stomach would betray his words, he dryly said, "I'm not hungry."

One of the men grabbed the bowl, took a bite, and then handed the bowl back to him saying, "Eat."

It didn't appear to have anything added to it and he needed to eat something. He took a few bites and slowly chewed. Although it looked like plain spaghetti noodles, it tasted completely different from the good ole American noodles he was used to. He ate it because he was hungry, but that didn't mean he liked it. Now, even a ration pack sounded good.

That afternoon, the guards came back and walked him out to a little balcony to get some fresh air for a few minutes. He heard the artillery bombing throughout the night and knew the troops were not far. The hot, cement rail burned his hands as he leaned out to scan the area around him. He was too high to jump, but the thought crossed his mind as he squinted down at a brown, dry hill in the near distance.

He looked again. It looked like… was it possible? Was the 7th Army's artillery dropping over the hill? Were they so close he could actually see them? A quick glimmer of hope made his heart race for the first time since he had been captured. It was quick lived, but it was still hope before he was taken back inside and locked in the cell.

From the landing in Fedala, he knew the enemy headquarters would be quickly discovered, and troops would arrive to gather any information left behind. As long as they didn't fiercely bomb it first, he had the possibility of being back with his company by nightfall. He didn't know Agrigento had been taken early that morning and many of the Germans had either already escaped or were captured throughout the area.

Chapter 10 – Captured By The Enemy

Although he was still under lock and key, he could tell there were only a few people left in the building with him. Eerily quiet with only an occasional soldier running down the hall, he could tell they were feeling the pressure. It wouldn't be long.

He pulled his *New Testament* out of his pocket and ran his hand across the smooth, dark cover with the gold lettering. A dim light came in from the hall, but he couldn't see the small words in the darkness. Yet somehow, the black lettering on the white pages provided a sense of comfort as he sat on the hard floor and waited. He put it back in his pocket—it was all he had to keep him sane.

Maybe they'll leave me behind and I'll be found by American troops, he thought as the afternoon sun faded from the hall. However, the enemy proved to fool him. In the cover of the darkening night, three Germans opened the door to his cell and motioned for him to go with them.

Out in the hall, he wondered for a brief moment if he could make a run for it. If he could get outside, he would be able to get to the troops—he was so close. But before he could move, two of them tightly hooked onto his arms and the third walked closely behind with a gun aimed and ready.

The men jabbered together and he wished he could understand what they were saying so he knew what was going on. Where were they taking him? They got down to the first floor and opened an old back door. He quickly understood the plan when he saw the waiting ambulance with several of the enemy's wounded.

They could get him out of Agrigento by putting him in the ambulance. Hate filled him for each one of those guards as the frustration of being so close took hold. Here he was sitting in an enemy ambulance with guards watching his every move and his troops were just around the corner—literally.

The ambulance bounced and jolted through the bomb-cratered roads, and deadly screams of pain and agony filled the tight space with each bump. Covering his ears, he desperately hoped to block out the frantic calls for help and mindless screaming. To keep his mind occupied, he closed his eyes and ran through the Lord's Prayer—*Our*

Father, which art in heaven, hallowed by thy name... but it wasn't working as the screams tore through his thoughts.

He could feel someone staring at him. Light flashed through the darkness and he could see the white of the eyes of an injured man lying close at his feet. Dark shadows trickled fresh from the man's nose and mouth as he moved his cracked lips. There were no words—only a low, guttural sound came from somewhere deep within before it stopped and the man's eyes closed as his head went back onto the hard ambulance floor.

He swallowed hard and closed his eyes again. The hot, stuffy air made his breath catch in his chest, and he felt like he was going crazy. If he got lost in the cries of misery, the sounds would bounce around his head and permanently leave its mark. It was bad enough he was riding with bleeding, injured men, but to hear their screams caused his blood to curdle and his mind to explode. *This must be what hell is like*, he thought. But he was wrong—this was only the entrance to hell as the ambulance lurched along the bumpy roads.

He didn't even care where they were going anymore. He would do anything to get off that ambulance. It was near midnight before they finally stopped in a tiny town and got him out. Completely lost, he heard something about Necchio, but that meant nothing to him. Wherever he was, the same hot night of Sicily greeted him as he was pushed across a dirt road and into an old, cement building. Again, his heart dropped. Another cell... another dark, disgusting, dirty cell even worse than the first—if that was even possible.

Exhausted in every sense of the word—mentally and physically, he resisted the initial urge to lie down on the wooden bed pushed against the wall. He didn't even need to see through the darkness to know it was full of dirt, bugs, and filth. A noise behind him made him jump as he turned around and saw a worn, stained blanket that had been thrown onto the dirty floor.

He coughed as he angrily looked at it and then kicked it. That was all they could do—throw a repulsive blanket probably covered in dirt and mouse droppings onto the floor for him. Even though there was no mattress or pillow to cover the hard, wooden bed, he wasn't going to use the blanket. He'd just leave it right where it was—on the floor.

Chapter 10 – Captured By The Enemy

He couldn't believe places like this really existed… but they did, and he was left to sleep in it. He sarcastically laughed at the thought… sleep? He was so tired, but with his head pounding from stress, fatigue, hunger, and an awful, putrid smell that began to radiate in the heat of the cell, sleep eluded him. Instead, he felt nauseous as he sat on the edge of the bed, coughed, and swatted off roaches.

He hoped his uniform would help protect his skin from the fleas, bedbugs, and lice as he finally lay down on the bare bed. Even with his mind running in high gear, he eventually gave in to pure exhaustion. After sleeping for what must have been only a few hours, he awoke to the crowing of a rooster somewhere in the distance.

Confused and half-asleep, he sat up and looked around him. The room was still dark and it took him a few seconds to realize he was in a prison cell. Oh yes, he had been captured by the enemy and was trapped in a nightmare that kept getting worse. Sitting on the edge of the bed, he scratched at his bug bites and rubbed his head with the palm of his hand. He had hoped the short rest would take away the headache, but it hadn't. His clothes hadn't protected him from the bugs either.

Before long, a couple of guards came in and got him. *Oh boy, here we go again*, he thought. The last time he almost got shot, and he had no idea what to expect from these guys as they took him to a dingy room where a dim light carelessly hung from the ceiling. An Italian officer was sitting at an old desk and several guards stood around the room. After they sat him down in a wooden chair in front of the desk, he waited for the ruthless questions to begin.

To his surprise, the officer didn't threaten him or yell, but began with a smile. "Well, you is young. How many years you have?" he asked. His English was better than the interpreter's was from the last place, but still broken.

Shocked by the difference in technique, he was careful not to get caught off-guard. He knew the officer was trying to slip him up by talking about things in general before adding in questions to get specific information. So he made his answers as brief as possible. "Twenty-four," he started.

"You out long?" came the next question.

He wasn't in the mood to play their games. "I can't answer you that."

"How many you say come over with you?" the officer asked.

"I don't know."

Undeterred by his lack of answers, the officer calmly continued, "Africa beautiful by Mediterranean Sea. You were to Africa?"

He was tired of answering these questions and stopped all together. *Come on; let's get this over with*, he thought since he knew they were wasting their time... and his. Once more, he looked at the officer and said, "I've done told you guys. I don't got the information you want."

"Of that you is sure?" the officer asked.

He remained silent as they continued asking random questions. Finally, the officer looked him in the eyes and said, "You believe we have New York and the Great Lakes?"

Carl looked the officer back in the eyes and boldly stated, "No."

"Why not?" the officer asked.

He had no way of knowing, but he hoped they hadn't as he answered with a lie, "Because I just came from there."

"Then answer me this," the officer said. "New York has been bombed?"

Agitated, he snapped, "No, and never will be!"

"You think you win the war?" the officer said with almost a look of pity in his eyes.

He didn't even have to lie about that, "Yes, I do."

The officer leaned toward him over the desk, "What make you think this?"

He shrugged his shoulders. "I don't know. You'll have to wait and see."

"Many troops come over with you?" the officer repeated.

The same questions were being asked, but a little more aggressively now, "You in Africa? Where you come from?"

"I don't know," he repeated to each one of them.

Frustrated, the officer gave up and confirmed what Carl already knew from the moment he was caught, "You to have your hair cut off and you to go to a camp near Palermo. You probably not see home again."

Chapter 10 – Captured By The Enemy

Sent back to his cell to await his haircut, he again kicked the blanket that was still on the floor. A small cloud of dust lifted into the air that he couldn't see in the dark the night before, and he was glad he hadn't used it. In the dim light, he could see the cement walls were covered in dirt and black mold. No wonder he was coughing throughout the night. With nothing to do but wait, he lay on the hard bed and scratched at bug bites that itched with no end.

Around noon, a small dish of noodle soup and a piece of bread were brought to his cell. This would count as his one meal for the day. Although he still didn't like the taste, it was food in his empty stomach.

Strange enough, they left him alone for the rest of the afternoon. Then, that evening, they came in holding a razor. If the prison camps were anything like these holding cells, being shaved would be a blessing. With less hair, he would have to worry less about lice and diseases passed through bug-filled hellholes like this. Part of him was ready to join others at the Prisoner of War (POW) camp, but the other part of him kept thinking he should be able to find a way to escape. In fact, escape constantly filled his mind, but so far, he was always under heavy guard.

The next day proved no different. Under guard, he was taken to another small camp a short ways from what he knew as Necchio. Although he wasn't in Palermo, he was questioned once again. He was tired of repeatedly being asked the same questions.

This time when he went in the room, the German officer asked for his billfold. He had almost forgotten he had it. Nobody had asked for it before. Sitting back in his chair, the officer flipped through it as the questioning started with an interpreter saying in good English, "You'll find it better if you answer our questions."

This officer wasn't brutish like the other Germans and said in heavy accented English, "Have a chair. Take a cigarette."

"I don't smoke," he said as he sat down and thought, *Ha, getting nice just to pump me. That's not going to do you no good.*

"No smoke?" the officer asked in disbelief. Then he asked, "Wine?"

"No, I don't drink," he stated.

"Oh, you married," the officer said, holding up the picture of Helen from his billfold.

Carl looked at the picture Helen had given him at the dance the last night he was home and answered with a sharp, "No." Irritated that the officer was rummaging through his things and there wasn't anything he could do about it, he added, "She's just a friend."

The officer took his time and slowly looked through the rest of the pictures of his family and friends. Unexpectedly, the officer then returned his billfold back to him. Dumbfounded that the officer had returned it, he didn't say a word. However, the next question from the interpreter didn't surprise him one bit, "Been overseas long?"

He looked up and flatly stated, "It's against military rules to answer your questions."

"Well, it may be best for you to talk. It's really nothing to us. We only want to notify the Red Cross so they can make a report on you to your home," the interpreter responded.

Like hell, he thought. It was almost as if the voice coming from his mouth was not his own anymore. Tired of the questions, he was becoming hardened and said, "I don't know anything."

His heart stopped when a guard standing against the wall unexpectedly made a fast move toward him with a bayonet, but stopped short. Inside he was shaking from the scare tactic used, but he didn't utter a word. After that, they gave up on getting information and the interpreter said, "We're sending you to a Prisoner of War camp. There you'll work according to the instructions given."

Maybe, he thought, but knew better than to say it aloud. Two guards marched him out and they began to walk under the hot, afternoon sun. After making it about a half-mile, they stopped in a wooded area where a lot of people had gathered. *Why were all these civilians in the woods away from their homes?* he wondered.

It didn't take him long to realize their villages and homes were being bombed, and the woods had become a place of refuge. "American," someone shouted, and people ganged around him by the dozens—especially worried, nervous women and little children. One woman came over and handed him a bowl of food. Excited for a change, he looked into the bowl and saw… floating pieces of spaghetti noodles for a soup. Although it wasn't what he wanted, it was beginning to taste good now and he was truly grateful for her kindness. Thanking her, he ate every last drop.

Nobody had much and it was with a sincere heart when food was shared with another. It was obvious the majority of people did not want this war and they were scared. A fairly well dressed man in his forties stepped forward and spoke to him in English, "American?"

"Yes," Carl answered.

The man nodded his head in approval, "I used to live in Boston! Nice America is."

Something told him it was another gag to get information. He didn't trust anyone as he said, "Yes, I like it lots better than here!"

The man's English wasn't fluent, but he could understand him as he continued, "I left there about ten years ago. Someday, after the war, I go back maybe."

"Wish I was that sure of things," he replied.

As they spoke, the man would stop to tell the others who had gathered around them what he was saying.

"Is it true New York is all bombed?" the man asked with a look of concern.

"No, that's just plain propaganda," he said, and he hoped it really was.

"How do you know?" the man asked. "How long since you been there?"

He didn't answer, but knew more military questions would follow. Sure enough, he was right. He must have answered "I don't know" a hundred times before the man finally got the point and moved on to ask something else. "Is it true the Americans will kill all the women and children when they get here?"

Surprised they would even think that, he said, "No! You'll find them to be very friendly. It's all propaganda."

The already nervous women became more anxious as they yelled out questions in Sicilian without waiting for the man to interpret them. Carl wished he could calm their fears with the truth, but could only say, "I'm sorry. No Italian."

The man said, "They want to know if the Americans will destroy our homes and take all our stuff?"

"No, I tell you. They're your friends," he tried to convince them.

It was no wonder the people were scared and anxious. With all the propaganda and lies being told about the Americans, they were petrified. After about an hour had passed, the guards led him down a small path. As he walked away from the group, he heard the man call out, "Hope they hurry and get here. Don't you worry; you'll be took care of good. Someday you go home again."

Sarcastically, he thought, *Yeah, what a morale builder with two guards on me and headed for a Prisoner of War camp.* Had that man been digging for information, or just curious? He didn't know, but he knew he could trust no one.

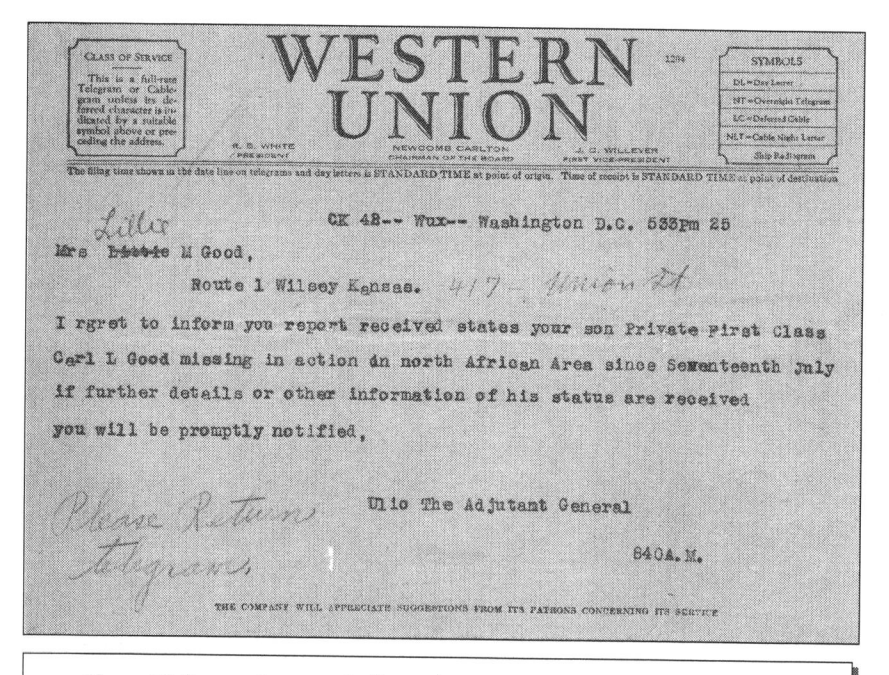

Figure 28: Post card sent to Carl's mother to tell her that Carl had gone MIA
*Note - Although he was captured on the 16th, it was reported on the 17th on some papers.

Chapter 11

LIVING HELL

SWEAT SOAKED THROUGH Carl's shirt as they crossed off the miles under the Sicilian sun. After about four hours of walking, a truck pulled over and gave them a lift. Thirsty and tired, he was grateful for the rest. After a while, the sun fell over the hills and he could see the lights of Palermo shrouded in the darkness.

However, there was not a Prisoner of War camp in the city. Instead, he was locked in yet another holding cell with those darn bugs. Red, itchy bumps all over his body made it look like he was covered with measles. He felt like it too the way he scratched like a poor, starving street dog with a million fleas.

Tired, hungry, and discouraged, he could no longer imagine a future. Before, once in a while, he would think about what it would be like when he got back home. Now, it was a matter of holding his head above water long enough to grab a quick gulp of fresh air to keep from drowning.

Early the next morning, he could hear voices coming toward his cell. The fact that the guards were casually talking and laughing made him so mad he could spit. How was it that he was so miserable, and they were happy and comfortable?

They opened the cell door and handed him a cup of coffee. *Sure a big breakfast*, he thought as he drank it. He knew it was all he was getting and tried to appreciate it, but he really couldn't. It hadn't even been a week since his capture, but he noticed his clothes were already fitting looser. He could literally feel the weight leaving him.

Although in good physical shape, the heat, mental fatigue, and lack of food, made the walk through the mountainous hills exhausting. After walking for quite some time, he saw the camp in a clearing in the distance. That had to be it. As every rocky step took him closer, he could see the barbed wire enclosure with old, large desert tents set up inside. Finally, when they were close enough, one of the guards pointed to it and jabbered something. He didn't need to understand the language to understand what he was saying.

Yeah, yeah, I know. This is it, he thought as he arrived at Camp 98[111] close to the village of San Giuseppe Jato within the Province of Palermo. His morale was already low and he didn't know it was even possible for it to drop lower, but somehow it did. Guards were standing along the outside, and they made it obvious there would be no easy escape. Solely at the mercy of the enemy, he walked to the headquarters tent. It felt like he was being buried alive—slowly and relentlessly.

Already feeling devoid of human rights or feelings, he officially became a nameless prisoner. His billfold was thrown to the side before they made him take his clothes off and placed them in a big barrel of hot water to delouse them. He hoped it would help. When he got his clothes back, they handed him a dirty blanket and sent him on his way.

Immediately, several other American prisoners came up to him, including one lieutenant. They passed several other tents before stopping at one. For some reason, there weren't many other prisoners there. He wondered if this camp was a death trap, or if everyone had been shipped out to other camps since the Allies were headed that way. Once inside the tent, there was room for about fifty men, but he could only see about fifteen.

Some of the dreariness of officially being labeled a prisoner left as he felt a connection with his new comrades—Pawnley, Trenin, Baker, Hamel, and Goldstein[112]. Indeed, the situation had not changed, but now he had people to share it with—they were all living the nightmare

---

[111] Some details of Camp 98 are from the memories of Armie Hill in a 1976 interview with his son, Dennis Hill
[112] Real names unknown

of being captured by the enemy. In fact, he didn't even need to know them—being American was good enough for him.

The lieutenant came over to talk more and introduced himself as 2nd Lieutenant Chansler[113] from 2nd Armor. Then he said, "This is a hellhole, but you aren't alone."

"I've seen a lot of hellholes lately," Carl said with a look around the tent. "Don't look like it's much different here."

Greeted by the same bugs and filth, he knew it was going to be a long road ahead—unless he could figure out a way to escape. It wouldn't be long before General Patton would make it to Palermo. In fact, he didn't know it, but troops were Truscott Trotting on their way now. In less than three days, they'd be in the city of Palermo.

The lieutenant walked through the tent with him and they passed some troops who were curled up motionless on the hard, wooden slats that made up the beds. Separated from the rest, they were against the far tent wall. One of them loudly moaned, and Carl asked the lieutenant, "What's wrong with them?"

"Dysentery mostly," came the cool reply.

He wasn't surprised. There was only one water source, and he had passed by the hand-dug, slit trenches that served as the bathroom for all. It was obvious it had been awhile since the prisoners had covered the old trenches and dug new ones. Flies took no time to feed on the bloody vomit and diarrhea and that was a good way to pass it on. The Army's saying of 'COVER', 'BURY', and 'SWAT THAT FLY' to prevent dysentery was no longer an option.

Continuing along those lines, the lieutenant said, "It's nasty as all get go in here and Lord knows we don't get much to eat. We're lucky if we get a few pieces of spaghetti noodles floating in the water they call soup and maybe a hard piece of bread for breakfast. Sometimes there might be a small piece of cheese or rotten oxen meat, but not often anymore."

"What about the Red Cross parcels?" Carl asked.

"Nonexistent," the lieutenant answered. "But these men here are the lucky ones. Several months ago, this place was full—holds about

---

[113] Name known, but changed for privacy

500. If you got too sick, you'd be sent to the infirmary. Rumor is those guys got the death needle[114]."

He hadn't heard of that before as he repeated, "The death needle?"

"Well, they pulled out a big syringe and injected them with something. You get injected, we never saw you again," was the lieutenant's reply.

Grim, he thought. Then asked, "So, where is everyone now? Why so empty?"

"They ship us out to other camps," the lieutenant said. "You had better not be too sick to ship off, or you'll die here."

After a brief pause in the conversation, Lieutenant Chansler looked directly at him and asked, "So, what's the news from the front?"

Surprised, he looked back at him and said, "You know we can't discuss military affairs here."

"I outrank you. I want to know what's going on," the lieutenant boldly stated.

He had enjoyed talking to the lieutenant, but that question immediately raised red flags… that and why the lieutenant was the only one who wasn't transferred out with everyone else. Then, for him to use the "I outrank you" card with an attitude. Carl was mad as he said, "I don't care if you outrank me or not. Look where we are. Do you think it matters?"

The lieutenant looked around, "There's nobody here who is going to hear us. Tell me what's going on."

"No," he said. "You know it's against Army policy. I refuse to answer your questions concerning military."

Not happy, the lieutenant retorted, "Well, you just wait. When we get back to the States, I'll have you court martialed for disobeying an officer in command."

He wasn't afraid of the lieutenant's threat. "You go ahead and do that. They done told me I wasn't going home."

With that, he turned around and walked outside. Baker and Goldstein were already out there, and he joined them as they walked a

---

[114] Referenced by WW2 People's War (The darkest hour - 5th Northamptons (part 2), 2003)

distance away from the tent. When he was sure nobody else could hear them, he asked, "Do you guys get the feeling Lt. Chansler isn't who he says he is?"

Baker looked at him, "The lieutenant's been here the longest of all of us, but don't know exactly how long that's been. Why? What'd he do?"

"He knows darn well what's going on around here, that's for sure. But he threatened to court martial me if I didn't give him news of the front, and it don't seem right to me," Carl said as they walked.

"That's not right. The lieutenant knows better than to ask those questions," Goldstein agreed.

Carl looked at them, "I know I haven't been captured long, but the thing that gets me is if he's trying to gather information for the enemy, then he's probably got on a dead soldier's uniform."

"Yep, it would be easy enough for them to do. Enemy don't got no respect," Baker said as the conversation died down.

He was shaking his head in disgust when he saw a second large camp surrounded by a barbed wire fence he hadn't noticed earlier. He walked toward the end of the thick rows of barbed wire that ran horizontal and vertical along tall, wooden posts that surrounded his enclosure to see the other camp better. A big group was gathered.

"What's going on over there?" he asked as he moved closer to get a better look.

"Civilian concentration camp from what we can figure. Sad—just look how skinny they are! They are treated so poorly," Baker said, dejectedly shaking his head.

It was obvious, but he couldn't help but say it, "They're slowly being starved to death, and they'll do the same to us no doubt. We got to find a way out of here."

Although the camps were totally separated from one another, he could get close enough to catch a glimpse of what was going on. A scream broke through the air. He peered through the barbed wire.

"You might want to turn around. Whenever there is loud screaming, it is unbearable to watch," Goldstein said.

Lost in the events, the words didn't register. He grabbed onto the fence, he couldn't believe what was happening. A mother was

187

clutching her sick, crying baby and the guards were pulling the child from her arms. She was held back screaming and one of the guards grabbed the baby and threw him into the air. The cries stopped on the end of his bayonet[115]. More screams filled the air as a group of women surrounded the sobbing mother and pulled her away.

He didn't even realize the scratch down his arm from the barbed wire fence as he fell to his knees. How could this be happening? Who could do that? He turned his head and dry heaved because there was no food in his stomach.

Still holding onto the fence with one hand he spit, he could see a few children staring over at him. Worn and torn clothes covered their boney bodies as they got as close as possible to the barbed wire fence on their side of the enclosure. They were small, bug bitten, dirty shadows of death, and he imagined the tear streaks running down their little faces today. It broke his heart to see those precious little children who wouldn't have a chance truly to live. If they didn't die there, their innocence was already permanently scarred.

A little girl stuck her hand through the wires and waved at them. He slowly waved back. Horrified, he saw a guard come along, knock her to the ground with the butt of his rifle, and yell something at her in Italian. Then the guard turned around and glared over at him before walking away. Tightly held emotions threatened to explode. Men, women, and little children were being kept like hogs in a dirty pen. They were being murdered, beaten, and yelled at, and there was nothing he could do.

He hadn't expected to see that, and he was unprepared to deal with the raw emotion that came with it as he quickly turned around and stormed away. There was no way he could stand there for another second. He wanted so badly to grab a gun, a club, or anything, for that matter, and give the guards some of their own medicine, but he was completely powerless and trapped. Once again, he felt a heart strand harden as he turned his empathy into hatred.

---

[115] True story Carl witnessed, although place is not exact. (This was one of the stories too hard to talk about, but passed on by a family member who found out about it.)

Yet one word constantly floated above the hatred—ESCAPE. More than ever, he wanted to be free—away from the dirty, methodical, dehumanizing guards... away from the hurt and pain... away from the screaming images. For now, he could only bury what he had seen, or he knew those images would bury him in return.

He felt he could trust everyone but the lieutenant, so he kept his mind busy by paying attention to every detail of what was going on around him so he could find a way out. It wouldn't be easy with the enormous cliffs that blotted the sun from shining into camp. In fact, it would only work if the Americans were truly on their way to Palermo. Last he knew, they would be unless they had gotten stopped along the way.

That night, he lay on the blanket that covered the wooden slats of the bedbug-infested bed and thought out how he could escape. He wasn't going to sit down and slowly die to the enemy's satisfaction. They had told him he wasn't going home and that was fine. However, one thing was for sure, it would be under his terms, not theirs. If they shot him dead, it was okay because he hadn't given in to them.

His stomach growled, and he thought back to what the lieutenant had said about the Red Cross parcels not making it to the camp. He was grateful for what the Red Cross[116] did for them, but he didn't understand why the parcels were dropped off away from the camp without making sure they got to the prisoners. Conditions here were so bad he bet the camp officer was keeping the Red Cross parcels for himself—not everyone played by the rules of war.

If they were to escape, they would need to find where the food was being hidden because there was nowhere close to get it—they were

---

[116] The Red Cross was linked to the Geneva Conventions (treaties and protocols that establish the standards of international humanitarian law regarding the basic rights of wartime prisoners and the protection for the wounded and civilians.) Not everybody signed up at the convention and that is why some prison camps or prisoners were worse off than others (Japan was one of the countries that did not sign.) Under the terms of the Geneva Conventions, the Red Cross was allowed to carry out its work of supporting those who were captured. Food and sanitary packages were part of this support from the Red Cross. Packages varied by country, and the American Red Cross provided aid both at home and behind enemy lines.

stuck on an island and it wasn't safe to ask. The question was how to get it. Those thoughts ran through his head as he tried to fall asleep.

When he awoke in the morning, he had an idea. The lieutenant was still sore with him from yesterday and stayed to himself. So as soon as he got a chance, he slipped out with Pawnley, Trenin, Baker, Hamel, and Goldstein to make a detailed escape plan without letting the lieutenant know—he didn't trust him.

The plan wouldn't take long to carry out, but they would have to act quickly. They had a better chance of making it back to American lines before the enemy transferred them to camps further into enemy territory. If General Patton were as close as Carl thought, they would be getting transferred soon.

As they worked on the plan, they had to be careful not to call attention to themselves as a group. Pawnley had snuck in a knife and it hadn't been discovered yet. They would each take turns using it and cut through the barbed wire fence. Once it was cut, they'd wait until night and quietly disappear.

Another prisoner had tried to escape like that before, but he was recaptured, tied to a flagpole in the middle of the camp, and left without food for several days. When the weak and mostly dead prisoner was untied, nobody ever saw him again[117]. The camp made the consequences of trying to escape a deadly offense, but Carl was determined at least to try.

They picked a spot in the fence that was out of the way. It had to look like they were just sitting there, not cutting on the fence. The guy with the knife would go cut for a bit and then bury the knife in the ground nearby for the next person. Before getting started, Carl told the small group, "This is it guys. We got one chance to make it work."

Since it was Pawnley's knife, he was going to cut first when the time was right. The knife was hidden under an empty bed away from where they slept. Given the go, he watched as Pawnley casually sat on the empty bed and reached his hand in between the slats to find the knife sticking in the wood. As Pawnley pulled on it, a group of Italian

---

[117] Story told by Armie Hill in a 1976 interview (Hill, Recollection of camps 98 and 59 from Armie Hill, 2008)

guards suddenly came into the tent to do a "random" search. Carl saw Pawnley freeze and quickly lie on the bed. A guard walked toward the rest of the small group and started patting them down. He hoped Pawnley did not have the knife in his hand. It was almost as if they were specifically looking for it.

Pawnley was spotted over on the empty bed and Carl held his breath. Luckily, nothing turned up. He didn't know if the guards got next to their plan somehow, or if the lieutenant had heard them, but either way, it was too dangerous to continue. They'd have to lie low for a few days, but he was disappointed. Somehow, their plan was knocked in the head before they had even made the first cut.

Before the guards left, one of them said in broken English, "Tomorrow... new camp. We leave early."

Carl clenched his fists. "Tomorrow?" he muttered quietly. "That don't give us enough time."

However, true to their word, early the next morning, the enemy came and got everyone who could walk and lined them up outside. Besides Pawnley, Trenin, Baker, Hamel, and Goldstein, there weren't many others. "Hey guys," he whispered, "You notice the ole lieutenant ain't here with us."

Sure enough, he wasn't. Bombing boomed in the distance and once again, the frustration of being so close took hold. He couldn't believe it! The Americans surely were taking Palermo, and they were being moved to another Prisoner of War camp further away.

He began to figure out another way to escape and make it back to American lines and shared his idea with the others, "There are six of us. We can overtake the guards once we're out of sight on the other side of the mountain. We could easily make it back to Palermo from there."

"I agree," Hamel whispered before they loaded up on a truck at the front entrance.

He noticed a few sick men who used every ounce of their strength to get on the truck. Nobody wanted to get left behind. It was a risky chance—they would die at the camp, or the Americans would soon move in and save them. There was no way of knowing which would happen first.

191

As the truck bounced down the other side of the rugged mountain, they looked around. There were nearly two guards for every one prisoner. The plan would not work—they were overpowered and had no weapons. Instead, they were taken to a railroad station and waited for a train to arrive. He couldn't help but feel apprehensive with the thought of getting into an enemy train with American bombings so close. After all, an enemy train was a desirable target.

When the train stopped to pick them up, he felt like they were cattle being sent to the butcher. He could feel the guards breathing down his back as he climbed into the dark boxcar and sat down against the hot, metal wall. The thud of the guards' heavy boots echoed as they paced the boxcar floor—stepping on or kicking anyone too weak to move. There was no mercy! He was glad he was only stuck in that camp a few days and still had some strength left. Had it been any longer, he could see what might have happened.

The afternoon heated up, and so did the boxcar. There were only a few holes for air and it was hard to breathe. He didn't know whether it was better to stay by the burn of the metal wall or try to catch a flow of air. Hot and thirsty, he thought maybe if he fell asleep, it wouldn't be so miserable. Although difficult to sleep in there, he thought of cooler places and closed his eyes.

The train jerked to a stop and he opened his eyes. He wasn't sure if he had slept or passed out from the heat and lack of air, and he had no idea how long the trip had lasted or where they were. He anxiously stepped out and took a deep breath of the warm air that greeted him before being taken into an old building. The cells didn't look as discouraging with the other guys nearby.

"I'm starving," he said through the bars in the cell. "I wonder if they'll bring us something to eat."

"Me too," answered Trenin from the cell to his right. "It's getting late. It doesn't look like anything's coming."

The night wore on and Carl finally got the attention of one of the guards. He tried to convey the message of needing something to eat by acting as if he was spooning something into his mouth. When the guard turned around and ignored him, he kicked the door. One meal a day was bad enough, but it looked like it might turn into one meal every three days. Before leaving the next morning, he was handed a cup of coffee—and that was it for the day!

Surrounded by guards, they walked out of the building. The town was busy with people going everywhere. The odd thing was it looked like they were going everywhere with no place to go. He wondered what they knew that he didn't. When the sound of bomber planes filled the air, he realized what was causing the stir. Nobody knew what to expect and the people were scared. The way they scattered in every direction reminded him of mice mindlessly running when a granary door was opened.

Fear drifted through the air, but with good reason. Their cities were torn from end to end, and they were left destitute and hungry. If a crumb dropped, it was snatched up quicker than a miser could pick up a hundred dollar bill. Some didn't have a chance to get out in time. This was a reality of war and he hadn't expected to see it from an inside perspective.

They made it through town, but some of the sick men were struggling to keep up. This was a rough trip and with no food, he wondered how long they would be able to do it. Baker and he hooked arms with one of the guys and helped him make it to where there was a small boat waiting. Pushed together in a small quarters, the hot, sticky air made him feel sick.

Word was they were heading to a camp outside of Naples, Italy[118]. So far, the enemy kept moving him one step ahead of the Americans,

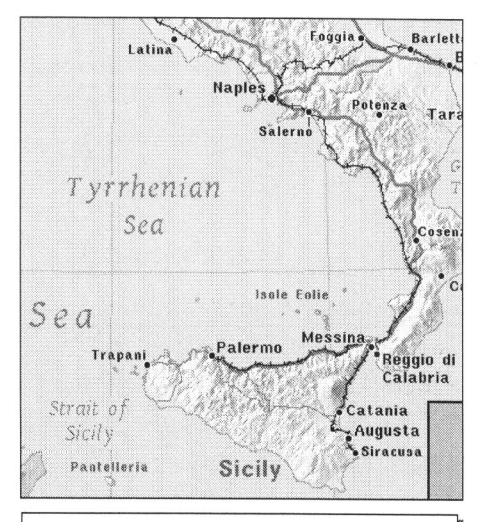

Figure 29: Map that shows Sicily and Naples, Italy
(PAT public domain maps)

---

[118] Based on letters and prison camp information, we know he was sent to transit Camp 66 near Naples, but we do not know for how long.

but he hoped it wouldn't be long before they caught up so he could return to his company. He wondered how much time had gone by since he was captured. He asked the other guys, "Does anyone know what day it is?"

Nobody was sure, but agreed it had to be the latter part of July. When they arrived at what they guessed were the docks of Naples, he wouldn't have guessed it was 2200 hours. Night was bright as day as bombs, flares, and enemy fire cut through the darkness. Once again, they would be stuck in the middle of it until the next morning.

When morning arrived, they began another long walk. Twisted train tracks curved toward the sky and bombed buildings lay crumbled along the road. It was evident last night's bombing had caused some major damage. Civilians lined some of the streets and watched them go by. Covered by guards as they walked, some of the people waved, but others were either too scared or weak to move. He could tell by the look of them that they were living in filth and starving. He and his fellow prisoners weren't the only ones being shoved around like dogs by the Germans and Fascists[119]. He hoped the Allies would be there to help them soon.

Weak and tired, he kept putting one foot in front of the other. What little energy he had left was quickly draining in the afternoon heat, and he wondered how much further he could walk with no food. He could feel the blisters on his feet as they rubbed against his boots. When he could hardly take another step, a horse and cart pulled up beside them and talked to the guards for a moment.

The back of the cart was filled with loose hay, and he couldn't believe their luck when the guards motioned for them to climb in the back. Even moving at a slow pace, the air felt good as he rested his feet. *Wait a minute*, he thought looking around, *where were the sick guys?*

He looked over at Baker and whispered, "What happened to the other boys. Last I knew they were walking behind us."

"I hope they were left at a hospital near Naples and didn't give out along the way," Baker whispered back. "I didn't see them leave either."

---

[119] A person who practices Fascism (radical authoritarian nationalism) * Explained in more detail in Chapter 12

Nobody knew, but he leaned back until he saw the new camp and its barracks in the distance. After several days of not eating, he was actually glad to see it. Of course, it was as nasty as the last and the smell verified that as they arrived. No sewers or running water played its toll and the stench covered the camp.

A few prisoners came over, gave them a general rundown of what to expect, and then added, "With all the stuff going on with Italy, this place has changed a lot. We get one meal a day, plus one Red Cross parcel a week. But don't get excited, there's never enough to go around. We end up sharing most things here."

"It's more food than we've been getting... even if we do have to share it," Carl said, knowing he needed the Red Cross parcel for survival.

Next, they went into the stuffy barrack where a few mice scurried across the floor and the smell of men who couldn't shower, but sweat all day, penetrated the area. Old beds made from 4x4 wood planks were inside. Although he already knew the answer, he still asked, "No blankets?"

"Nope. Only an old mattress filled with fleas, bedbugs, and lice," came the reply.

After a while, he went back to his bed. He was exhausted as he lay down and fell asleep. Strangely, his toleration for such revolting conditions was growing.

The next morning, everyone was required to get up and go outside. In long rows, they lined up to participate in roll call and to be counted like sheep. *Only a sheep would die in a hellhole like this*, he thought as he waited for his barrack's turn. For the first time, he saw everyone, and there were hundreds of them—Americans, British, South Africans, and French to name a few.

After several hours of roll call, he met up with the guys from the last camp and said, "Looks like a small cup of coffee is our breakfast."

"Beats having nothing," Hamel said as they found the line and waited.

To pass the time after "breakfast", they talked to the prisoners who had been there for a while. It was easy to make a quick friend in a place where everyone was in the same miserable situation. Even

195

though all of them were captured and subject to the will of the enemy, they could keep their minds busy and free through shared thoughts, ideas, and books.

Finally, the chaplain's words made sense. The chaplain had said if he kept the *New Testament* with him, he'd be sure to go home. It was a matter of keeping his mind busy and retaining hope—both things needed for survival. The greatest danger of being held captive was to become inactive. Inactivity led to a vicious cycle starting with self-pity and ending in death from the crushing blow of feeling overwhelmed by the adverse conditions[120]. Although he may not have realized it at that moment, that was the difference between being a survivor and being a corpse.

In fact, as the long days passed, he saw it happen around him. Self-pity snuck up on those who least expected in the form of dysentery, malaria, and starvation. Death was always close by, and it was plastered on the faces of those who had already given up. Where there was no will to survive, there was death. It was that simple, and he wasn't planning to give the enemy the satisfaction of seeing him dead.

A full day's meal consisted of a morning drink, a small cup of watery soup, and a piece of bread so hard it couldn't be eaten in one hungry gulp. At night, when he lay down, he was beginning to be able to count his ribs easily. He looked forward to the weekly Red Cross parcels to keep from starving. Although the sanitary supplies were usually missing, he waited for the small cans of food that had to get them by until the next week.

Sharing with Goldstein, he pulled out a can of meat. The can was poked full of holes so it would immediately spoil if not eaten. He showed it to Goldstein, "Looks like they don't want us hoarding food. That might be a problem if we weren't already half starved."

"Must've been a problem before," Goldstein said as he hungrily ate his equally divided part of the meat.

They were so hungry they hardly noticed a short-lived argument that broke out nearby between two men about who got what. Every

---

[120] Referenced by WW2 People's War (The darkest hour - 5th Northamptons (part 2), 2003)

man made sure he got his fair share of everything. In fact, scales in the thousandths of ounces could not have measured it any closer—fair was fair.

"It definitely ain't a problem now," Carl said as he carefully ran his finger along his side of the can to make sure he caught every particle belonging to him. When he was done, he could see his own reflection in the empty can and carefully set it to the side. Things he once would have considered trash quickly became useful tools within the camp. Ingenuity flourished and nothing went to waste.

He got up and looked for loose pieces of the brown, twine rope that bound the Red Cross packages. As he picked one up from off the ground, Goldstein asked him, "What are you saving the rope for?"

"I'm going to make me a broom… or rather a brush, to sweep with," he answered as he looked at the small pieces of rope in his hand.

"What are you going to sweep?" Goldstein asked as they walked toward the barrack.

"My bed and stuff. I might be stuck here, but I don't have to live in this filth. This way, I can brush my things off," he answered as they walked through the door.

It didn't take him long to figure out a way to tie the pieces together and try it out. Dust floated into the air as his rope brush hit the bed. Goldstein was impressed with the idea and asked, "Hey Good, you think I could borrow it for a minute?"

"Sure, but bring it back," he said as he got out his soup bowl.

It wasn't time to eat, but he filled it with a little water and carried it back to his barrack. He wet down the floor by his bed. It didn't really do much, but at least it looked cleaner. Goldstein used the brush and brought it back to him. Carl put it away and they walked back outside and met with a small group of Americans.

Before long, a few guards came around yelling, "Double rations, double rations, volunteer for double rations."

Somebody called out, "What for?"

"Filling up bomb craters," came the reply.

The idea of double rations, even for one day, was tempting, and a few men joined the guards. He looked at his small group and said, "Not me! If they don't want them there, let them give up."

"Yeah, I don't care what they give me. I wouldn't help them," said another.

Most of them felt that way. After the volunteers left, they walked around. He saw Trenin playing checkers on a hand drawn checkerboard in the dirt. Trenin moved a small rock on his turn and then looked up at them, "Did you guys hear the guards giving double rations for volunteering?"

"We sure did," Carl said, "but they ain't going to get us out there helping the enemy. Some Americans went though. We got to convince them it's not worth it when the guards come back looking for volunteers tomorrow."

Everyone agreed and helped spread the word. No matter what was offered in return—it wasn't worth it. The next day when the guards came to get volunteers, not one American went. It had worked.

The days in the August heat passed without much new happening. In this camp, he received one lira[121] a day for being held prisoner. He counted twenty-two[122] lire and knew it had been over a month since he was first captured. Finally, he could buy a toothbrush. He couldn't wait to brush his teeth with a real toothbrush again!

Of course, even with the time passing, he still had escape on his mind. It was what he looked forward to as he spent the days reading and talking to others. Sometimes, he would trade his *New Testament* for another book, but he always made sure to get it back. It didn't matter if the other person was religious or not—in these situations, most everyone became a little religious. He was sure first prayers were uttered from the mouths of disbelievers in war more than once.

Talk and speculation about what was going on around the front rampantly moved throughout the camp as the number of planes flying overhead increased. Not long after, two heavy bombardment Air Corps guys, Sergeant George Tucker and Sergeant James (Jim) Kingsland[123], were captured and said Sicily had been taken on

---

[121] Italian money: lira is singular and lire is plural
[122] Number of lire as remembered by Carl
[123] Real names—although Carl remembered the name James Kingsley, records prove James Kingsland was on the same plane with Tucker when it went down and his records match the rest of the information Carl remembered.

August 17. It could only be assumed an attack on Italy wasn't far off. Especially, since the Germans had managed to get troops, supplies, and weapons back to Italy even though the rush toward Messina was achieved in good time.

A few days later, August 25[124], the day started hot with roll call and count as usual. It was an ordinary day in camp until he felt his barrack shake as bombers roared through the morning sky—a little too close for comfort. The scenes of destruction he had witnessed from bombings flashed through his mind, and now they were flying above him—and he was on enemy territory.

Surely, the bombers would recognize the prison camp and stay away. Although he knew nothing was guaranteed, he went through his day. At or near high noon[125], he stood at the front of the barrack waiting for his afternoon meal of soup. Kingsland and Tucker were nearby when the sound of a plane made Tucker run to the door. Turning around, he yelled, "They're coming in. Get down!"

There was no time to process what Tucker had said as a bomb hit a trainload of ammunition along the railroad a few hundred yards from camp. Explosive energy radiated outward in all directions as it traveled above the speed of sound. Even though the overpressure from the blast only lasted a few milliseconds, it was long enough to blow out the windows and take the end of the barracks out. Without time to think or take cover, he was picked up like a rag doll and thrown half way across the barrack from the force of the explosion.

Explosions from artillery shells continued, and he knew he had to pick himself up and get to a safer place. Feeling dizzy and foggy, he dragged himself out and crawled into a drainage ditch as the roofs continued to blow off latrines, barracks, and other buildings. All afternoon the explosions continued, and he kept close to Mother Earth in the ditch. His head pounded and his body ached, but he wasn't going anywhere.

---

[124] True event as written in Carl's memoir. However, it is unknown if these explosions were at Camp 66 or Camp 35 near Salerno because letters addressed to Carl at both places were returned to him after the war.

[125] Carl didn't have a watch with him and told the time by where the sun was positioned in the sky. When the sun reaches its highest point, it is high noon.

Not only was his body suffering from the compression of the explosion and the depressurization force, but also from the blunt-force trauma from face planting into the hard floor. In and out of consciousness, he struggled to stay awake. The words of Psalms ran through his mind—*The Lord is my shepherd; I shall not want. He maketh me to lie down in green pastures: he leadeth me beside the still waters. He restoreth my soul: he leadeth me in the paths of righteousness for his name's sake. Yea, though I walk through the valley of the shadow of death, I will fear no evil: for thou art with me; thy rod and thy staff they comfort me...* and he passed out again before he could finish.

He didn't know how much time had passed when he felt pressure on his legs. There wasn't enough ditch for everyone, but that didn't keep people from squeezing in if there was a spare inch. He tried to move his legs, but there was nowhere to put them.

A feverish chill ran through his body as he lifted his head to look around him. Wincing in pain, he slowly raised his hand to touch the side of his head. It was as sore as a boil! Warm blood ran from his nose and down his throat. He coughed and tried to swallow, but his throat was sore and dry. At death's door, he waited to pass out again from the loss of blood.

A blood-curdling scream awoke him. Confused, he looked around. Where was he? Another scream made him jump as it echoed through his mind. It appeared he was in some sort of hospital, but how did he get there? He remembered nothing after the bomb exploded, but he wasn't alone. He could see rows of beds and most of them were full. Another scream and he realized there were no anesthetics. He looked down at his legs... they were both there.

A nurse came by with water when she noticed he was awake. "So, you decided to join us," she said with a smile. "Here, drink some water."

He put his hand on his throat and tried to speak. His throat was swollen and his words only came out in a hoarse whisper, "It hurts."

"Yes, it's going to hurt for a while," she said as she put a cool rag on his burning hot forehead. "You are lucky to be alive."

Before leaving, the nurse held the cup to his sore, cracked lips again. It took every ounce of strength to choke down a few desperate drops. Never before had he felt so exhausted and weak that he could hardly move. His nose was still bleeding and the loss of blood was overtaking him.

He tried to sleep it off, but even that was painful as he woke up throughout the night shivering from the high fever that burned within him. Too weak to find another blanket, he shivered. The excruciating pain from his throbbing head made him nauseous. He wondered at what point it was better to die.

Low flying planes made their presence known, and he knew the chances of making it through a second bombing were zero to none. He wasn't the only jumpy one though. At one point, a guy ran past him wildly searching for a place to take cover. If he had the energy, he might have done the same.

After three days in the hospital, he still felt miserable and began to wonder if he would ever get his strength back. To make matters worse, he received word all prisoners were being sent to a new camp in northern Italy. Now he was one of the sick ones, but there was no way he was going to get left behind while everybody else moved on. He pushed himself to get up and pretend he was well enough to go.

Within minutes of leaving, he wondered if he had made the right decision as he struggled to keep up. His body ached and he had zero energy to walk under the August sun. It felt as if a furnace was blasting in hot air with no thermostat to control it. Not a single breeze relieved the struggle as he carried the one box he had been given. He had to keep going, even if it meant dragging one foot in front of the other across the dry, dusty road.

One mile, then two, and on to the third, he didn't think he could do it anymore. He had tried, but he began to feel like he was completely going to give out as he fell to the rear one by one. Death would have been a pleasure right then, but once again that stubborn part of him kicked in and refused with every ounce of his being to die and give the enemy that satisfaction. That thought alone kept his feet moving as he completed the fourth, fifth, and sixth mile.

When they were within a half-mile of the train station, a sound made his heart jump—low planes were passing overhead. The guards all started talking at once as they pushed everyone off the side of the road into the cover of an olive grove. The planes disappeared in the clear, blue sky and everyone picked up their stuff.

Already at the end of the line, he desperately tried to get back on his feet—but he couldn't. He pushed himself to his knees, but he could get no farther. Drained, he fell forward onto his hands and put his forehead on the ground. When the guard saw he wasn't getting up, he came at him with his bayonet to poke and push at him.

He raised his head and tried to focus through a blur of fading color. The guard's mouth was moving and yelling, but the words faded into a new peace that enveloped him in silence. On the line of life or death, he really didn't have the energy to care what was being said to him. He finally had reached the point of giving up—not because he wanted to, but because his body had reached its limits.

In the moments he struggled, Baker, Tucker, and Kingsland had walked back to him. Baker picked up the box he was carrying and Tucker and Kingsland grabbed his arms and pulled him up between them. They had been in the blast too, but Tucker and Kingsland knew what was coming and had gotten down fast. Since they were newly captured, they had more energy than the rest.

Still, he looked up at them and slurred, "Leave me here. I can't do it nomore."

"Come on. You're too close to quit now. We're almost there," Kingsland said firmly.

He wanted to, but he whispered, "I can't take another step."

"Come on. We'll help you," Kingsland said as they helped him move forward.

Every yard felt like a hundred yards. Every breath felt as if it was his last. Finally, he heard Tucker say, "Only a few more steps."

Without a bit of strength left in his body, Kingsland and Tucker lifted him onto the crowded boxcar and sat down nearby. It was impossible to get in a comfortable position, but he stretched out on the floor as much as possible. The train lurched forward and headed north. Nightfall approached and the train stopped. All the guards got out.

"What's going on," he whispered, but nobody could hear him.

Tucker looked over at Kingsland and said, "They're going to lock us in here overnight so they're not around if the train gets bombed."

Twisted, broken tracks... the bombed train by the prison camp that nearly took his life... it was a sickening thought that they had been left in the hot, dark boxcar possibly to die. The guards would have a chance to escape if the planes showed up, but nobody else would. There was nothing to do but wait and pray the Allied bombers wouldn't find them that night. For once, he was relieved when he heard the guards open the boxcar door and climb in before the train jerked into motion early the next morning. They had made it through the night.

That afternoon Tucker and Kingsland helped him out of the boxcar and onto a truck that took them the rest of the way to the new prison camp—Camp Servigliano number 59. Weak and tired, he stumbled through the gates. Several prisoners came over to greet them and anxiously hoped for updates and news. Too tired to participate in the conversation, he listened as they talked about the camp. One of the guys who came over said, "I've been here two years now. It's not as bad as some of the camps out there."

Carl hadn't even been captured for two months, and he was barely hanging by a thread. Maybe this camp *was* different. Although the stench was the same and it was still a prison camp with bugs and filth, the atmosphere was noticeably different as they walked through the camp toward their barrack. They passed guys playing cards or checkers in the dirt, others exercising, and one group even building some clever creation out of scraps. It was as if everything ran smoothly and the feeling of desperate hopelessness didn't overtake every prisoner.

"Almost there," Tucker told him as he helped him along.

He was tired, but he knew he could make it that last little bit. Maybe if he didn't think about the walk and listened to the guy talking, it would be less painful. The guy hadn't stopped talking and was saying, "There are roughly 2,000 of us here now. However, we keep it organized and there are many groups around to make you feel comfortable. With limited water and rations, it's certainly no place to call home, but we make the best of it. As long as you follow the rules, you'll be fine. The camp commander isn't too rough, but he has a way of making sure everybody knows who doesn't follow the rules and the consequences that follow through public display or solitary confinement."

They finally reached their barrack and went in. A mouse scurried under one of the wooden, stacked bunks. Unfazed by the mouse, Carl just wanted a bunk so he could lie down. The bedbugs were so thick he could see them climbing the posts of the beds. In these conditions, a shower once every two weeks (if he was lucky) was not enough. He felt dirty and sick.

"Don't get comfortable, Good," he heard Kingsland say. "We're taking you to the camp hospital. If you don't start eating, you're going to starve."

To be honest, he didn't feel hungry anymore and even soft food felt hard. Water burned his throat as he swallowed, and it was less painful to sleep through it. It could take weeks slowly to starve to death, but only days to dehydrate and die of thirst[126]. Kingsland was right. He needed to see the camp doctor, Captain Millar[127].

If the rumors were true, Italy wasn't going to last much longer as an Axis partner. Although they didn't know what that meant for them, he was already thinking of how to escape into the Tenna Valley in the Marche and into the Sibylline Mountains[128]. In a camp this size, there were other groups constantly thinking the same thing—and he needed his strength to be able to do it!

---

[126] As a general rule, depending on many other factors, it is said 3 minutes without air, 3 days without water, and 3 weeks without food will cause a person to start dying from the lack of aforementioned items.

[127] Captain J.H. Derek Millar was a British chief medical officer at Camp 59 and referenced by Dennis Hill (Hill, Captain Millar—valor in the hour of crisis, 2011)

[128] Part of the Central Apennine Mountains.

Chapter 11 – LIVING HELL

Figure 30: Camp 59 near Servigliano, Italy
(Permission granted by Associazione Casa della Memoria)

CHAPTER 12

NARROW ESCAPE

IMMEDIATELY, CAPTAIN MILLAR began treatments as he handed Carl a cup with purple liquid and said in his British accent, "Here, have a gargle with this."

It didn't look so bad, but when he put it in his mouth, he gagged—it tasted rotten! It took every ounce of self-discipline not immediately to spit it out. Noticing his reaction, Captain Millar put his hand on his shoulder and said, "Not to worry, mate. You'll get used to it."

He didn't know about that, but as the days passed, it was helping his throat heal. Although he still wasn't able to take advantage of the full portions given in the hospital area, he was gaining his strength back. After ten days, he could even eat the bread if he soaked it in his soup to make it soft enough to swallow.

He was getting well enough that Captain Millar told him to come back every third day instead of every day. Grateful for the good doctor's help, he walked back to his barrack. In a week and a half, he was getting a good idea of how things worked at the camp.

The next evening[129], he slowly walked outside with a group of buddies he had come to trust. Along with Tucker and Kingsland, there was Joseph Altomari[130], James (Jim) Snodgrass, and James (Jim)

---

[129] September 8, 1943
[130] Carl remembered the name Joseph Olinix, but there are no such records. However, Joseph Altomari was in Camp 59 and escaped. He was also on the same paper of those who made it back to Allied lines along with Snodgrass, Martelli, and Carl.

Martelli[131]. They all agreed—escape would be the only way out and it filled their minds.

In midsentence, Carl stopped talking and held up his hand, "Do you guys hear that?"

They all stopped and listened. It sounded like a commotion was coming from the direction of Servigliano—a village less than a mile away[132]. "It doesn't sound like a sad cry of distress, rather a happy uproar," Tucker said.

They nodded their heads in agreement, but they hadn't heard any new information that would cause the villagers to shout out like that. In the prison camp, it had been another routine day—September 8. They joined with another group who had obviously heard it too. "What do you think is going on over there?" Carl asked.

"No idea, but we're hoping it's good news," one of them said.

They talked about it until it was time to return to the barrack. Once inside, they were locked in and nobody was allowed to talk. With so much going on, it was hard to keep quiet and a few guys kept talking. Suddenly, the night guards barged into the barrack[133].

Everyone lay quiet as the guards took a wild guess at who was talking and grabbed a sleeping man from his bunk and yelled out, "Solitary! Solitary!"

The two guys who had been talking burst out laughing at the notion the guards had grabbed someone sound asleep. The guards grabbed them too, and walked out with the three of them headed for solitary confinement. Although solitary confinement for something like that was usually only one or two days in a separate area without food, it was not something he wanted to experience from himself—especially if he was innocent.

The next morning, he got up as usual, but before long, another loud roar came from Servigliano. Everyone stopped what they were

---

[131] Real names as remembered by Carl unless otherwise noted
[132] Events of what happened inside Camp 59 as pieced together by Giuseppe Millozzi (Hill, Captain Millar—valor in the hour of crisis, 2011)
[133] Solitary confinement and other aspects of Camp 59 described by Armie Hill from interviews with his son, Dennis Hill, in 1976 (Hill, Recollection of camps 98 and 59 from Armie Hill, 2008)

doing and listened. He looked over at Kingsland, Tucker, and Martelli, and the four of them joined groups of prisoners who were being drawn to the main gate. "Can you see anything?" he asked them as he stood on his toes to try to see through the crowd.

It was a silly question since Martelli was only 5'6—more than three inches shorter than Carl was. Martelli didn't seem to think twice about it and answered with a quick, "Nothing." With his Brooklyn accent, it sounded more like nottin'.

As they stood there trying to figure out what was going on, a low cheer started at the front and grew louder as it moved through the crowd. The guys in front of them turned around and yelled, "We're free! Italy packed in and the Allies are coming!"

Guards walked through the crowd, and one of them shook Carl's hand with tears in his eyes. Was this really happening? Could it be true? The excitement radiating through the air said it was. A guy ran through the crowd picking up random people in a giant bear hug, spinning them around, and then moved on to the next person with a laugh.

Nobody minded it today as they moved in mass toward the parade area. Music filled the air and national pride glowed through the prisoners as various national anthems played. When the first notes of the *Star-Spangled Banner* began to play, he felt the music flow through his body and carry him home. What a day! They were free!

There weren't many details, but hearing Italy had packed in was enough. All the planning of escape was being fulfilled on its own. In no time at all, they would be set free and returned to their companies. They would no longer be trapped in these mice-infested, bug-ridden, disease-covered barracks. Now, they only had to wait at the camp until the Allies came in and liberated them as ordered.

That night, everyone was out walking and talking before it was time to return to the barracks. Anticipation radiated out of each prisoner as they speculated how the release would work. The talk was some of the Italian guards, who didn't want to be there in the first place, had already vacated their posts with the news. Captain Millar was taking charge of keeping things in order while they waited.

Chapter 12 – Narrow Escape

"If that's true, we can use the weakened security around the prison to our advantage and escape if we have to," Carl said as he talked with his group.

"You're not goofin'. We need a plan," added Martelli. He spoke fast and his Brooklyn accent made his words sound like they blended at times.

"We don't have time tonight, but let's see what tomorrow brings and go from there," Snodgrass said as they walked into the barrack.

However, the next morning was the same—no news. The excitement began to die down when the second and third days came and went. They couldn't be let out to wander the Italian mountains, but where were the Allies? Why had no one come to get them yet? Enough time had passed for them to be rescued—or had it? Something wasn't right.

Concerned talk over what should be done was the main subject of conversation. Once again, opinions were divided. A variety of statements flew around:

"We should wait. There are a lot of camps. They haven't made it this far yet."

"I smell a mouse, something ain't right."

"If we try to escape, they will shoot us."

"Nobody will shoot us. Unless they're Fascists, they don't care."

"No, the ones who don't care already left. The ones left will kill us."

"What will we do if we get out?"

"Well, where are they?"

There was too much confusion not to be prepared. They didn't have any weapons, but they gathered some rocks. If it came down to it, they could use the rocks to throw at the guards as they ran out the front gate. If enough of them escaped at the same time, they would be able to make it—well, at least some of them would.

It sounded simple enough—Italy folded and they should be free. However, there was a lot going on in Italy they didn't know about. It had been a little over a month since the head leader of the Fascists and dictator of Italy, Mussolini, was arrested and overthrown[134]. However,

---

[134] July 25, 1943

Mussolini's replacement, Prime Minister Pietro Badoglio, was slow to take charge as needed. It didn't take long for the Germans to quickly use it to their advantage and start taking control.

The Italians didn't know who they should be fighting—the invading Allies or the Germans who were occupying key points and headquarters, cutting telephone lines, and passing around misleading propaganda. The Italians had already signed a secret armistice with the Allies on September 3[135]. However, it was so secret the Italian armed forces didn't even know about it until September 8 when the Allies published it with their planned landings in Salerno set for the next day. They needed to push the Germans back.

Hitler wasn't going to lose a second foothold without a fight. He needed Mussolini out of prison to regain the support of Italy's strong Fascists. The Fascists would help spread fear among the Italians who didn't agree and make the general public afraid to help the Allies. Four days later[136], Hitler had Mussolini rescued by a special force and immediately sent him to northern Italy to regain those valuable connections.

So much happened so fast that nobody knew what was going on! One day they were being told Italy had folded and joined with the Allies, and then in the next few days, they were being told Italy had surrendered to Germany. The camp commander was confused along with everybody else—no matter which side he took, he could end up dead.

The next morning was the 13th and Carl was due to see Captain Millar for his medical visit. Large groups of prisoners stood together talking as he passed by. He knew he would hear some good information while he was at the hospital. If a mass escape were going to be put in order, it would come from Captain Millar.

Sure enough, when he got there, he heard a senior British officer had been sent to the camp forbidding an escape with a stay put order. The officer had emphasized the last thing they needed was a massive, disorganized massacre.

---

[135] When the Allies first landed in Italy
[136] September 12, 1943

Nobody wanted a bloody massacre, but nobody wanted to get transferred to Germany either. The stay put order would be taken into consideration, but ultimately, Captain Millar was going to do whatever was best for everyone in the camp. There were other things to worry about—like why the Allies were not moving in and the rumors of Germans taking nearby POW camps were becoming more common.

Upon returning to the group, Carl shared what he had heard and then added, "There's no question in my mind; I will die trying to escape rather than be taken to Germany. I done had my feel for what it was like to be with those Krautheads, I'm not going to their motherland no matter what!"

Although most of them agreed, there were a few who weren't sure. One of them said, "If there is a stay put order, then we should wait. There's nothing to worry about. The Germans will be too busy fighting to worry about us. They'll keep us here where at least we're protected."

Carl was in no mood to argue, but he couldn't agree with that logic. "No, no... we can't stand around waiting. There's no time. If the other POW camps are being taken, then what makes you think they won't come here?"

"Look around," the other argued pointing to the thick stonewalls topped with broken bottles and glass that angled inward. "How can we escape a prison camp like this? There's not a chance."

"Well, you can stick around, but I'm not," he said. "Where there's a will, there's a way, and I got the will. If there is a mass escape, I'll be one of the first ones out of here."

Of course, he knew it wouldn't be easy to escape, especially in his weakened condition. He had studied the camp many times, and he knew there were guard towers on each corner, searchlights directly lighting the camp at night, and guards on watch duty. By now, the guards who had left were quickly replaced under the new German power.

It might be near impossible to escape the camp under normal conditions, but with all the confusion, it could be a possibility if Captain Millar led them in that direction. Although it wasn't confirmed, it definitely felt like the push was headed that way. Especially when Red Cross parcels were handed out—just in case. It wouldn't be much, but it would be enough food for roughly ten days if he ate it sparingly.

Before dawn, September 14, the rumors were moving like an untamed wildfire. He heard yelling outside and tried to hear what was being said. Someone opened the barrack door and yelled, "The Germans took a POW camp nearby, and we're next! Get prepared! We're leaving tonight with or without the commander's help!"

He knew what was meant by "with or without the commander's help." There were rumors the guards would let them go before the Germans got there. However, nobody knew if the rumor could be trusted. Some of the guards who had bailed from their posts earlier had ended up dead, and similar threats were being dispersed among all the people. He doubted if the guards would put their lives on the line for them.

The day quickly passed with anticipation of what was to come. By 1700 hours, he stood in front of his barrack to hear the final news from Captain Millar. Were they leaving or staying? Upon hearing the words *get ready to escape*, his blood pumped faster. He had waited for those words since the day he was captured. Today, they were really going to do it, even with armed guards on watch.

Everyone in the camp had to decide right then and there to go or stay. Nobody would be forced to escape. Either choice was risky, but Carl wasn't about to pass the opportunity—no matter how dangerous it was. They had already planned an escape group of six—Kingsland, Tucker, Altomari, Snodgrass, Martelli[137] and him, and he was confident his group had no hesitations.

As they got ready, Kingsland said, "Captain Millar said not to do anything foolish before or after the escape. Don't forget we're unarmed."

"All we got are the rocks we collected. Keep them close by and grab your stuff," Tucker added.

Somebody ran by yelling, "The Germans are getting closer!"

That one sentence added fuel to an already raging fire. The prisoners' force and desire made the plan for escape irreversible at that

---

[137] All real names of the people in his escape group

point. The evening sky darkened and the tension continued to rise. No longer able to wait, newly captured British Special Air Service (SAS) men got together and began chiseling a large hole in the stonewall[138] surrounding them. Whether it was through the front gates or not, they were NOT going to be taken to Germany.

The hole was busted out, and a few prisoners went through it. Gunshots rang through the night as they escaped. Carl grabbed a few good throwing rocks and ran through the darkened chaos with his group. This was their chance! After getting through the hole in the wall, they made it to the second perimeter fence. Another hole was already cut there and they slipped through it.

More gunshots rang out as prisoners poured through the hole in the darkness. Those bullets were either to produce fear but not intentionally kill, or make it look like the guards resisted against the escape even though they didn't really care. Either way, he quickly crawled into the underbrush toward the mountains.

Figure 31: The hole in the wall from which Carl and his group escaped Camp 59 (Permission granted by Associazione Casa della Memoria)

Nobody in his group had a map like some of the other groups. They would have to make an educated guess as to where the safest place would be—away from the Germans. Snodgrass and Altomari had been in the camp the longest and Snodgrass whispered, "Based on hearsay, there are basically three options. We can go down the hills to find the Adriatic Sea and try to make it south to where the Allies are fighting, head north for the neutrality of Switzerland, or try to hide in the protection of the rocky valleys and hills of the mountains nearby until the Allies arrive."

---

[138] From a book about the SAS (Dorney, 2005)

They didn't have time to think about it long. From where they were, they heard the camp's loudspeaker as a flustered Italian voice boomed across with instructions for the guards to cease fire. Had the rumors been true but the guards misinformed, or had Captain Millar talked with the camp commander and taken full responsibility for the escape?[139]

Figure 32: Map showing their starting point near Servigliano
(PAT public domain maps)

Shortly after, around 2230 hours, many more prisoners and Italian guards ran through the gates and doors around the prison camp when someone went running through the camp yelling, "The Germans have come to take us to Germany!"

Now, there were more than 2000 escaped prisoners in the darkness trying to figure out where to go next. He could feel it getting crowded around them. "We got to keep moving. Getting far away from this camp will be our best chance to not get recaptured when the Germans move in, and I have a feeling they're right around the corner. I've always looked at heading toward Switzerland," Carl whispered.

---

[139] Captain Millar signed a declaration taking full responsibility for the escape as explained by Giuseppe Millozzi

Snodgrass whispered back, "I've heard there's a river[140] running between the wooded areas here. We can stay in the woods and head that way."

Martelli spoke fast and low in his Brooklyn accent that seemed to cut the "r" and "g" off the end of some of his words[141], "No matta' the direction, we'll need the protection of the woods. Headin' toward the mountains is a good idea, plus we'll have wata' nearby."

Tucker and Kingsland started out and climbed through the brush first. Out of the six of them, they were still the strongest. After only walking about a fourth of a mile, Carl had to stop and catch his breath.[142] Nobody complained. They were all weak from the prison camp—some more than others.

He knew their rests had to be short. He didn't want to be anywhere near the camp by morning, but he could only handle about a fourth of a mile before needing to stop again. Snodgrass was wearing out too, but they kept going by the light of the moon. After stopping for a breath, Snodgrass sat down and leaned against a tree. When they started out again, Snodgrass didn't get up.

Carl went over to him and shook his arm. "It looks like Snodgrass is completely passed out," he quietly said.

Snodgrass was the one in the Army medical department, but at this point, they were all on an even playing field. Carl wondered if his body had finally succumbed from being in the camp longer than the rest of them. Lightly slapping him on the face, he said, "Wake up. You can do this. Come on."

It was hard to see him in the dark. "Come on. We got to get out of here, Snodgrass," he urged as he felt for a pulse along his neck. He felt one.

Snodgrass wasn't dead—only exhausted as he slowly blinked his eyes open and looked around. They didn't have time to wait it off and

---

[140] Tenna River
[141] There is much more to a Brooklyn accent, but for reading purposes only a few characteristics will be used
[142] Story of escaping through the hole in the wall and what happened after was written by Carl in his memoir and is a true account. Conversation and details have been added.

several of them helped pull Snodgrass to his feet again. Carl's own close call with death still hung fresh in his mind, and he hadn't been left behind—much thanks to Tucker and Kingsland. Although weak himself, it was his turn to repay the favor.

The mountains were his focal point and they climbed through the darkness, up the rough, rugged terrain all night. Higher than the camp below, he looked back. He saw what looked like little fires burning below them. *What's burning?* he wondered, but it was too dangerous to ask it aloud.

Before long he realized the fires were coming from large, loose stacks of hay—dangerous hiding spots for escapees who didn't think about them becoming quick infernos. With the light of a match, the dry hay started on fire and the prisoner either burned, or was shot upon exiting. It was cruel, but after what he had seen earlier, it was not surprising.

Completely exhausted, they made it a little less than ten miles before the morning sun began its daily ascent into the blue sky. Happy with their progress, they hoped they hadn't pushed too hard. It would be too dangerous to move in the light of day, so they could rest it off as they hid themselves in a low, brushy area within the municipality of Monte San Martino. It wasn't the safest place, but safer than being out in the open.

Figure 33: View of Monte San Martino landscape in 2015
(Pictures taken by Vanesa and Ricardo Funari)

Chapter 12 – Narrow Escape

It was interesting how the tables had turned. Now, he was the rabbit being hunted. Only difference was he had hunted rabbits for food and necessity, and the Germans were hunting him because they wanted to recapture or kill him.

It felt like the crosshairs of a gun scope continuously were on his head. If he moved in the wrong direction or talked to the wrong person, he could be shot. To further the danger, the Germans and Fascists quickly made it known that anyone caught helping the escaped prisoners would suffer the consequences of death.

The friendly Italian *contadini* (farmers) were becoming afraid of their own shadows and had become prisoners in their own country. They were also suffering under the hands of the Germans and hoped it would end soon. The problem was figuring out who the Fascists were. Not all Italians were there to help and would turn them in without hesitation. There was nobody they could fully trust—nobody.

After going all night, he slept through most of the morning. By afternoon, he couldn't sleep. It was too hot and gunshots unceasingly rang through the air. It was too dangerous to move, but he was glad to have the Red Cross parcel with him. He quickly realized he was the only one in his group who had secured one, and it wasn't going to last very long between the six of them.

After a few hours, the sun began to set in the western sky, and they got ready to move. This time, they headed down hill instead of up, as they stayed hidden in the woods. Suddenly, he stopped and everyone else did too.

It was important to carefully watch each other and react accordingly when it was too dangerous to speak. He pointed to something, or someone, he saw in the dimming light. Behind some bushes, they watched and waited. When they saw it was an old, Italian woman walking near a humble home, they put their heads together and whispered so quietly they could hardly hear each other.

"Maybe we could get a bit of something to eat," Carl started out.

"Does anyone speak Italian?" Tucker asked.

Martelli nodded his head, but looked unsure. Everyone was surprised. Martelli hadn't mentioned that before. Then Martelli quietly added, "My parents were both born in Italy. I was raised speakin'

English with my brothas and sistas in the Italian part of Brooklyn, but it won't be fluent... if it's even the same dialect at all."

"Doesn't matter. Let's try," Kingsland whispered.

Everyone agreed.

She froze in place when she saw them come out and walk toward her. It wasn't completely dark yet, but it was getting hard to see. Martelli stepped forward and tried to speak, but the woman blankly stared back at him. "Forget about it," he said in one breath that sounded more like fuggedaboutdit. "She doesn't understand me."

It was okay. They could still get the message across as they acted as if they were stuffing food in their mouths. Looking at them, the woman said, "*Páne?*"

He recognized that word from the Soldier's Guide. It was one of the words he had practiced. "Bread," he guessed.

"I think you're right," Martelli agreed.

She said a long sentence including the word *páne* as she turned around.

"I think she said to wait for bread... or somethin' along that line," Martelli told them.

It was not easy to trust people—especially older people who may favor the Fascist ideology. Germans were everywhere and they didn't know if she would turn them in or not.

"Um... should we wait here in the brush and see how quickly she returns?" Altomari nervously asked in an accent similar to Martelli's. Turned out they were both from Kings County, New York. However, he was quite a bit older than the rest of them—eleven years older than Carl was.

Before they could decide, the woman came back out with a small loaf of bread. It was hard to ask for food when they knew the people didn't have a lot to give. Humbled by her generosity, Carl looked at her wrinkled, aged face and said the other word he remembered from when he helped the man with the mules up the ditch, "*Grazie! Grazie!*"

They equally divided the loaf between the six of them without dropping a crumb and kept walking. A mountain peak in the distance was their guide for that night, and they hoped to make it by morning.

Once the sun was gone, the chilly, mountain air crept alive around them as the sound of night took hold under the moonlit sky.

Silently walking, they heard a noise and took cover in the mountain brush. They waited, but nothing appeared. Constantly on the lookout, they walked along a small path they had found along the southern boundaries of the Municipality of Monte San Martino. Off in the distance, there was a hamlet with three farmhouses, and they crept in that direction. Most likely one house belonged to the owners of the land and sharecroppers used the other two.

Through the darkness, they saw an Italian man working outside in the cool night air and chanced to talk to him. After all, there were six of them and the man was alone from what they could see. Martelli tried to speak. He started it out with a simple phrase, "*Buona sera, signore*[143]."

Stopping his late evening work, the man looked at them and smiled, "*Buona sera.*"

After exchanging simple pleasantries, they learned his name was Giovanni Straffi[144]. He seemed glad to see them as he pointed down to one of the houses they had seen earlier and said something about *casa mia*.

"He said somethin' about his house. I think he wants to help us," Martelli said as he looked back at them.

Eventually, they would have to trust someone, but all six of them were plenty leery as they quickly conversed.

"Will he help us, or turn us in?"

"It's too risky."

"This could be our chance to get somethin' solid to eat."

"The nights are getting cold. He might have some hay for us to rest on."

"I say we go with him, but don't let our guards down even for a second," Tucker said, ending the conversation.

The possibility of food and a place to sleep for the night outweighed the risk, and they walked down the dry, dusty road with Giovanni.

---

[143] Good evening, sir.
[144] Real name of farmer—Verified through the help of Ian McCarthy and Antonio Millozzi

Carl guessed Giovanni was in his late fifties from the look of his tough, wrinkled, sun-soaked skin, but his gentle smile radiated kindness. If they had to trust someone, he looked like a good man to trust.

They intently listened as Giovanni gave them a run down on what was happening around them. Martelli figured out part of what was being said, and Giovanni acted out the rest. From what they could piece together, he had gone to town that day to get the latest updates and everyone was talking about the prison break. The Germans and Fascists were hot in the area rounding up as many prisoners as possible and spraying the brush with gunfire as they went along.

Giovanni stopped walking and stretched out his hand as he pointed around him in the darkness. Carl figured he was giving them a layout of the area. After he pointed to the same area several times, Carl asked Martelli, "Why is that area so important?"

"I think he's sayin' we'll be safer there, but he wants us to go with him tonight," Martelli said. Looking back at Giovanni for confirmation, he asked, "*Domani*[145]?" and pointed to the canyon area.

Giovanni nodded his head yes and motioned for them to follow him as he continued talking and pointing out empty fields of stolen animals and grain. They could tell this war had brought nothing but misery to these people. Abruptly stopping, he pointed to their uniforms while sweeping over the area with his hand. Then he held up three and then four fingers as he repeated, "*Tre o quattro giorni.*"

"Is he saying he hopes they will be liberated by the Allies in three or four days?" Kingsland asked, looking at Martelli.

Martelli nodded his head yes, "I think he is."

"Three or four days sounds about right to me," Carl said, looking at the others. "We can wait it out."

"Oh yeah, after what we've been through, that's a drop in the bucket," Kingsland agreed.

After another brief walk, Giovanni stopped by an old chicken coop within a couple hundred yards from a tall, rectangular house. It was odd how the house was divided. It looked like it was two stories, but animals lived in a section of the bottom half to keep the top half

---

[145] Tomorrow

warmer during the cold winters. Giovanni said something to Martelli as he pointed at the coop.

Martelli stopped to figure it out for a minute and said, "We can stay in the chicken house for tonight."

"Well, based on what we have gathered from Giovanni, the enemy is swarming around here looking for us," Kingsland said. "So, is it more dangerous to trust someone like him or stay on the open roads?"

"Er... wouldn't the chicken coop be the first place they look? I mean, if they find us, they'll send us back to Germany or shoot us," Altomari said with a glance down the dark, country road.

"Either way it's a gamble," Carl said. "The obvious answer is to say no, but it don't matter where we go, we'll have to get food from somebody. In my opinion, the less exposure to the enemy, the better."

He felt like he was putting poker chips marked with his life on black and wildly spinning a roulette wheel. If it landed on red, he lost. If it landed on black, he still had a chance to make it until tomorrow. There really wasn't a safe place anywhere, and as far as he was concerned, getting recaptured wasn't an option.

"Valid point, Good. We don't know who will help us or who will turn us in. It's safer to trust Giovanni here. Tell him we'll only stay until things settle down," Tucker said, looking around to see if anyone disagreed.

Nobody said anything although Carl could see Altomari uneasily biting his lower lip. Martelli passed along the information. Giovanni smiled, put up one finger as he said something, and walked to his house. A few minutes later, he came back out with his wife walking behind him. She carried a pitcher of fresh wine made from the surrounding vineyards.

"Now that's what I'm talkin' about," Martelli said, rubbing his hands together.

After everyone but Carl took a large drink, Giovanni's wife looked at him and said something about *vino* while shaking her head no.

Carl knew what she meant and Martelli verified it when he said, "She wants to know why no wine. It's good."

Shaking his head no, Carl pointed to the nearly empty pitcher, "No thanks. I don't drink w—"

Before he could finish, the group burst into quiet laughter. Giovanni's wife looked surprised, but laughed something in return. He didn't understand her words, but he had a pretty good idea based on her expression. In an area of vineyards, who didn't drink wine? With a smile, he shrugged his shoulders and repeated, "No wine."

Again, everyone quietly laughed as Giovanni and his wife wished them a good night and headed back to the house. Alone in the darkness, they made small beds of straw in the empty chicken coop. There were no chickens because Giovanni said the Germans and Fascists had already stolen them along with anything else they wanted. If that were true, Giovanni could most likely be trusted—he probably hated the enemy as much as they did.

However, in the back of Carl's mind, he still worried. What if Giovanni turned them in for some kind of much-needed reward? They'd have to take turns sleeping while one person stayed awake and listened, and they'd have to be absolutely silent. Although they were on a country road, they couldn't chance being heard by a passerby—their English words would be easily detected.

Kingsland volunteered to stay on guard first as Carl lay down on the prickly straw. It felt soft compared to the hard, wooden beds in the prison camps, and they were protected from the chilly, night air. Bugs, smell, night noise—nothing mattered for a brief moment as his body relaxed as much as possible while on the run.

A few hours later, Martelli's Brooklyn accent broke through the silence as he bumped Carl's arm, "Good, it's your turn to listen."

He sat up. *What time is it?* he wondered as he looked out a small window at the moon. He didn't have a watch, but he could get an idea by reading the moon as long as it wasn't cloudy. Although harder than simply looking at its position in the sky like the sun, he could read the line where dark and light met. Then he checked its position to figure out how much time they had until sunrise. It looked like they still had a couple more hours before they needed to leave.

Giovanni had told them to be out of the chicken coop before sunrise in case the enemy passed nearby. That was why he had been pointing to the deep canyon area last night. It was low, remote, and a ways off the main road. A river cut across the countryside where thick

Chapter 12 – Narrow Escape

timber brush and high grass grew. Giovanni hoped they would be safe there.

After an estimated hour, Carl lightly tapped Snodgrass. "It's your turn for guard," he whispered as he lay back down on the warm straw.

It wouldn't be long before they needed to head out, but he thought that at least another hour of rest sounded good. It felt like only minutes had passed when he heard Altomari whispering, "Come on. It looks like we need to head out."

Through the chilly, early morning darkness, they crept through the damp grass into the canyon. When they stopped in some heavy brush, they got together. Tucker whispered, "It's too dangerous for us to all stay together now. We'll have a better chance if we break into smaller groups."

"I was thinking the same thing," Carl whispered back. "I was thinking we shouldn't risk more than two in a group."

They would all still stay in the same area, but moving around in a group of two was safer than being in a large group. He knew Tucker and Kingsland would pair off, and that left Martelli, Snodgrass, and Altomari. It didn't matter to him and Altomari and Snodgrass had been together at the camp longer, so he joined with Martelli.

"Let's stay hidden in the brush and head down toward those trees in the valley," Carl suggested as they split off from the others. The trees were part of a green, leafy apple orchard. "Look at that," he whispered in surprise. "I never saw grape vines growing up the trunks of apple trees before."

The long, green vines spilled over the branches and there were grapes ripe enough to eat. He knew the picking time for apples depended on the variety, but when he lightly pulled on one and it came off in his hand, he took a few. With the enemy moving around the area, he didn't figure the fruit would last long.

Martelli came over to where he was eating an apple and whispered, "You'd betta' eat up. I'll bet you dollas to doughnuts there won't be many more chances like this come along."

Carl laughed at the odd expression. He hadn't heard "bet you dollars to doughnuts" before. He caught most of what Martelli said,

223

but sometimes he had to listen closely to understand his expressions or the different way he pronounced words.

He ate the sweet fruits, but they weren't heavy enough to satisfy his hunger. He only grabbed a couple apples to take with him for the afternoon though. Somebody worked hard to get that fruit to grow, and he didn't feel right taking it. He needed food to survive, but he wouldn't get greedy. If he didn't know the Germans would probably steal the fall fruit anyway, he would have felt too guilty to eat any of it from the Italian orchards.

Further down in the orchard valley, they came upon a water well. The sweet fruit made him thirsty, and they stopped to get a drink. In the dim morning light, he sat at the edge of the well and listened as birds welcomed the new day. Then turning his head, he thought he heard something else—like a gentle laugh. He looked over at Martelli who was carefully listening too.

Quietly, they moved back into the cover of the trees. From where they hid, Carl saw two girls balancing large water vessels on their heads as they went toward the well. The girls quietly talked as they lowered the vessels. He looked at Martelli and with a nod of the head suggested they go out. Startled, the girls looked up when they saw them. Carl pointed to his uniform and asked for some *páne*.

The girls nodded in understanding, pointed to a house on a hill, picked up the empty vessels, and walked in that direction. "Do you think they'll come back?" he whispered to Martelli.

Martelli nodded yes. From where they were hidden, they could see the house as they waited. He saw the girls go into the house and reappear with the same vessels minutes later, but it didn't look like they had any bread. Maybe they had nothing to give, or maybe their family was afraid to help them.

When the girls got back to the well, they lowered the large vessels and pulled out spaghetti, bread, and wine. They had hidden it so they weren't seen with food out in the open. Impressed with their cleverness, Carl said, "*Grazie*," and gobbled it down.

Before long, he noticed an older man coming down the hill toward them. Carl looked at Martelli and they got ready to run, but the girls repeated something about *papá, papá*. Hesitantly, they waited.

Chapter 12 – NARROW ESCAPE

The man, who they figured was the girls' dad, was happy to see American soldiers. Like Giovanni, he made it clear he couldn't wait for the Allies to get there and set them free from Axis control. He pointed to his two daughters and put up three more fingers while pointing at Carl. They guessed he was saying he had two daughters and three sons.

The man feared for his family, but indicated he would help them out when he could. Pointing to where the food had been hidden in the vessels, he wanted to make sure everything stayed hidden. Everyone knew the consequences of helping an escaped prisoner. The Germans had been making life difficult for the Italians for some time, but since the escape, it was ten times worse.

They certainly didn't want to put anyone in danger. If they hung out in the canyon and kept a close eye out for the enemy, they could wait for the Allies arrival and not stay in one place too long. However, after three long days passed, there were still no signs of advancement from the Allies.

On the other hand, the enemies were passing so close they could hear them day and night. A full week passed, and he was beginning to wonder how much longer they could dodge the bullets... and the autumn weather as the nights out in the open got colder. He looked down at his thinning uniform. Was it really thinning, or was it getting colder as the end of September crept nearer? Most likely, it was a combination of both.

One thing was for sure; he'd have to find a way to get new clothes soon. It was risky to take off the American uniform if the Allies did come along, but at this point; it felt safer than wearing it. Where were the Allies? Why was it taking them so long to get there?

Carl didn't know the Germans had created several strong lines throughout Italy and it was going to be a fight for the Allies to move through—let alone make it to the rough, mountainous terrain where they were trapped. However, he did know things were noticeably getting worse. There were still lots of prisoners roaming the mountains, and the Germans and Fascists were stopping at nothing to recapture or kill them.

Whenever they ran into fellow escaped prisoners, they shared valuable information like best friends. It was as if there was an instant bond of trust between them. He was learning lessons by the dozen as they whispered together about the tricks and trades being used around the area.

"Have you heard the Germans have threatened to destroy the homes and kill any family found helping us? They've already done it to prove their word. There's even talk of public hangings."

"They're also sending beautiful girls to houses around the area to see if prisoners are being kept in the house, or if they know where any of us might be hiding."

"I heard the same thing, but with people going around selling eggs and stuff, but really looking for evidence of prisoners in the area."

"Oh, there are even men going around giving away shoes and money to anyone who goes to get them—for a reward on our heads, of course."

"You know, there's a few people we think we can trust, but with the enemy offering them the stuff they need most—money, food, and clothes, it makes you wonder when they might turn you in."

"You're right about that. There are plenty of Italians who need money and will do near anything to get it. If they get paid for each one of us, they can clean up pretty good. What's there to stop them?"

"Watch your step. They're staying close to the roads for now, but don't get too comfortable."

All of it was true. If the poor Italian families were afraid before, they were petrified now And they had good reason to be. The Germans had committed untold horrors around the area from raping the women to killing babies.

However, there were still families who believed in regaining liberty for Italy. Orchestrated by Giovanni, three families made sure Martelli and he had a little food to eat daily—a small piece of bread, fresh sheep cheese, macaroni, or ground-cooked corn.

It wasn't much, but it kept them from starving to death. They were forever grateful because they knew those families were giving their all—including a death sentence if they were discovered helping them. He wondered why Giovanni was risking so much for them.

His question was answered when Giovanni pointed to him one day and said, "*Mio figlio Carlo.*"

Chapter 12 – Narrow Escape

Carl looked at Martelli for help.

"*Figlio* is son. He has a son named Carlo."

Martelli was beginning to understand Giovanni's Italian dialect better as he added, "I think his son was captured and sent to a prison camp in the U.S. He says he lost a Carlo and gained a Carlo."

"That explains a lot," he said under his breath as Giovanni went on to tell them he had two sons captured while fighting for Italy. His other son, Edoardo, was sent to Germany where he complained of always being cold and hungry. At least Carlo was being taken care of in the U.S. prison camp. Maybe that was why Giovanni felt a connection with them and was willing to give them as much as he could. In return for Giovanni's help, they would help him out with the farm whenever the Germans were out of sight.

First, they needed to trade their uniforms for some civilian clothes so they could be out in the open without it being so obvious they were American. The clothes were old and worn, but they'd have to make do. They would serve as a source of being hidden when they were really in plain sight as long as they didn't speak. Second, they would no longer call each other by their last names. That disappeared with the uniform—from now on, he was Carl and Martelli was Jim.

According to Giovanni, Italy officially declared war on its former Axis partner, Germany, on October 13, so it shouldn't be long before the Allies moved in and things would settle down anyway. After all, almost an entire month had passed. They were optimistic until things began taking a turn for the worse as Germany and the Fascists kept tight control through fear and punishment.

It became too dangerous to stay in one place. They had to move around the area near the homes of the families

Figure 34: Photo of the Monte San Martino landscape (used on cover) (Permission granted by photographer, Ibrahim Malla)

they trusted. Every day Giovanni kept them updated with whatever information he could get in Monte San Martino, but they didn't know when an unexpected visit from the enemy might occur. After all, even if they couldn't see them, the enemy was everywhere.

Chapter 13

COLD

MORE DAYS PASSED and Carl and Jim kept low—still waiting for the Allies to arrive. One evening, before the sun dropped behind the hills in the west, they cut across the tall grasses and weeds of an open field looking for food. They were off the main roads, and it had been quiet all day.

The unexpected sound of truck motors broke through the calm air, bringing with it a wave of fear. They looked at each other and instinctively dropped to the ground. The trucks stopped. Through the grass, Carl could see what looked like a hundred men getting out to search the area. He felt a surge of panic as he quietly lowered his head to the ground. The sound of German words drifted across the wind from both sides of him. He was boxed in—just as he was when he was captured the first time.

Without warning, the talking stopped and the sound of deadly machine gun fire took its place. The Germans sprayed the tall weeds where their silent bodies lay hidden, and he dared not breathe as death reached closer and closer. With his eyes shut tight and his jaw clenched, he prayed extra hard.

Nevertheless, by the look of things, it was going to take more than a prayer to save him this time. He began to accept that this was it—this was his call home. *It is better to die than to be recaptured*, he told himself as the shooting was within a measly hundred yards of where they lay. Suddenly, the shooting stopped and the men turned around. Their voices faded back into the distance, and the sound of trucks moved on down the road. Carl couldn't believe it—they were so close!

Mentally fatigued, neither one of them moved. The chill of the evening wind blew over them, but the sound of gunfire in the distance meant the Germans were still raiding the area. He was pretty sure the Germans were not only looking for prisoners, but also for 18 to 25 year old Italian men who might be fighting against them.

It was another near miss to add to his list—that was for sure. Now, he prayed for the safety of the families who were so good to them. He was glad he was nowhere around them when the raid happened, but he worried someone might have turned the families in for helping.

After the second hour passed, they stood up. It was dark enough they felt safe to move, and the sound of bugs in the country air meant things were getting back to normal. "Let's check on Giovanni," he whispered, and Jim nodded in agreement.

Crouched in the weeds, they passed by Giovanni's house. A small light shone through a window and things appeared to be okay from the outside. Everything was in place and it didn't look like a confrontation had taken place there. The two boys Giovanni had living at home were still too young to get involved, so they didn't worry about them as they moved on and found a place to sleep in the canyon brush.

At sunrise, they stayed away from open fields and roads as they made their way back to find Giovanni. They saw he was already working outside, but the way he was looking around made them nervous. "You think he's lookin' for us?" Jim whispered.

"There's only one way to know," Carl whispered back as he made a sound to make Giovanni look in their direction. If Giovanni were alone, he would let them know. If it were a trap, he would ignore them. That's what he hoped anyway.

Giovanni looked their direction and smiled as he walked to where they were hiding. He gave them a big hug and told them what had happened the night before. His family was okay, but there was a family in the area that lost a son and several others who were injured in the ordeal.

Carl knew the death would shake the area with fear. While Jim talked with Giovanni, he sat down on a big rock and waited. He ran his dirt-smudged hand through his hair and wondered how much longer it would last? He sighed knowing a death procession would move through the area soon. Unfortunately, he knew what to expect, and it would cut through his soul to watch the hardworking families mourn for their loved ones. Clothed in black, the mountain air would be filled with heartfelt wails of despair and pain.

Death had become a piece of everyone's life in one way or another and the ugly color of black signaled it. He wished the pain and war were over. He wished he would never have to see the color black being worn again.[146] He was tired of seeing the people suffer.

Yet the enemy had no plans on stopping the relentless terror they were causing. He wasn't sure how much longer they could survive the wait for the Allies as the fall days got colder. The sun provided some warmth during the day, but in the cloak of night, the cold air wrapped its cool breath around them and blew into their bones, making them shiver from the inside out. He pulled weeds around him and shivered.

Not only was it getting colder, but two of the three families feeding them dropped out in fear. Giovanni took them on by himself, but there wasn't always enough. Rumbling stomachs made them go out and search for anything edible when they felt it was safe enough to do so.

Raw acorns were quickly becoming a staple. The bitter aftertaste made him want to spit, but it was a small price to pay for some much needed protein. He was so hungry almost anything tasted good—even raw acorns.

Late one evening while searching for food, they heard a branch snap a few yards over in the woods. They stopped and listened. The light click of two sticks being tapped together was hardly noticeable. He let out a deep breath, and they walked to where the noise was coming from.

Kingsland, Tucker, Snodgrass, and Altomari were all four together. He hadn't seen them in a few days and smiled while saying in a hushed voice, "Glad you guys are okay. Anything new?"

Kingsland shook his head no as he whispered, "We're going to try to make it back. It's getting too cold to make it through the winter. You guys coming?"

"It's still too dangerous," Jim whispered in return.

---

[146] This so greatly affected him that even over fifty years later he asked the author why she would want to wear the color black

"Talking to the Italians, if this winter is anywhere near like it was last year, we'll all freeze to death. That is if we don't starve first," Kingsland countered.

"You know the Allied lines are stopped several hundred miles from us, and the enemy is still red hot looking for us. If they find you, it's a one-way ticket to Germany..." Carl paused before finishing, "Or to your grave."

This time Tucker joined in, "Don't matter. We'll find a way out."

"You guys are committing suicide if you leave now," Carl argued.

"We've already decided," Snodgrass said. "We're leaving tonight. If you guys don't come, you'll freeze."

Carl noticed Altomari didn't say anything, but he seemed to be going along with the others. "Good luck then," was all he had left to say because he wasn't going. He looked at Jim who was also shaking his head no. They were both staying.

In the dark, they watched as the four of them turned around and crept through the brush. Perhaps they had a chance, but Jim and he agreed it was too dangerous to go now. It felt odd knowing they were the only ones left from their group of six, but he would risk a cold winter and starvation over being captured by the Germans on down the road. In fact, he had already made up his mind, if it came down to it—he wouldn't be taken alive a second time.

Early the next morning, a noise drifted into his dreams. His eyes popped open. Stock-still, he listened from the brush where they were hiding. Jim hadn't moved, so he tossed a small pebble at him to wake him up.

He heard it again. This time he was sure it was the whine of a motorcycle engine, but he couldn't tell from where it was coming. He peeked out only enough to see the main road. His heart dropped. An Italian Fascist known as Roscioli[147] was searching the area. Everyone knew who Roscioli was based on the "honored" reputation he had built in the area for having captured or killed over fifty[148] prisoners by himself.

---

[147] Settimio Roscioli was a notorious Fascist in the area well known for hunting down and killing escaped prisoners

[148] Number as remembered by Carl

Carl ducked back down and looked at Jim as he mouthed, "Roscioli."

They'd have to keep low and out of sight for the rest of the day for sure. Sometimes he felt like Roscioli was specifically looking for them. There was always the fear that somebody would turn them in. So far, they had managed to stay out of sight of him and his Fascist workers—usually only by a hair.

But living with the knowledge of being hunted was exhausting! It was like being strapped in an electric chair and seeing the warden's hand on the switch all day—waiting and expecting the final jolt, but not knowing when it would come. Then, if the switch wasn't pulled that day, he was released to survive the night where others were waiting to make the kill instead. The next day, it repeated[149]. It was a constant battle and he was tired of mentally expecting to die and the physical stress and pain that came from it. However, he had no choice but to wait it out and not go crazy in the process.

After lying low for a few more days, he went with Jim to Giovanni's. Giovanni apologized he didn't have more as he handed them a small wooden bowl with a piece of fresh sheep cheese and a chunk of bread. Equally splitting the food, Carl savored his portion of the soft, delicious cheese. Such food had become a delicacy to him.

Upon returning the empty bowl with thanks, Giovanni looked at them sadly and shook his head. They waited for the bad news that would unquestionably follow. Although Carl didn't understand what Giovanni said, he heard a few Italian words he had come to recognize—*four, five, miles,* and *I'm sorry.* The first thought that raced through his mind was Kingsland, Tucker, Snodgrass, and Altomari. Since the four of them had left, the number of enemies in the area had only increased.

"Was it about the boys?" he asked.

Without looking up, Jim said, "No way to know who, but a couple guys were captured five miles down the road."

"Does he know if it was them?" he asked, but he knew the chances of it not being them were slim to none. Without waiting for the

---

[149] Haunted (Ells, 2005)

answer, he kicked the dirt and said, "Darn it! Why didn't they listen to us? We told them it was too dangerous. What happened?"

Giovanni shrugged his shoulders when Jim asked, but added he had heard only two were taken prisoner again. What did that mean? He assumed it meant two of them were killed[150], but he wasn't sure. He hated not knowing.

It only took one mistake, one tiny mistake, to end up dead. When was the nightmare going to end? When would they stop searching for them? It was hard to remember what it felt like to be carefree and relax. He was jittery and deep sleep was something long forgotten, but the enemy stayed strong around the rural mountain area month after month.

At first, he wondered why, but then he realized there were bands of partisans[151] who were forming in the area as time went on—up to one hundred of them! Partisans wanted a free Italy, and they were willing to fight against the German and Fascist armies to get it. Having them around the mountainous area was like bringing flies to honey—one of the reasons the area constantly buzzed with activity.

Carl got to thinking. Maybe they could use it to their advantage and join with a band of partisans who were gathering in the mountains above them. "Let's go find them," he told Jim, and they set out.

Figure 35: Leader of Gruppo 1 Maggio, Decio Fillipponi (Photo from Gino Pallotti's collection)

The partisan band they came across was named Gruppo 1 Maggio. A few British escapees had already joined so they stopped and talked to them for a minute. "You need to meet with the band leader, Decio Fillipponi, first. He's over there in the white sweater," one of them said, pointing to a man talking to a small group.

---

[150] Kingsland's report shows he was recaptured and returned to Germany
[151] Member of an armed group of fighters who fought secretly against the occupying force, in this case, Germany and the Fascists

Chapter 13 – Cold

Carl and Jim walked toward Decio and stood to the side until he finished talking. The other men left and he looked at them through black-framed glasses. He was clean-shaven with a deep cleft in his chin. He stood out from the rest in his thick, white sweater.

In broken Italian, Jim told him they wanted to join and fight with them. After asking a few questions, Decio nodded his head in understanding and called over two boys with short, black mustaches who looked about their age. He introduced them as Riccardo Funari[152] and Gino Pallotti[153] and went off to consult with a few others. They figured out Riccardo and Gino lived in the Monte San Martino area near where they were hiding. Both had left the Italian Army after being injured.

Riccardo had a scar across his face from getting shot through the jaw in Greece. It didn't stop him though. He believed in the fight so much he gave up a life of comfort and took to the mountains with his friend, Gino. His parents couldn't understand why he would risk his life again, but Riccardo was a born fighter who believed it was his duty to help free Italy. He was energetic and friendly as they talked. "Don't worry," he said in Italian, "If you don't join us, we'll keep an eye on you. I have a big family[154]. I'll get them a message to be on the watch for you."

Decio came back. It was too risky to have them without the language skills. A misunderstood error could lead to a quick death. He ended by saying, "We'll let you know if something comes up and we need your help. Riccardo and Gino will check on you when they go home."

Disappointed, they went back down the mountain. Winter was coming and they needed a more permanent hideout that could help protect them from the weather. It didn't look like the Allies would be there any time soon, and they needed protection.

---

[152] A Monte San Martino hero for what he gave to his country. Story verified and supported by Umberto Funari's (Riccardo's brother) surviving son (Ricardo Funari) and granddaughter (Vanesa Funari) 2014
[153] In 2015, author contacted Gino, who was doing well and living in Rome. Gino reported he remembered Carl very well.
[154] There were eleven children in the Funari family

Over the next few days, they searched for the perfect place. An Italian boy stopped to talk to them and they wondered if he was one of Riccardo's brothers. Jim explained the need for a more permanent hideout for the winter, and the boy motioned for them to follow him.

They walked down the edge of a big ditch hidden in the timber a ways off from the rural road that passed nearby. There they would be protected from the approaching cold, winter wind. They could see a large house 200-300 yards across the road. It was the Funari house.

It was perfect. The only way to get to the ditch was by walking, yet they still had a view of the narrow, dirt road nearby. If they looked out, they could see a lot of the surrounding country, but most importantly, they could see the main road that ran below. They could also keep in touch with Riccardo about what was going on with the partisan groups because they'd be across the road.

Figure 36: Landscape looking away from the Funari house 2009 (Permission granted by Vanesa Funari—great niece of Riccardo Funari)

Smiling, Carl gave the boy thumbs up. It was better than he had imagined. The boy nodded and began building a small shelter out of wicker plants. He didn't say much as they helped him, but they were grateful for his knowledge. The plants made it look like there was nothing there if a passerby happened to get off the road and look in the ditch.

A couple days later, they ran into two other American prisoners by the river. One looked excited as he rubbed his hands together and said, "We're planning a raid in town with a group of rebels. You should join us."

"What's in it for us and who's all going?" Carl asked.

"We're joining about a dozen Italians who say we'll find loads of shoes, clothing, and needed supplies being hoarded by a Fascist storeowner."

Carl looked at Jim who nodded his head yes. "What time?"

"Meet us in the woods near the main road at dark... around 2000 hours. The Italians are supposed to bring extra weapons."

"We'll be there," Carl said. "We could use some new clothes and supplies."

That evening they got to the meeting place just as the sun was setting. There was a small group gathered, and he saw the two prisoners from earlier that day. The cold air nipped at his ears, and he rubbed his hands together to keep them warm. All he had to wear was a light pair of pants, a thin shirt, and a little suit coat. A nice cap and gloves would be worth the trip across the rough terrain. Light snow was already in the air, but it wasn't sticking yet.

Before leaving, someone handed him a club. It wasn't much, but it would do. Besides the clubs, there were a couple shotguns and pistols. One of the pistols didn't have any ammunition, but they could still use it to produce fear if the need arose.

By the time they were organized and made the trip into Monte San Martino, it was nearly 2300 hours when they arrived at the storeowner's house. The old house they stood in front of was cold and dark. "Are they sure this is it?" he whispered to Jim.

Jim nodded, "I hope this isn't no weasel deal, but they say this is the place."

If this was it, why were the Italian rebels standing back? "Come on," Carl whispered to the Americans. "We didn't come all this way to stand back in the shadows and chicken out now. I'm going with or without them."

Jim and the other two Americans moved across the street with Carl as they eased up to the old, wooden door. They stood behind him with their weapons ready as he tried to open it—it was locked. The echo of his club boomed into the air as he beat on it and Jim joined him by hitting it with the butt of the pistol he carried. They were making too much noise. He held up his hand to stop.

"What's a matta' for you?" Jim asked as his words blended and sounded like whatsamattaferu. Carl knew he was asking what the problem was.

"We're only asking for somebody to shoot us out here like this. We got to get in."

He could see the rush of adrenaline as their warm breath sent white puffs into the chilly night air. Jim stepped up and yelled through the door in his best Italian, "Open the door and don't try anything! We are rebels, but we won't hurt you if you obey!"

A shuffle across the inside floor could be heard, then a click of the lock. The door creaked open and a stooped, old gent stood in front of them saying he had nothing of value. They stormed into the house. Jim sat the man down in a chair by the door and told him their business as he kept the gun on him. Just because the man was old, didn't mean he was harmless.

Carl and the two others started searching the house from top to bottom. "I'll search the closets," he called out as he went from room to room, opening every door he could find.

The other two looked under furniture and searched for hidden doors. "There's nothing here! Where's all this stuff he's supposedly holding?" Carl yelled out.

"The man keeps sayin' we're wastin' our time cause he don't have nottin'," Jim replied.

Carl tapped the club against the floor and said, "I'm beginning to believe that. If he does, he must have hidden it awfully well because there's nothing here."

Discouraged, they went back outside. The group of Italians anxiously waited to hear what they had found. Irritated, he said, "Tell them if they want to know, they should've come in with us. What now?"

"These guys are a bunch of scumbags, but they're talkin' about tryin' a couple more places. Maybe we'll have betta' luck at one of them," Jim said, looking at him.

Carl was annoyed with how the situation was playing out. "Well, we're already here. Are they going to help this time around?" he grumbled as they walked to another two houses in the predawn coldness.

His question was silently answered as the Italians hid behind a bush, and the four Americans did the dirty work—again. Based on the moon, it looked like it was near 0300 hours when they came out of the third home, and they were still empty handed. They needed to start back.

Chapter 13 – Cold

An ache ran through his ears from the cold wind as they walked through the mountains. Irritably, he whispered to Jim and the other two Americans, "What a bunch of crap! These rebels are worthless. They only had us come along so they could leave us with the sack if anything bad happened, but you can bet they'd of benefitted if we'd found anything. I say from now on, it's all Americans or nothing!"

Irritated, everyone agreed.

Then Jim quickly added, "Not for nottin', but we shoulda known better. Those shems[155] just wasted our time... saying they were goin' to keep chicky[156] cause they were too scared to help."

"You can bet I'm not doing that again," one of the other escapees agreed.

When they got where they had met earlier that evening, they shook hands with the other two Americans and went their separate ways. Carl took the club with him as they made it back to their hut in the ditch. Without the blowing wind, it felt warmer than he expected. He lay back to back with Jim for added warmth and covered his ears with his arms. They were both so skinny it didn't make a huge difference, but the extra body heat had to help a little.

It seemed like only minutes had passed when he thought he heard his name softly being called. At the edge of the ditch, he could see Riccardo and Gino. It was great to see them and get the latest news. Jim joined him as he walked over to where they stood. Riccardo handed them each a small bowl of spaghetti and excitedly told them Decio was opening the German confiscated granaries in Monte San Martino that morning. They were all headed there now.

This was a chance for Jim and Carl to help and possibly get some grain out of it. They both felt like they could trust Decio's band, so they agreed without hesitation—even after the bad experience last night. There was something satisfying in simply knowing the stolen grain would get back to the people after the Fascists, working under High German command, had confiscated all the gathered grain and

---

[155] Jerk or stupid person
[156] Keep chicky is to stand guard while doing something mischievous

food from the farmers. The poor Italian people had been left with nothing to survive the winter. This was too good to miss!

Before heading back to where they had just come from, they grabbed an old ox cart from Giovanni's. The roads were still pretty quiet, and they hoped to blend in with their civilian clothes and ox cart. Although the cold had prevented them from being able to bathe in the river for some time, they had been able to shave a few days ago so they didn't look too straggly. The bathing part wasn't so noticeable because most of the people in that area lacked indoor plumbing and they fit right in. Still, they couldn't afford to call unwanted attention by looking like disheveled prisoners.

When they got to town, they found Decio keeping order at the opened grain bins as the grain was unloaded and carried to a nearby train track. Riccardo and Gino waved them over when they saw them. They loaded the cart and took loads of grain to the large crowds of hungry Italians waiting at the track.

Within hours, the granaries were completely emptied, but Carl and Jim were able to grab two hundred pounds of wheat to take back with them as they blended in with the crowd and headed back through the mountains. He pulled the loaded cart over the rocky, dirt path and Jim pushed from behind. They struggled to catch their breath as they went uphill, but it felt good knowing the granaries had been emptied of thousands of bushels. It was about time the Germans were rightfully cheated of their stolen grain.

Giovanni saw them coming down the dirt road and ran out to meet them. Upon seeing the wheat, he turned teary eyed with gratitude. They gave all of it to him, but they knew he would share with others—after all, that was a sharecropper's life.

Repeatedly thanking them, he said something with the words *páne* and *domani*. He knew Giovanni was saying there would be bread to eat tomorrow. The very thought of a loaf of fresh, baked bread made his mouth water.

Winter was kicking into high gear and food was scarcer than ever. It didn't help the matter any when there was snow on the ground. If the enemy was anywhere near, it became too dangerous to leave the protected hut and risk leaving tracks. During that time, sometimes

Chapter 13 – Cold

they ate—sometimes they didn't. The stored acorns offered some nutrition, but they weren't enough to fill their empty stomachs and make them feel full.

The days passed and the winter temperatures continued to drop. Had they made the right choice to stay and wait it out? Maybe… just maybe, the others were right when they said waiting through the natural progression of winter was too dangerous. Things appeared only to be getting worse instead of better as they slept on the cold, hard ground in their thin, patched up clothing. Without a blanket, the nights were long and miserable.

Unable to control his shivering one night, his teeth chattered as he whispered to Jim, "Maybe we should try to leave. It's only going to get colder."

Through clenched teeth, Jim whispered back, "I've been thinkin' a lot about that. Just haven't figured out the right time yet. You comin' if I try?"

"Giovanni will give us the newest updates in the morning. He'll let us know if it's safe."

"I think I'm goin' to try no matta' what. My hands are so cold I can't feel them half the time and I'm tired of bein' hungry all the time."

"I know. Me too," Carl sympathized as he tried not to think about the cold and relax his aching body.

The next morning, there was a skiff of snow on the ground. Carefully stepping in areas that were yet bare, they climbed out and headed to Giovanni's house. Where there were patches of snow, they walked backwards. That way any prints found would lead the follower in the opposite direction of where they were going.

The early air was chilly, but the sun brought some much-needed warmth to the day. Giovanni wasn't outside, so they grabbed an ax and started chopping wood. Not only was it a way they could pay back Giovanni for his help when it was safe enough for them to be out, but it also got their blood pumping to keep them warm.

Neatly stacking the cut wood, they saw Giovanni walking down the road. He must've gone into town for updates. Now was the perfect time to ask about trying to escape before it got too cold. He joined them by the wood and sincerely thanked them for their work. After he gave them the rundown, Jim asked about conditions to escape.

By the worried look that crept across Giovanni's face, Carl knew it was too dangerous to try to leave. Disappointed, he thought, *Too dangerous? When will it not be dangerous?* Months had already passed and nothing was getting better.

It appeared Jim was unfazed by Giovanni's words as he stared at them and said, "Not for nottin', but I'm goin' to try anyway."

"What?" Carl said in surprise. "You heard him. It's too dangerous."

"I'm tired of waitin'. It could still be months before somethin' changes. You comin' or not?" Jim asked, looking at him.

Giovanni put his hand up to stop them. He assured them they would not die under his watch. He would continue to help them.

Carl paused. He knew Giovanni would help when he could, but he didn't want to put his family in danger either. He thought about it before saying, "Giovanni's right. We should wait a bit longer."

"But how much longa'? I'm leavin' as soon as this snow clears up."

"Well, I'm staying," Carl said as he placed the last pieces of wood on the pile.

After a few days, the ground was clear of snow. The moon was shining bright in the sky when Jim looked over at Carl and whispered, "I got nottin' to lose. I gotta get back home to my wife and baby."

"I think you should wait," Carl whispered one more time.

But Jim had already made up his mind as he turned and crept up into the darkness. Carl watched him get on the road near them and disappear into the shadows. It felt strange knowing he was gone. Tomorrow, for the first time in months, Carl would be alone. He wasn't sure what he would do as he fell into a light sleep with the normal night sounds surrounding him.

Early the next morning, he decided to take a walk down to the valley. It was pretty calm and it appeared safe as he quietly walked through the damp, morning chill. In his mind he knew Jim had left, but he still turned to look for him every once in a while.

The morning dew seeped into his worn shoes and chilled his sockless toes. Although his socks had been gone for a while now and his toes were used to feeling numb from the cold, it was still uncomfortable. He stopped and shook off his foot.

Chapter 13 – Cold

When he looked up, he saw the figure of someone herding sheep down in the valley. It was a typical job for an older woman or child, so he didn't feel threatened. Much of the land was cultivated, making it difficult to find patches of feeding grass, so it wasn't unusual to run into herders in the middle of nowhere.

He kept walking in that direction and realized it was Giovanni's wife who was out there. She saw him. "Carlo, Carlo," she called out, waving him over. He could see something in her hand that looked like sticks.

Curious he walked over to her. Once he was closer, he could see she was not holding sticks, but long, wooden knitting needles. He was impressed by the way families in this area were so knowledgeable in living off the surrounding plants and animals. It required hard work, but they found ways to provide for their needs.

She pointed down to his sockless feet and said something. He looked down at his old, worn shoes. Was she talking about his feet being wet and cold? He didn't understand. He was getting where he could understand a word here or there, but the language barrier was still a problem and Jim wasn't there to help him out.

She stopped talking and grabbed a piece of spun wool from her knitting. Running the yarn down his foot, she measured it. "*Domani... domani*," she repeated, pointing to the grassy spot where the sheep were grazing.

"You want me to come back here tomorrow... *domani*?" he asked, pointing to himself and then to where he was standing.

She nodded her head yes, and he nodded back in agreement. If it were safe, he would go back tomorrow. He waved goodbye and went on to look for food. Although unsure if he had understood, it looked like there was a possibility he'd be getting a warm pair of socks tomorrow. The hope carried him through the rest of the day and into the chilly night. The hut was extra dreary without Jim, and the only noise to break the silence was his growling stomach from not finding food.

Even though Jim and he didn't talk much because they didn't want their English to be heard, there was something comforting about having a friend go through the same hell. Sure, occasionally they had split up and gone their separate ways, but they had worked well together. Maybe he should have gone with him.

Those thoughts drifted through his mind as he fell into a light sleep with one eye opened. Especially now, he had to be on high alert—even in his sleep. It was a way of survival, a way to rest, but not enough to risk getting caught. He had trained his mind always to be aware—to hear, see, or even smell anything unusual. Although exhausting, it was the only way to survive the hunt. He had already made it longer than most of those who had escaped, but he didn't know how much longer he would be able to keep going. Some days were worse than others.

In the morning, he went back to where Giovanni's wife had told him to meet her. The cold didn't seem to bother him as much today as he anticipated the warm socks. He could see her sitting on a large rock as the sheep munched on the wet grass around her. She smiled up at him when she saw him walking toward her, but her hands never stopped moving as she finished the last few stitches with precision and speed.

She handed him a pair of long, woolen socks and pointed to his feet. He plopped down on a small rock beside her and pulled them on. They went over the calf of his legs and were exactly what he needed. The warmth from the socks felt better than putting on a brand new pair of shoes. He couldn't believe she could make such a wonderful gift by only measuring his foot with a piece of yarn.

At that moment, as he sat there, he was sure he looked awful. He hadn't been able to shave for several weeks and his hair was long and overgrown. Skinny, dirty, hungry, and tired, he realized that even in the most difficult situations, there were still tender mercies sent from heaven. He was familiar with hard times all right, but living like this really put hard times into perspective. It was impossible to imagine unless it was lived firsthand—and he was living it every day.

A few more days passed, and the wind blew colder bringing with it the chance for snow. He hunkered down in the hut and hoped all of this would soon become a distant memory instead of a looming reality. A noise broke through his thoughts and he listened. There it was again—a clicking sound like the one Jim and he used when hiding

Chapter 13 – Cold

and it was too dangerous to communicate. Why would he be hearing that when Jim was gone?

He heard it again—closer this time. Hidden in the shelter, he grabbed a rock from a pile he kept beside him. He always knew what was around him in case he needed it—rocks, sticks, clubs, pitchfork, hoe, or anything else he could quickly grab. Leaves crunched and a twig snapped, meaning somebody was off the road and headed directly toward him. Prepared to attack with the rock, he heard a familiar voice whisper in a Brooklyn accent, "Psst… Hey, it's me, Jimmy."

"You son of a gun. You almost got a rock to the head!" he angrily whispered back.

Jim shrugged his shoulders, "I tried to let you know it was me."

"I didn't expect you'd be back. What happened?" he asked as he took a deep breath.

"Oh, there's no way!" Jim said, shaking his head. "It's solid."

By the look on Jim's face, he could tell something had happened—and it had shaken him up pretty good. Carl didn't want to press for details, and Jim didn't offer them, so he changed the subject. "So the German lines are solid and the Allies can't push through. That just supports the fact that we'll be left to face the full force of winter with these rags we got for clothes," he said, pulling on the thin material of his shirt. They had worn the same clothes every day since they had traded in their uniforms, and the threads were light and worn.

Sure enough, as the days passed, there were times when the bitter cold made his ears ache, his eyes water, and his nose run, all while the icy wind burned at any exposed skin—especially his face and hands. The only option was to stay in the protection of the hut, but he couldn't stand lying around all day. The desperation to get out and move pushed him into the open despite the low temperatures and the chance to be spotted. Besides getting food and water, he also needed to breathe the fresh air and feel alive.

One particular day, the temperatures plummeted. The hut didn't seem to offer its usual protection against the wind. Carl blew his warm breath into his hands and rubbed them together. "We got to go out and meet with Giovanni. Two days have done gone by since we've ate anything solid."

Jim agreed, and they headed out. If they ran, they would call attention to themselves, so they walked fast. Giovanni saw them coming and went out to meet them as he shook his head and said something about *freddo*.

Freddo meant cold and Carl could only imagine the temperatures would continue to drop throughout the night—low enough that freezing to death could become a reality. He tried not to think about that. There was no extra energy to waste on worrying. They would do what they'd been doing all along—survive the night the best they could when it came that time.

Giovanni took them to where the oxen slept in an old stall under the house. The straw on the ground was old, smelly, and dirty, but he pointed to it and offered to let them sleep there that night. Carl could smell the strong stench from where the oxen lay even though he was left with a poor sense of smell from the explosion. However, that was of no concern at this point. It was a warm place to sleep and they crawled under a bit of dingy straw and huddled down beside the warm bodies of the two oxen. They wouldn't freeze to death after all, at least not that night.

From then on, staying there was an available option if the enemy wasn't concentrated in the area. However, it was a last resort—saved for when their choices were limited to that or freezing. When they did stay, they arrived late and left early, making sure to cover their tracks. They would never do anything to jeopardize the safety of Giovanni and his family. Just in case, there was a pitchfork within reach if he needed to use it as a weapon.

The winter days were short and the nights long, but they were making it through them. A few days of bright sunshine came here and there, and one such day led him on a walk to a clear, running creek that ran through the area. He could see his breath in the cold air, but the sun made up for it. Jim had stayed behind, so he was flying solo for the day. He walked along the banks until he came to spot where the water slowed to a ripple. *Ahh... a chance to wash my feet and break up any possible tracks should someone come along*, he thought as he rolled up his pant legs and took off his shoes and socks. After being out in the cold for so long, it wasn't a shock as he

Chapter 13 – Cold

stepped into the water and chunks of snow flowed down the creek past him.

A darkened circle formed where he stood as the dirt washed off his feet, and it felt good to have his feet clean. While he was there, he decided to go ahead and wash his socks too. They were even dirtier than his feet. He washed them until the water wrung clear. Satisfied that they were as clean as he could get them, he saw a sunny spot on a rock a few feet up the bank where he could lay them to dry. He carried his worn shoes and walked back through the water as it calmly ran over his feet.

The calmness suddenly exploded with the thumping of his heart when he heard a noise in the brush directly across from where he stood. He stopped dead in his tracks for only a second before panic swept through him as he thought, *My gosh, they're across the creek from me!* There was no time to turn around and grab his socks. Instead, he quietly waded up the creek so there wouldn't be any footprints.

After going about a hundred yards through the water, he carefully climbed up the bank and put his shoes on. Spots of snow still covered the ground, and he walked backwards in the snow until it was safe to turn around. Relieved to make it out alive, he went back to the hut and quietly told Jim what had happened. He had mixed feelings as he said, "I can't believe I lost those socks, but to the heck with them. I had to get out of there!"

"There's a chance to find them if we go back later," Jim sympathetically offered.

"I wish I would've left them on my feet or carried them along with my shoes instead of laying them out to dry," he said sadly. "But it's too dangerous to go back. Someone will take them or the enemy will use them as a trap."

Once again, he was left without the warmth of socks, but he hoped the worst part of winter was over. If they were extremely lucky, they might even get an early spring. However, it was only wishful thinking as the sky clouded over and threatened snow again a few weeks later.

Giovanni confirmed his worry. The biggest snowstorm of the year was headed their way. Giant flakes of snow began to swirl through the air as they spoke, and Carl wondered what they would do. They couldn't stay in their hut in the ditch—it would be too dangerous to leave, as the thick snow would not allow them to hide their tracks. Not to mention, they had no food. If the snow lasted too long, they could die. He noticed nobody was speaking. Everybody must be thinking what to do.

When Giovanni spoke, the only word Carl understood was *tedeschi*. That couldn't be good. He looked over at Jim and asked, "What about the Germans?"

"He don't think they're be comin' by cause of the snow," Jim answered. "No goofin', he thinks it'll be safe for us to sleep in the house."

"In the house? That's too dangerous. Don't you think we should sleep with the oxen?"

"Tracks in the snow could be more dangerous," Jim countered. "The house will be safer."

"I suppose you're right," Carl agreed. "But we'll need a plan to make sure his family stays safe if those Krauts decide to show up."

It was hard not to feel guilty when he knew he could be putting Giovanni's family in grave danger. He was tired of depending on them for his basic survival—especially when it came to eating the only food they had left. Sure, he worked hard for Giovanni when he could, but he knew there was so much more being put on the line. They had all seen the Germans in action. There was no justice for an act such as this—only punishment.

Giovanni eagerly took them inside, and that night Carl tightly pulled the wool blankets up to his chin and slept on a real bed. Almost two years had passed since he had slept in a bed, and he basked in the glory of the warmth and softness that cradled his exhausted body. Such a luxury almost made the war feel like it was coming to an end… but he knew better.

Although protected from the outside elements, he remained aware and on edge. He couldn't waste a minute thinking the enemy had given up on looking for them. It was as if his life, and the lives of the other escapees who had made it this long, had become the enemy's sought-after prize. They had become the ultimate capture.

He would play their little game because he had to, but for him it was about making it to the end before time ran out. As long as he stayed one step ahead, he would only have to wait. The Allies would make it through, he was sure of that. He just wasn't sure when.

A cold gust of wind rattled the house as giant snowflakes continued to fall outside and cover the frozen ground. He was glad to be inside, but he knew they had to be careful. It only took one mistake and everything they had suffered up to this point would be in vain.

Although it made him nervous to be there, he enjoyed spending time in a family setting. The meals around the table, the conversations (even if he didn't understand), the laughing, he had missed it all. However, after a few days, the snow began to melt, and Giovanni heard Germans were moving toward town. Their time indoors quickly ended.

It was a nice break, but he was glad to be back outside where he wouldn't be putting Giovanni's family in as much danger. Before they left, Giovanni gave each of them a wool blanket and assured them spring was on the horizon. If anybody knew how to read the outside earth, it was Giovanni. Maybe they'd be the ones to prove everybody wrong and make it through the winter after all.

It was a good thought, but that night it was hard to keep that in mind as he tightly wrapped his blanket around him and covered his head. Jim was at his back, but the cold from the frozen earth seeped through the blanket. A shiver ran through his thin body as he moved his numb fingers and toes back and forth. They felt stiff and swollen and he missed his warm socks more than ever. He hoped tomorrow would be better, but with the Germans near town, he knew it wouldn't be.

It should be getting easier by now, not harder. Discouraged, a scripture from his much read *New Testament* ran through his mind reminding him he had come too far to give up. The scripture was about not fearing his enemies because the strength of God was greater. Although a comforting thought, it was hard to let it sink in with the reality of constantly being on the run.

He was nothing compared to the strength of the enemy! Literally, he could do nothing as he watched people die—innocent children die—due to the strength of the enemy. Nevertheless, those words were all he had left. He needed that belief to survive every single day—to not give up, even when it was dreary enough to do it.

Maybe if he closed his eyes tight enough, he'd wake up from this nightmare in his bed at home. But when he woke up the next morning, he was disappointed. He was still in the mountains of Italy—cold, hungry, and wet.

CHAPTER 14

TAKING A CHANCE

AFTER ENDURING MONTHS of cold, one morning Carl woke up to birds chirping in the fresh, cool air. It was the sweet sound of spring. Spring brought rain, but if he could survive the snows of winter, he could most definitely survive the rains of spring. Besides, the rain made things grow, and there would be plenty of work for them to do around the farm to help Giovanni.

He wasn't mistaken there—lots of backbreaking, tedious, and exhausting physical labor was the only way things got done around there. It was amazing how much easier and faster farming was with the help of tractors and farm machinery back in the States. It took days to do what could be done in hours back home—like plowing a field.

When he saw Giovanni had the oxen yoked and a ten-inch plow connected behind them, he offered to help. He had never plowed a field with oxen before, but he wasn't afraid to try. The plow pulled through the dirt as he held on to the handles that curved back. It was hard and bumpy, and he wasn't sure how he was doing.

A few hours in, Giovanni came back and took over. He tried to be nice about it, saying he was doing a good job and he trusted him, but he was afraid someone might see him out in the open field. The oxen were important to their survival and the more he had thought about it, the riskier it seemed.

Was he making straight lines? Was he moving too slowly? Carl wondered if those were the real reasons Giovanni wanted to take over and finish. It didn't bother him or hurt his feelings any. He didn't want to jeopardize Giovanni or his oxen. He knew how much they depended on the animals they had left, and he definitely didn't want the Germans getting ahold of them.

After a long day, they were given some bread and spaghetti. Everyone, including the neighbors, had been out working and they gathered to eat together. Giovanni stopped plowing long enough to join them—he wasn't even halfway done with the large field.

Carl showed them the blisters on his hands from the plow. "In America, this work is easier," he told them with a smile as Jim joined in telling them about tools and machinery from back home. The families couldn't believe it! The farmers were working at what seemed a hundred years behind, and they didn't even know it. They worked the land as they always had and used what was available to them to do it. They didn't complain—that was the way of life and they were okay with that even though it was hard work.

Not everybody in Italy was the same, or even understood the farmers' way of life. In fact, the educated, book-smart, city folk considered them only to be poor, uneducated, country people of the mountains. However, what those "educated" people didn't know was how incredibly knowledgeable the farmers were—only in a different way.

It was something Carl saw every day as the farmers worked hard and provided for their every need. Whether it was carrying heavy earthen jars on their heads for clean water, working by the clock of the sun, taking care of their animals that in return provided for them, growing food, or helping neighbors, they worked in unity and skill. This brought a whole new meaning to life—it wasn't about being educated, religious, or wealthy, it was about truly living no matter the circumstances.

One night, after a long day of planting, Carl said to Jim, "Ya know, sometimes I wonder why they are working so hard when they know good and well the enemy will reap the benefits of their hard work by stealing their food and animals."

"It's their way of life," Jim said. "It's what they do every spring."

The enemy couldn't change that with tactics of fear and death. And so, Carl and Jim worked along with them. For Carl, the fresh air

Chapter 14 – Taking A Chance

and hard work was relaxing. It felt good to be able to help Giovanni since his older sons couldn't. Jim had worked at a factory before leaving for war, and he needed to keep busy too, so they worked well together. Of course, they always had to keep a keen eye out for the enemy. They could never think they were safe because they weren't. However, they tried to blend in with the Italian farmers the best they could as they worked.

After the planting process, they prepared manure to use as fertilizer on the plants. Giovanni pushed the cart along, and Jim and he put it down. It was still warm as they scooped it out and spread it over the plants. On a hill, they looked down the rural road and saw a small group of German S.S. troops headed in their direction. They had the advantage of being able to see them first, but they didn't have time to run.

Giovanni's eyes opened wide and he quickly motioned for them to lie face down on the ground next to each other with their arms over their ears and crossed above their heads. He wasn't sure what Giovanni had in mind until he felt the warm manure plopping over him. Completely covering them, Giovanni left the cart in front of the heap and moved several feet ahead as he worked the ground on his hands and knees.

There wasn't a minute extra to spare as the S.S. troops passed by on the road. Giovanni could feel their eyes staring at him, so he looked up and gave a nod. For a brief second, it looked as if they were going to stop, but they didn't. He held his breath as they marched by parallel to the cart and went on down the road.

When Giovanni was sure the Germans were gone and there weren't more coming, he told them it was safe to come out. Clumps of manure dropped off them as they stood up and took a deep breath of fresh air. The smell was suffocating under the manure, but it had served its purpose and had hidden them.

"*Grazie*, Giovanni," Carl said. Then, looking at Jim, he added, "That was sure a close one."

Jim ran his hand through his hair and shook the manure to the ground saying, "Let's help get this mess cleaned up so we can go down to the river and wash off before the sun goes down."

They got on their knees and scooped the manure back into the cart by the armloads. When they were done, Giovanni shooed them toward the river covering his nose in exaggeration. There was certainly nothing to smile about, but Giovanni's expression was unexpected.

When they got to the river, the water rushed by as they stood on the bank. There was no way to get clean other than by jumping in—shoes and all. The cold water took his breath away for a brief moment as he went under. Pieces of manure floated up around him and were carried downstream. He put his head back and combed through his hair with his fingers. Then, he rubbed his neck and ears extra well. That was going to be as good as it got. He climbed out and joined Jim who had found a sunny patch along the bank. After sitting a few minutes, he said, "I'm going to head back to the hut. I think I'll dry faster walking."

Jim got up. "I'll go with you."

The words blended into one sentence and Carl didn't hear him. "What?" he asked.

Jim was already up and walking so he didn't bother to repeat himself. Instead, he said, "Fuggedaboutdit. Let's go."

"Do you think there's more Germans coming, or there'll be just a few small groups here and there?" Carl asked as they walked.

"Not sure, but either way, we should probably play it safe for a few days," Jim said as they neared the hut.

He agreed. They'd give it a few days and then try working out in the fields again. When there didn't appear to be much movement, they ventured out to help hoe. There was a bit of a breeze, but it seemed the hoeing went nothing but uphill. He stopped to wipe his sweaty brow and leaned against the hoe for a moment. Giovanni came along using the hoe like a skilled tool as he moved ahead of him. How was it possible for a man more than double his age to do so much? The work was exhausting, and there wasn't much food to build energy.

If he made it home from this war, he hoped he could work hard in the things he loved. If things went his way, there would definitely be farming involved, and he wouldn't take machinery for granted. A smile crept across his face as he thought about working his own ranch. For now, he continued hoeing after Giovanni—all uphill.

Chapter 14 – Taking A Chance

Every day brought something different when it was clear enough to be out. Although much of the food planted was similar to what he was used to at home—wheat, corn, oats, and garden foods, there were some new things he was learning as well. The citrus orchards, olive orchards, and vineyards growing throughout the apple orchards were unfamiliar to him, but he was learning how to trim the curled grape vines as they spread throughout the apple trees in the most peculiar way.

A few garden foods were nearly ready to eat, and he found one plant particularly interesting. It was some sort of odd-looking bean he had never seen before. About the size of a pecan, it could be eaten as a fresh-shelled bean or used in soups, stews, and salads. Curious to know the name, he asked Giovanni, who said, "*Al fava*[157]."

Confused, he repeated, "Alfalfa?"

Both thought the other was saying the correct word, or close enough to it, so they nodded in agreement. *How odd for a bean to be called alfalfa*, he thought, but didn't think much more about it. At least he'd be able to remember the name in Italian.

Rumor had it that the Germans were finally being pushed back by the Allies. While this was good news, it also meant there was a greater chance to have Germans around their area at any time. Still, they kept working outside as much as possible.

On an especially nice day, Jim and he were pitching dry straw onto a cart. They needed the fresh straw for the oxen stall. Just as he loaded his pitchfork and prepared to fling the straw over, he caught a glimpse of two soldiers walking their direction on the country road. He kept working and muttered under his breath, "Two Krauts coming our way."

Maybe if they kept working, the soldiers wouldn't bother to take a second look and walk on by. His sweaty hands turned white as he tightly grasped the sharp pitchfork as he stabbed at the straw. When they were parallel from each other, he briefly looked up and nodded his head. Still a ways off the road, the soldiers returned the nod and kept walking.

---

[157] A bean

He watched them pass and wondered if they had recognized them as American escapees. One of the Germans looked back at them and made eye contact before saying something to the other. "They know," he whispered to Jim. "They'll be back with more men if we don't do something... now."

Jim nodded. The sad reality was they were in war, and the enemy had seen them. They had no other choice but to attack with the strength of what they had—the pitchforks. "We gotta be quick and direct," he whispered as they crept silently through the brush to intercept the soldiers up ahead.

They knew the roads and brush like the back of their hand, so when the soldiers turned a curve in the road, they were there waiting. Adrenaline took control, and they did what they had to do. It had to be done or else they were risking their lives and the lives of everyone who helped them, especially Giovanni's family since they were working in his field.

"We gotta get them off this road," Jim said as they looked down at the two lifeless bodies.

"Hide them under the brush," Carl grumbled as he pulled on one of them before adding, "I hate this war!"

Even though he hadn't gotten covered in blood, he felt dirty. He had killed a man at close range[158], and he felt guilty and disgusted with the whole war. The look of death, the facial expression, the last words... it was something he would never forget. "Let's take these pitchforks down to the river and clean them so we can get them back to Giovanni. I want to wash off too," he mumbled, picking up the bloodstained tool.

It made his stomach churn, but there were two less Germans to worry about. He knew the enemy would have no problem doing it to him, but it was still haunting. He needed to bury the memory—never think about it again. Headed toward the river, he looked at Jim and said, "Nobody needs to know this ever happened. Don't even tell

---

[158] Carl never directly spoke of this incident, but due to flashbacks he had after making it home, his nephew, Jerry, said two Germans were killed in self-defense with pitchforks

Giovanni. If they find the bodies, they'll have no way of knowing who done it."

Jim agreed. There were some things nobody needed to know. It wasn't worth the risk. Who knew, maybe they could even be charged for it fifty years down the road. They were justified in their doings, but nobody else was there to verify that.

After cleaning up, they hurried back to the field and grabbed the cart to take back to Giovanni. He thought about what to say to Giovanni since they'd be staying low for a while, but when they got there, Giovanni rushed out to them breathlessly saying, "Germans are all around. Go and hide. We'll get you food when we can."

Before they left, they grabbed some beans to take with them. After months of eating acorns, they tasted pretty darn good straight out of the pod. It was no different from eating fresh peas or green beans.

It had become too dangerous to get out much as the weeks passed. They could make it to the gardens at night sometimes and get beans, but with the number of planes constantly flying through the sky, the enemy was squeezing tighter. Everyone was feeling the pressure and the enemy threatened, killed, and stole more than ever. Once again, a shadow of fear fell over the people, but the hope for a free Italy kept them going.

Spring marched forward like the soldiers around him. One early morning, rain dripped into the hut and woke him up. He lay awake and thought about his situation. His clothes were really only patches upon patches, his shoes were nearly gone, his mind was always running, he was jittery from always being hunted, and his boney body was tired, cold and hungry. Trapped in a wet ditch, he told himself one more time, *Hang in there. It'll be over soon.*

But who was he fooling? The closer the Allies got, the worse things were getting. He was stuck in the middle—the Allies were close, but not close enough to get to them. He became restless. He wanted to leave. Things were heating up enough he thought if he played his cards right, he could make a run for it soon. It was a matter of taking a chance at exactly the right time without risking it all.

The last night of April came. The rain splashed around him and it looked like a long, wet weekend was in store. He heard someone on the road near them. He made eye contact with Jim. Neither hardly breathed as he slowly reached for his club with one hand and a heavy rock with the other. Jim did the same, and they waited.

Then he heard Riccardo's voice. He let out a deep breath and stood up. They were seeing Riccardo more than usual since he was recruiting much-needed fighters from around the area. Whenever Riccardo went home, he crossed the road to bring them news and food.

They stood in the protection of the ditch and talked to him. He told them he had come from visiting his girlfriend and was going to sleep at home for a night before meeting back up in the mountains. For a brief moment, Carl envied the idea of going home to sleep in a nice, warm bed. It sounded too good to be true—going to a place called home, out of the weather, with the comfort of family, and a warm meal. He wondered when it would be his turn to do the same—if ever. In fact, if he were in Riccardo's shoes, he would have done the same thing.

Riccardo got ready to leave and said in Italian, "See you tomorrow."

Carl waved. "*Fino a domani il mio amico.*" Although he was sure his accent was off, it was one of the small phrases he had learned in the last seven months, meaning "Until tomorrow, my friend."

He shook off his wool blanket and lay back down. Riccardo confirmed what Giovanni had been telling them. It was worse than ever and that was why Riccardo was back recruiting more fighters. Carl knew the Allies had a punch the enemy couldn't hold much longer, but he was growing evermore desperate and anxious to leave. A light sleep carried him into the early morning dawn when a sudden scream cut through the air. He sat up wide-eyed and looked at Jim. His heart was racing. "What was that?" he mouthed.

Jim shrugged his shoulders, and they both sat listening as the noise picked up in volume—screaming, yelling, banging, trucks running. What in the world was happening? He grabbed his club and Jim grabbed a heavy rock as they quietly crept over to the edge of the ditch and peeked over.

The commotion was coming from across the road. Big trucks were in front of Riccardo's house as a squad of Fascists loaded everything the family owned—furniture, food, and livestock. Riccardo had been discovered as a partisan and somehow the enemy had found him at home.

There was nothing they could do but watch as the enemy cleaned the house down to the bare floors. He could hear Riccardo's mother loudly sobbing and he searched for Riccardo. There he was. He was being forced to watch as they stole everything from his family.

Everyone knew what was coming next, but Carl prayed the enemy would just take everything and leave. *Wishful thinking*, he thought. He knew the enemy would not stop there. He could feel his face getting red and hot as his blood boiled within him. At that moment, he wasn't sorry for killing those two German soldiers, and he wished he could shoot every one of those Fascist pigs down there. His body was telling him to respond—to do something, but there was absolutely nothing he could do.

Figure 37: Pictures of the Funari house 2015 (Taken by Ricardo Funari—Riccardo's nephew)

Once again, he was helpless. If he ran down there, he would be committing suicide. It would be like a rabbit running directly into a pack of wolves—there wasn't a chance. His head pounded and he felt nauseous as he tried to think of something. He rested his head on the cool, muddy ground in front of him. He could not bear to see one more person killed in front of him. He could feel himself hardening against the unbearable pain, and he was afraid it would take him over. If he gave in to the pain, he would die. Instead, he had to block it.

He lifted his head and mud ran down his face. The Fascists had now lined some of the Funari family up along the side of the ox stall. From what he could see, it looked like one of his brothers first, then his mother, then Riccardo, and then his father[159]. Riccardo's mother was still sobbing, but the men stood solid and solemn. They were only able to shoot hate from their eyes and nothing more—hate for the war, hate for the Germans and Fascists, hate for this happening to their family.

Flashbacks of being in front of a firing squad gripped his mind and numbed his body as his heart pounded loudly in his ears, and he struggled to catch his breath. The black scarf, the men lined up to shoot him, the dark room... he nearly fell to the ground with the haunting memory. His fingernails dug into the mud at the edge of the ditch, and he struggled to stand as a shot rang through the clear mountain air followed by an unearthly scream that sounded like it carried ten miles or more. Riccardo's young body crumpled to the earth. It was done—they had found Riccardo and killed him for defending his country.

He watched. There was no more room for sadness in his heart—only anger. He supposed he should be used to it by now, for this was just one more tragedy to add to his collection of many. The loaded trucks pulled away, and Riccardo's mother was left screaming and

---

[159] This is as recorded by Carl. However, it was passed on to the Funari family that the Fascists would not allow Riccardo's mother to watch and threatened her with death if she watched from the window where she stood. Then they killed Riccardo in front of the ox stall. Carl recorded the incident in 1945 and specifically listed the order in which they stood before Riccardo was shot.

crying on the ground beside her son's lifeless body. Her pain was deep and her agony could be felt across the road.

Had the enemy thought to investigate the other side of the road, they would have been discovered too. Once again, they had been spared as the trucks drove on to their next stop on the main road below. They could still see the trucks as they stopped again and the Fascists got out at another small house.

They saw a boy run out the backdoor into the thick brush up the mountain. They had heard that the boy who lived there had deserted the Italian Army. Apparently, this was his punishment—a shot in the back. The boy fell to the ground and the Fascists took what they wanted from the house and continued down the road.

This was getting more serious by the hour. Two killings he had personally seen that morning. News traveled fast and Riccardo's death sent a wave of panic plowing into the Monte San Martino area as friends and neighbors visited and checked on the family. Carl and Jim had to be careful to stay hidden with so many people passing on the usually quiet, country road.

When Giovanni went to check on the family, he stopped at the ditch before leaving. They were glad to see him and he filled them in on the latest news. He sadly shook his head and said in Italian, "It's a shame. This war is destroying us." He pointed back to Riccardo's house and added, "Poor lady… to lose her son. She was so distraught she left fingernail marks down the wooden floors. I saw them with my own eyes."

Jim helped translate and Carl didn't doubt she had left scratches across the floor. He had seen and heard her woe when it happened. By this point, it was far too dangerous even to go out. Every day of May felt like it was getting longer as they waited for things to cool down, but it didn't. Sometimes they got food, sometimes they didn't. Giovanni couldn't risk his family's life when the enemy was always watching through unseen eyes.

Yes, the same unseen eyes that had tracked Riccardo. But how? Was it the two men claiming to be British escapees who had seen Riccardo at his girlfriend's house the night before, but hadn't taken the invitation to stay and get out of the rain?

Jim and he had plenty of time to think about it, as they waited—wet, hungry, and tired of the constant struggle. June arrived and Allied forces were getting closer—he could hear the sound of their artillery, he could see their fighters patrolling the sky around them, and he heard the Germans were beginning to retreat even more. The lines were being pushed back and the Allies were moving in. "We got to find a way to get out of here before the retreating enemy reinforces right here in the open countryside," he whispered as they lay in the hut.

"No goofin'," Jim agreed. "This area could easily become a battlefield, and we'd be stuck worse than we are now. Things could get off the hook[160] in a hurry."

He was used to Jim's Brooklyn way of talking and most of the time he didn't even have to think twice about it anymore. "Yeah," Carl agreed, "this rough terrain here would work perfect for combat… and we wouldn't stand a chance."

"But there's also a chance the Allied forces would get here first. We just got to finish waitin' it out," Jim said, running a stick through the dirt.

"Yeah, but for how long?" he asked. "We've already been here almost nine months now… nine long months of seeing death and cruelty while being hunted, hungry, and cold. Giovanni said U.S. forces just took possession of Rome a few days ago[161]."

Jim's sentence ran together as he said, "What about Terni? By the time we get there, the troops should be movin' in."

Carl shrugged his shoulders and said, "It don't matter where we go. Right now, we're stuck behind German lines. You know as well as I do that there ain't a safe route. At one point, we'll have to cross those lines to make it to the Allies."

Things were moving, but the Germans and Fascists were not giving up without a fight. Carl looked over and said, "You're right. With the Germans being pushed back, we might be able to make it through to Terni now. I say we try before it's too late. If the Germans concentrate troops here, we don't got a chance."

---

[160] Get off the hook is like saying out of control
[161] June 4, 1944

Chapter 14 – Taking A Chance

Nodding his head in agreement, Jim said, "Let's go talk to Giovanni and let him know we're leavin' here."

That was the part he dreaded. It was hard to say goodbye, but Giovanni needed to know. Early in the morning, they went to his house. When Giovanni saw them standing there with the two wool blankets he had given them, he knew something was up.

They told him they were leaving and Giovanni called out to his wife. A tear ran down her sun marked cheek, and she begged for them to stay. She kept saying it was too dangerous to go and they'd get killed. Jim and he had become like sons to them, and they worried about their safety. Giovanni assured them they would be okay if they stayed and waited.

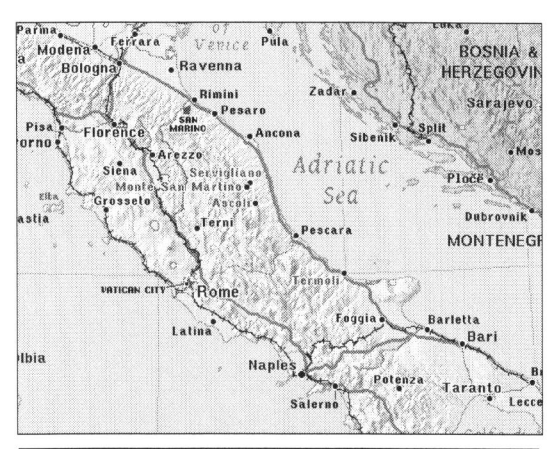

Figure 38: Map that shows Monte San Martino, Rome, and Terni (PAT public domain maps)

Carl had heard his division was moving through Italy and all he could think about was getting back to his company. His mind was made up and there was no holding back. They were heading to Allied lines and they'd be leaving tonight. "Please tell her we will be okay. We will make it through. I will give them my home address and they can write," he told Jim. "Tell them thank you for helping us all these months."

What else could he say? How could he thank someone for saving his life? He had nothing to give them in return. The only comfort he had was knowing he had worked hard for them.

When Giovanni's wife saw there was no changing their minds, she went into the house and brought out a bit of bread. Her face was tearstained as she handed it to them and preformed the sign of the cross. They would need all the blessings they could get.

Before it became harder than it already was, they turned and walked away for the last time. He couldn't bear to look back or wave as they kept to the shadows of the trees and far away from the main roads. They were too close to let their guard down now and the enemy was everywhere around them.

They saw another man walking along the edge of the road ahead. Paranoid, the man kept looking over his shoulder. Prepared to fight if needed, they quietly approached him. When he saw them, he raised his hands and said, "I'm American."

"Where you headed?" Carl asked.

"The name's Charlie[162] and I'm not sure where I'm going. My buddy was killed, and I'm done with this war."

"We're thinking to head to Terni," Carl said as Charlie joined them.

It had been cloudy all morning, and the heavens began to rumble. "I'll bet you dollas to doughnuts we're goin' to get some rain," Jim said, looking into the sky. No sooner had the words left his mouth than large, wet drops plopped into the dry, dirt road and started turning it into mud.

Another sound suddenly broke over the falling rain. Carl stopped to listen. "Engines! Vehicles are headed our way."

Careful not to leave muddy tracks along the road, they looked around and got covered under some wet brush. If the enemy didn't stop and check the area, they would be okay. He doubted they would stop with the rain, but his heart still beat fast in his chest as he waited for the last vehicle to pass. He hesitated to move. Were there more coming?

He didn't want to be waiting—he wanted to be walking. He wanted to be getting closer to being free. No, they had to play it safe. After waiting what felt like hours, they slowly got up. Wet and muddy, they continued walking.

Before making it a full mile, they heard the sound again. It must be a second convoy to the first. Maybe Giovanni was right. Perhaps they should have waited. The enemy was everywhere and they were right in

---

[162] Real person, unsure of name

Chapter 14 – Taking A Chance

the midst of them. One faulty move and the game was over—the wolf would finally get the rabbit.

After the last vehicle passed, they waited for a few minutes to make sure there weren't any stragglers. The mud seeped into the parts of his shoes where the leather had split as he started walking again. They had made it nearly eight miles, but in the rain, it felt further.

The rain started to let up, and they heard a third convoy coming. *Good golly,* he thought, *we must be right where the enemy is trying to reinforce.* Again, they holed up in the mountain brush. They'd push for a few more miles before stopping for a rest.

Evening approached and a cool wind picked up. It was June, but as water dripped down his bearded face and his wet clothes blew against him, he shivered. Ten miles—they had roughly made it ten miles. Maybe a countryside farmer would be kind enough to give them something to eat, but they had to be careful whom they asked.

"There's a house over there on the hill," Carl pointed out in a whisper.

Jim nodded and said, "I was thinkin' that house looked like a safe bet. Let's watch it a bit and see if there's any movement."

"I hear you," Carl said as they settled behind some bushes. It was getting dark, but they could still see well enough to tell if there was any unusual movement in the area. A calm breeze blew through, but other than that, it was quiet. After at least fifteen minutes, they nodded at each other.

He hesitated at the front of the house. When they asked for food, the farmer would either help them or shoot them. They had a fifty-fifty chance. This time around, it was all about taking chances and the sound of his knuckles knocking on the wooden door echoed through the quiet darkness as the three of them nervously waited.

An Italian man about his size opened the door and looked out at them. No words were needed—it was obvious who they were. The man quickly stepped outside and clasped his hands around theirs saying how grateful he was the Allies were near.

They didn't want to push their luck by asking for too much, so they kept it simple and only asked for a bite of bread. They only needed enough to keep them going. The farmer appeared to be sincere, but Carl had to wonder if the farmer was going in to get bread or a gun.

Relief came in the form of a smile as the farmer came back with a plate of bread, sheep cheese, and a little spaghetti. It was the best meal they had gotten for a while and it didn't take long for every morsel to disappear. They thanked the farmer for his generosity before turning to leave.

The farmer put out his hand and said to follow him as he took them to a shed full of straw. He pointed inside and told them they could rest there. It wasn't the safest place, but it couldn't be any worse than sleeping out in the open. Plus it would be warm and dry, so they accepted his kind offer.

Even in wet clothes, the exhaustion of the day carried Carl away as he lay in the warmth of the straw. He wasn't sure how much time had passed, but a sound snapped his eyes open. It was still dark. It took him a second to figure out where he was as he heard the sound again—closer this time.

Someone was coming toward the shed. He could hear footsteps getting closer. His heart raced as he sat up. He always had something nearby to use as a weapon, but in his exhaustion, he hadn't grabbed anything. Jim and Charlie sat up. They had heard it too. The door to the shed creaked open and Carl jumped up. Through the moonlit morning, he saw it was the farmer. It was about 0430 hours, and the farmer had come out to warn them things were getting hot in the area—they needed to leave. Before they walked away, the farmer handed them a small breakfast and said in Italian, "Be safe and be careful who you trust."

They didn't "trust" anyone, but they would still have to find people who might help them. Even if the person appeared to have good intentions, they knew better than to fully relax. The road ahead was going to be dangerous... no, it was going to be more than dangerous. It was like walking across a thin sheet of ice that could crack at any moment and drop them into the icy water below to drown.

After walking for over twelve hours, they saw a village down the mountainside. Maybe they could stop there for a few hours and rest, but they needed to know if it was safe. They saw an Italian man walking along the narrow, dirt path near them. Carl whispered to Jim, "Let's ask him. There's three of us and only one of him."

Jim stopped the man and asked if there were Germans in the area. The man didn't appear surprised to see them as he looked Jim straight in the eyes, pointed his walking stick toward the village, and said in Italian, "It is safe. No Germans there."

The man walked on down the path, and the three of them looked at each other. "Something feels off," Carl said. "Let's get over to that ridge so we can see down there for ourselves."

One thing they had learned was even nice and helpful people couldn't be trusted. It was unfortunate, but everyone was wearing the same mask. There was no way to tell who was secretly Fascist and who was willing to help them.

They left the mountain path and cut across toward the ridge. When they saw a small boy herding sheep, they stopped to talk to him. The boy looked to be about ten years old, and they knew they could trust the words of a child more than those of an adult. However, they still had to be careful. Children didn't play favorites—they would also tell the enemy whatever they wanted to know

Jim asked the boy the same question as they had asked the other man only minutes ago. Excitement lit the boy's face as he said something with a smile. Carl only understood two words—*tedeschi* and *cavalli*.

That was enough. Obviously, the village was full of Germans and their horses. He looked back toward the narrow mountain path. The man who had told them it was safe was long gone.

He walked with Charlie over to the ridge while the boy talked with Jim. In the village below, they watched as the German Calvary hid their horses in the barns and covered them up. "Well, looks like the boy is right—the village is chock-full of Germans! If we would've trusted that old man, we would've walked straight into the hot oven," he told Charlie.

"We're too close for that to happen," Charlie said. "Another close call to remind us why we can't trust anybody!"

Jim joined them and they made an unplanned detour across the mountains to get as far away from that village as possible. Only stopping for a quick rest in the brush that night, they were up and going with the sunrise the next morning. Their legs cramped and ached, but they kept walking. Unseen willpower pushed them forward as things got more precarious with every step.

They didn't talk much or take any unnecessary chances of exposing themselves. They avoided all contact unless they needed information. Even then, they usually did the opposite with whatever information they gathered. It was impossible to know who would help them.

The enemy appeared to be hanging fairly close to the roads, so they snuck through the off beaten paths hidden in the rough, steep terrain of the mountains in the direction of Terni. They walked until they saw a small village nestled in the valley below. It didn't seem to be buzzing with any unusual activity, but enemy eyes could be anywhere.

Headed toward the village, they ran across a couple sheepherders off by themselves. It looked like the herders immediately recognized them as Americans and waved them closer. "What do you think they want?" Jim whispered.

"Maybe they can give us some information," Carl whispered back. "Besides there are only two of them and three of us."

Charlie didn't usually say much, but added, "We got these walking sticks if we need to use them as weapons."

They agreed and went over to the herders who seemed glad to see them. According to them, the village was safe. Then one of the herders took the crook he held and pointed to a mountain behind the village and said there were several other escapees hiding in caves around there. They thanked them for the information and headed toward the village. "I hope it ain't a trap," Carl said as they edged closer. "Maybe we can get a small bite to eat and then head for the mountains."

Loud explosions boomed in the distance and confirmed they were getting ever closer. "Will these people risk helpin' us now that we're so close?" Jim asked as they looked down on the village, making sure there weren't any Germans down there.

It looked safe from a distance. "I guess there's only one way to find out," Carl said as they walked into the village at dusk.

After the first person turned his back to them and acted as if he hadn't heard, Carl noticed others gong out of their way purposely to avoid them. It was obvious the village people didn't want anything to do with them. Nobody dared offer a helping hand—the enemy could be watching from anywhere. The closer they got to the lines, the harder it was going to be. Fear had set in and nobody was willing to take a chance.

Carl's stomach rumbled—they hadn't eaten for two days and his energy levels were near zero. Not to mention that his feet ached from walking the rough terrain in shoes that could no longer count as shoes. "There's got to be someone around here who's not afraid to help us," he grumbled.

Jim agreed, "Let's try the farmers outside of here. They seem more willin' to help."

For whatever reason, based on their experience, it was true. So they stopped at a small house away from the village. The farmer opened the door and took a good look through the darkness before walking them down a worn path to an old barn. "Wait here," he said in Italian, "I'll bring you some food if it's safe."

A few minutes later, the farmer came back with some spaghetti. Explosions boomed in the distance, and the farmer hurriedly turned to leave, but quickly added in Italian, "Keep in mind, you may be close, but the enemy is always closer."

Jim told them the farmer's parting words and they knew exactly what he meant—the Allies were close, but the enemy was closer. Right up in enemy lines, they still had to get across to the other side. Close at this point, wasn't close enough. There were no deep sighs of relief, only the urge to keep going.

An explosion shook the barn. "Gosh, we're right in it. This probably ain't the safest place to be," Carl said, getting up and looking out the barn door as explosions lit up the darkness.

"No doubt we'd be safer in the hills," agreed Jim.

Charlie nodded his head and followed them as they crouched low until they could get in the cover of the brush. Up at sunrise, they headed to where the herders had said the other escapees were hiding in the mountains. It was too dangerous to keep going, and Terni seemed as far as it was when they started.

"How are we ever going to find those guys up here?" Charlie asked.

Carl was wondering the same thing, but as luck would have it, they ran into a couple of them who had come down to get information. They talked and each of them shared what they knew with the other. "You guys are right," one of them said. "It is too risky to travel any longer. Follow us. It will be safer up in the caves."

They followed them to a quiet area off the path and up a steep side of a cliff. There was a group of caves that had become hideouts. Carl leaned over to Jim and whispered, "What do you think? I think we should stay a few days while the enemy's so hot down there."

"Well, the caves are dark and they'll keep us off the main trails and out of the summa' rain," Jim whispered back.

"My only concern is if the Fascists ever check up here. There ain't no back doors or windows to jump through to get away," Carl said with a look around. "But I guess we got the view from the mountain. Just keep an eye open for trouble."

Jim nodded his head in agreement. They didn't have any guarantees it would be safer there, but right now; there weren't any guarantees for anything. At least a few of the guys had been there for a while and had things worked out pretty well. Even a few of the peasant families from the valley below occasionally brought food up for them to share.

It wasn't so bad and soon five days had passed. While they were there, Carl gathered as much information from the other escapees as possible. He had wondered if they should have waited like Giovanni had said, but at this point, it was too late to doubt their decision.

Besides, after learning more about what was happening around them, it looked like heading toward Ascoli would be closer, faster, and safer than Terni. Rumor had it that the Allies were near there now. It was only a matter of finding the right time to leave.

After a few more days of waiting, one of the boys came running over to where they were quietly talking. Fascists were spotted not too far off. If they came up any higher, they might discover them in the caves—and it looked like they were headed their way.

Everybody split up and hid in the darkest corners of the different caves. There was no getting used to feeling the pressure of the hunt, and the hunt was on as Carl heard Italian voices getting closer. A bead of sweat rolled down his face as he thought, *I have come way too far to be caught like this, darn it.*

One of the Fascist stepped in the cave where he was hiding. He instinctively pressed his body hard against the rocks and ground. He could feel Jim's body near his as they tried not to breathe.

The Fascist took a quick look around, but saw nothing in the dark. Had he waited for his eyes to adjust to the darkness and then looked around, he probably would have found them. It almost seemed as if he wasn't really expecting to find anybody and didn't look too hard. Either that or he didn't really want to give them up.

It didn't make any difference to Carl. He had managed to get by one more time—barely. Not believing their luck, they waited for a long time before moving. His body ached and his head pounded from the stress, but the Fascists were gone—and they hadn't taken anybody with them. After that, Carl was ready to go. It was too dangerous to risk a situation like that again. He knew the next time things wouldn't go the same way as they had that day. They had stayed up in the caves for eight days—it was time to leave.

The other escapees weren't ready to go. They still felt like it was more dangerous to leave. They said, "Wait a bit longer. The Allies will get here soon enough. If you try to risk it now, you'll be caught."

It reminded him of the day he had tried to talk Kingsland's group from leaving the Monte San Martino area, and he wondered if they were right. He wondered if the same fate would fall upon them if they left. Charlie agreed with the others saying, "Let's stay a bit longer. Those Fascists won't be back up here for a while."

Carl thought about it—he seriously did, but he looked over at Jim and said, "I'm leaving tomorrow morning. I know we can make it to Ascoli. If nobody wants to go, I'm going alone."

Jim didn't think long before saying, "I'm goin'!"

Nobody else spoke up from the group, and he looked at Jim and said, "Well, it looks like it's the two of us again."

That was fine with them. It would be easier to get food and shelter that way. Imagine how hard it would be if several of them would have wanted to go. Besides, with their worn clothing and long, dirty hair, he was sure they looked rough. It was most likely less threatening to see only two of them anyway. The escapees told them where to go. It wouldn't be easy by any means, but they were ready to be done with this whole ordeal.

Early the next morning, they said their goodbyes and started down the steep cliff to the dirt path below. Low clouds still hugged the glistening green valleys of the warm earth and the tranquil scene hauntingly appeared unreal as the sounds of nature appeared oblivious to the reality. How could the beautiful Italian landscape be involved in such a calamity? He had asked himself that question many times, but he still didn't have an answer. The Marche region was one of the most beautiful areas he had ever been, but the circumstances didn't let him enjoy it.

Right now, the challenge was making it to Ascoli and *that* was all that was on his mind. Not only would they have to stay hidden, but the mountainous terrain was rough and unforgiving in some places. Nevertheless, they were getting along.

After walking several hours, they stopped at a small stream for a drink of water. He sat down for a minute and looked down at his foot poking out from his broken shoe. He was surprised at how tough his feet had become from all they had endured in the last several months. From the cold, to having no socks, to turning blisters into calluses, his feet had stayed strong.

A cool breeze picked up as a few clouds blew their way and covered the sun. "Guess we should get moving. Looks like we're going to get some rain again," he said as he stood up.

Jim took one more drink before catching up with him saying, "Looks like it, but maybe it'll blow on by."

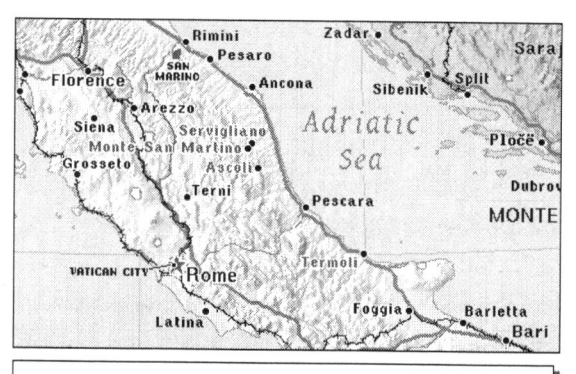

Figure 39: Map that shows Ascoli (PAT public domain maps)

Chapter 14 – TAKING A CHANCE

That was a nice thought, but it looked like they were walking toward it, not away from it. A few hours later, he heard thunder in the darkening sky and knew they would be walking with the company of rain soon. At least he would get a quick shower out of it. Not being able to bathe regularly was one of the hard things about being captured and living as an escapee. He hated the feeling of being dirty all the time.

The first few raindrops splattered against him, and he looked up toward the heavens and opened his mouth to catch a drop or two. Rain or no rain, they were not stopping. The rain soaked through his clothes and ran down his face, but he kept trudging forward. Through the mud, through the wet grass, through the fields, they walked. After being so wet, it didn't really matter anymore that the rain continued to fall.

Several hours later, he saw a small village in the valley below. There didn't seem to be anything unusual going on down there as they watched it from the brush. They walked toward it with caution. Upon arriving, he could tell the people recognized them as prison escapees by the looks on their faces, but they weren't afraid to talk to them. In no time at all, they were told the Allies were indeed taking Ascoli. For some reason, he believed them this time. In fact, several different people said the same thing.

It had to be true, but their words came with one precaution—watch out for snipers. Not everybody was happy the Allies were there. Even with the warning, he felt a new life come over him—they were closer than ever.

Suddenly, he felt like he could keep on walking. Although he was tired and jittery, the news was enough to keep him going. Then, hearing a plane overhead, he looked up and saw the shine of a big white star. "An observation plane," he said under his breath as if it had fallen directly out of heaven for them.

They stopped and waved their arms up at it. "Do you think they saw us?" he asked Jim as a wave of energy flowed through his tired body. "We're right at it. Them boys can only stay out two hours and they got to go back in and get filled up. I'd say we ain't too far from the troops."

"I think you're right," Jim agreed.

The rain stopped, making it easier to get through the valleys and hills. They reached a small path and could see the main road. In the early evening hour, he opened his eyes wide as his heart beat faster—this time from excitement, not from fear. In front of them they could see Ascoli—a city now under control by the Allies. Although there was still a lot to get through to get down there, they were finally close enough to see it.

Headed toward the main road, they saw an old, small building that looked like a shed. When they passed by it, an old, Italian man stopped them and asked if they wanted a bite to eat. Ascoli was still off in the distance, and they didn't know how long it would be before they would get there. His stomach growled and he looked at Jim and said, "It might be our only chance."

He hoped this was the last person they'd have to trust as they stepped into the shed to keep from being seen from the main road. There was a little window on the sidewall where a small stream of evening light brightened the dingy floor. However, it wasn't long after the man closed the door that there was a sound that made his stomach drop. It was faint and hard to hear, but he instantly knew what it was as he whispered to Jim, "He locked the door. Let's get outta here."

Jim had already turned and was opening the window. If there was anything good from being nearly starved to death, it was that they were so thin they could slip through the small window and run. Forget the food. Forget it all. They were not going to get turned in now!

Dropping to the ground, they turned and ran down a slope on the other side. He wasn't sure if the man had heard them or if he could see them as they ran, but Carl wanted to get as far away as possible. Down the rocks and mud he slid until the shed was out of view. He didn't know if the man had a gun, but the thought of being so close and then being shot in the back kept him going until he had to stop and catch his breath. He bent over with his hands on his knees and muttered, "Boy, that was another close one. Son of a gun, when do we get a break?"

"We're almost there, but this isn't over till we're home," Jim said as they started walking again.

Chapter 14 – Taking A Chance

He kept walking even though his calves ached. Faster and faster until they were almost jogging. At the top of another hill, they looked down into the valley where the most beautiful sight welcomed their weary bodies. There, within a few minutes jog, were Allied tanks, jeeps, and tents. He blinked his eyes and hoped the scene before him would not disappear before he could get down there. "We finally made it!" he told Jim with a smile before using every ounce of strength he could muster to sprint toward the Allies.

When they got down there, they came across a few British troops who were still securing Ascoli. They pointed them in the direction of a British captain giving orders to his men. They got over to him and saluted, "We are American prisoners of war, sir."

Just by looking at them, there was no doubt that they had personally visited hell. Dismissing his men, the captain stood in front of them and sternly said with a strong British accent, "I know all about you boys. Well, you're free! Go and have a good time."

Carl looked at Jim. Where were they supposed to go? The captain looked back at them and said with a laugh, "I'm only joking. Welcome back, boys. I'll get one of my officers to have you looked after tonight and tomorrow we'll send you to an American Air Force base down in Bari."

Time stood still for that moment as it was carefully etched into his war-broken soul—June 21, 1944, at about 2000 hours. They had made it to the Allied lines! Not discrediting the greater power who got him there, he was incredibly thankful. He had waited and prayed for this great day for over eleven months. He was FREE—such a wonderful word he could never take for granted.

Now, if only he could convince his mind to believe it. He knew he was free, but he couldn't help but feel the sense of danger and panic he had depended

Figure 40: Postcard Carl picked up from Ascoli when he made it back to Allied lines

on to survive. He tried to push it aside—he could only take one step at a time.

It was too late to get much to eat, but they were satisfied with whatever they could get for the night. When the officer handed them a special release Red Cross parcel for escapees, Carl looked down at the contents. There was a razor with blades, shaving cream, a toothbrush, toothpaste, a comb, a pair of socks, and a few other items. At that moment, it felt better than Christmas.

"Take a quick shower and change those clothes," the officer called out to them. "Looks as if they're about to rot off you."

I'll be happy to do that, he thought. It was his first hot shower in months, and he wanted to soak up every hot drop as it ran off his unrecognizably thin body. He shaved his sunken, bearded face and saw his reflection in a mirror for the first time since he was captured. *Oh my gosh*, he thought, *what has this war done to me?* And that was only what it had done to him physically.

After getting cleaned up, the officer took them to where there was a group of partisans in the mountains, saying in his British accent, "Don't worry. You'll be safe here until they get you to the American base in the morning."

Tonight, he could finally sleep with both eyes closed—or so he hoped. With so many experiences and emotions trapped inside his mind, he realized the war would hold him prisoner until the day he died. It was a matter of dealing with it without letting it eat him up from the inside.

The next morning, he was surprised to find that it hadn't been a dream. However unbelievable it felt, it was really happening. After a small camp breakfast, he got ready to leave.

A Polish woman got in the truck and motioned for them to get in. Immediately, he realized the trip across the narrow mountain roads was going to be long and rough when she turned so tight against the mountain the truck scraped against it and threatened to push them down the steep drop on the other side. There was no extra room and if another vehicle chanced to come along, the only way through was for one of the vehicles to move back in reverse until the road widened again. Fresh bomb craters also pushed them precariously close to the

Chapter 14 – Taking A Chance

ledge as pebbles tumbled over the mountainside. It was going to be a long, rough ride to Bari.

His body was tense as he tightly held on to the seat as they bumped along, but the woman driver had a grip on it. She handled the roads until several hours later she had to stop at a railroad track that couldn't be passed. They all got out of the truck and walked by the twisted, broken track blocking their way. She pointed down the tracks and said in broken English, "Is there."

Figure 41: Map that shows Ascoli and Bari (PAT public domain maps)

Sure enough, he could see planes coming and going from the Air Force base down in the valley. He nodded his head to show her that he understood. They said thank you and started down the track. As they got closer, they saw a major standing out on the track to meet them. "That lady must have radioed them and told them we was coming," he said to Jim and they jogged to where the major stood.

The major greeted them with a big hug, "Welcome to the 12th Air Force! We are glad to see you boys make it back."

An American flag blew in the wind and made his heart proud. The first thing he thought to say was, "My outfit shouldn't be far up the road. I want to get back up there with them."

The major looked at him and said, "You forget your outfit. You aren't fit for anything."

It was true. He was nothing but skin and bones. However, the major's next words stung even deeper, "You wouldn't know anybody from your outfit anyway. Probably not the same men from when you were there."

Had the fighting over the last year been that bad? It made him wonder what would have happened to him if he hadn't been captured. What about Rodriguez, Bethem, Nyleve... it was too much to think

277

about. He was still trying to process what was happening now. They walked back toward the camp when the major said, "Don't you boys worry. We'll get you cleaned up and taken care of. Then you'll be on your way home."

Without thinking, Carl retorted, "Oh bull! I ain't going home. We've heard those stories before."

He had convinced himself home was an evasive place impossible to reach. It sounded too good to be true, and one thing he knew was if it sounded too good to be true, it usually was. How would he be going home when those left in his outfit were still fighting? The war wasn't over. In fact, based on the fight for Italy, there was still a long ways to go. Italy was only one small part of the equation for winning the whole war.

"Let me show you boys something," the major said as he took them down a little ways to the airfield.

The sound of bomber and fighter planes coming and going exploded through the air. It was an amazing sight he would never forget as the bombers continuously loaded, delivered, and reloaded. Somewhere it was raining hell, and he was glad he wasn't still stuck in their path. As one plane returned noticeably damaged, the major yelled over the roar, "They aren't all fortunate, but we're having pretty darn good luck."

After watching for a few more minutes, the major yelled out, "Now, let's get you boys something to eat. I bet you're starving."

The major had used a common expression, but the truth was they were starving as they left the airfield and walked toward the camp's kitchen. The cook had set out a large banquet of food for them—American food. Everything looked so good!

He heaped his plate full, but after eating two small sausages, a helping of mashed potatoes, a piece of bread, and a glass of milk, he couldn't eat another bite. He wanted to eat, but he couldn't even though it was sitting right in front of him—tempting him with what little he could smell. When the major saw they weren't eating more, he said, "After all that time, I thought you'd be hungry."

Disappointed, Carl said, "Me too. I guess my stomach is shrunk tight. I haven't ate like this in months!"

Chapter 14 – Taking A Chance

"Don't you worry," the major said reassuringly. "We'll get you boys fed and taken care of while you're here. As soon as possible, we'll be putting you on one of them B-25s and sending you to Africa so you can get checked over to go home. For now, we'll work on getting you some supplies. You boys go take it easy. There's a large group of other escapees who are waiting along with you."

When they found the other escapees, he was surprised at how many there were—there had to be more than fifty. He looked around the room. He stopped and stared at a couple faces he thought he recognized in the crowd. Jim was looking at the same guys. They were skinnier than he remembered, but they all were. Could it be they weren't killed after all? He had assumed when Giovanni had told them only two were recaptured the other two had been killed, but apparently not. He walked toward him in shock and Jim followed. "Snodgrass? Altomari?"

Snodgrass and Altomari stood up and gave them a brotherly hug. They all sat back down and talked about what had happened since they last saw each other. Everything was so surreal. For the first time in months, they had clean clothes, a full stomach, and a shaven face. After talking for about an hour, the major came in looking for Jim and him. "Let's go get you some pay," the major said as they followed him to the pay office.

The major handed each of them $100 and said, "The first thing I want to see is you don't spend a dime until you go get a haircut."

"No complaints there, sir," Carl said with a smile.

Although he had shaven his face the night before, his hair was still long and he couldn't wait to cut it all off. It was only five cents for a haircut, and he closed his eyes as the hair limply fell down his face and onto the floor. He couldn't help relate it to the end of that part of his life. Never again, under his control, would he let his hair get long.

Over the next several days, he watched as the rain splashed outside. The bad weather was causing delays with bombing missions, not to mention the trip back to Oran, Africa, where they'd be quarantined for a couple weeks before being sent back to the United States. At least he was waiting in comfort this time. They had been

279

given a complete uniform, shoes, and socks. It was more than he would have asked for.

It took a few more days, but finally the weather was good enough to leave. The orders were issued from Headquarters on July 3—*Happy birthday to me*, he thought as they climbed into a B-25. Although making it home had been their goal, they hadn't talked much about it. Instead, the idea sat quietly in the background of each act that could lead them there. Even now, as the plane engine roared, he still couldn't conceptualize that it was happening. In fact, he knew they weren't out of the woods yet. Anything could still happen between here and there.

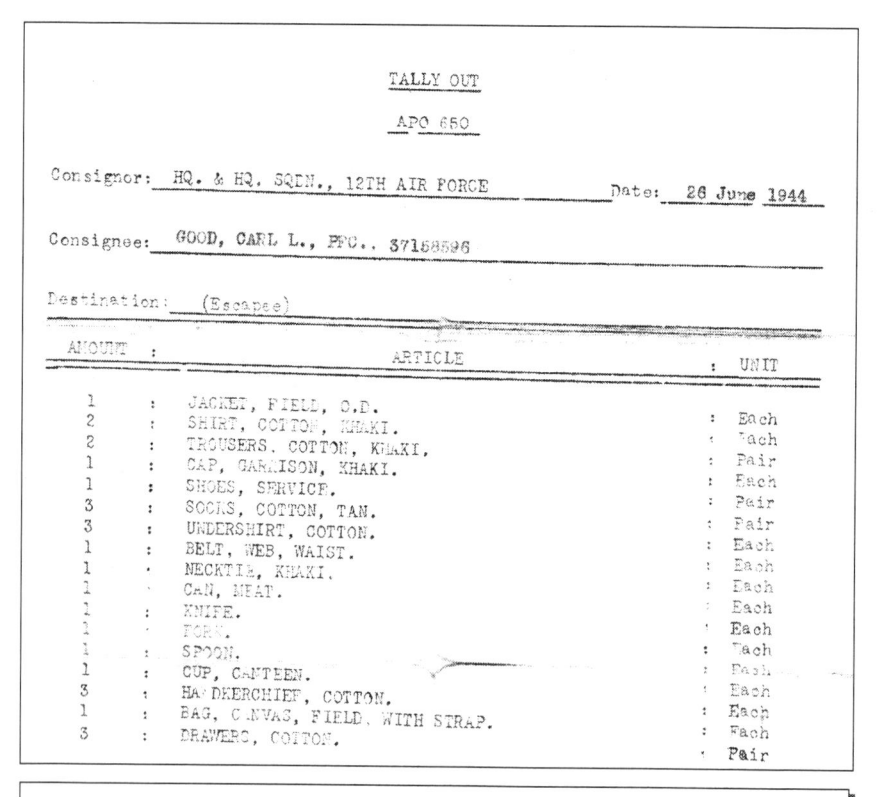

```
                         TALLY OUT
                          APO 650

Consignor:  HQ. & HQ. SQDN., 12TH AIR FORCE        Date:  26 June 1944

Consignee:  GOOD, CARL L., PFC., 37168596

Destination:  (Escapee)

AMOUNT  :               ARTICLE                    :  UNIT

   1    :   JACKET, FIELD, O.D.                    :  Each
   2    :   SHIRT, COTTON, KHAKI.                  :  Each
   2    :   TROUSERS, COTTON, KHAKI.               :  Pair
   1    :   CAP, GARRISON, KHAKI.                  :  Each
   1    :   SHOES, SERVICE.                        :  Pair
   3    :   SOCKS, COTTON, TAN.                    :  Pair
   3    :   UNDERSHIRT, COTTON.                    :  Each
   1    :   BELT, WEB, WAIST.                      :  Each
   1    :   NECKTIE, KHAKI.                        :  Each
   1    :   CAN, MEAT.                             :  Each
   1    :   KNIFE.                                 :  Each
   1    :   FORK.                                  :  Each
   1    :   SPOON.                                 :  Each
   1    :   CUP, CANTEEN.                          :  Each
   3    :   HANDKERCHIEF, COTTON.                  :  Each
   1    :   BAG, CANVAS, FIELD, WITH STRAP.        :  Each
   3    :   DRAWERS, COTTON.                       :  Pair
```

Figure 42: Supplies that were given to Carl by the 12th Air Force after he made it to Allied lines

When they were in the air, the pilot looked back at his cargo of men and shouted out, "Well, you boys suit yourself if you want to put your chutes on or not. We'll be flying so low across the Mediterranean

Chapter 14 – Taking A Chance

for identification that I can tell you right now they won't do you any good if you have to bail out."

Nobody moved or grabbed a parachute. It obviously wasn't worth the trouble if they were flying too low to use it anyway. When they were flying over Sicily, a loud explosion shook the plane. "What was that?" Carl asked as the pilot yelled out that a large ammunition dump exploded right beneath them as they passed.

Here we go, he thought as he grabbed for whatever was around him and held on tightly. He had thought about this possibility, but had dismissed it in order to get one step closer to home. Now, he could hear the shrapnel flying up and hitting the plane. A few men screamed and jumped up in panic to grab a parachute, but he knew there was no point. His mind blocked out the chaos and he felt numb as he braced for impact. The turbulence settled down as they passed through the worst of it, but a small hole had broken through the metal of the plane and they began to go down, down, down…

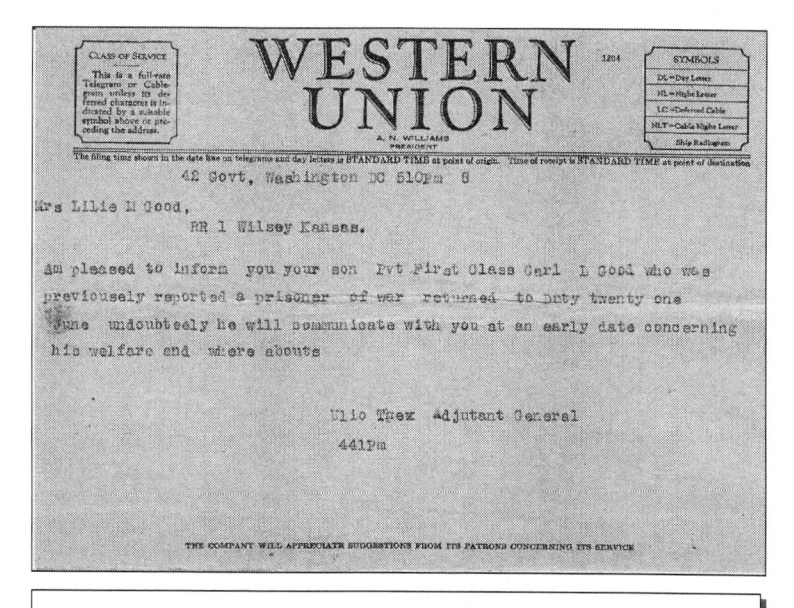

Figure 43: Post card sent to Carl's mother to inform her that he had made it to Allied lines. However, his mother did not get it right away because it was sent to the wrong address.

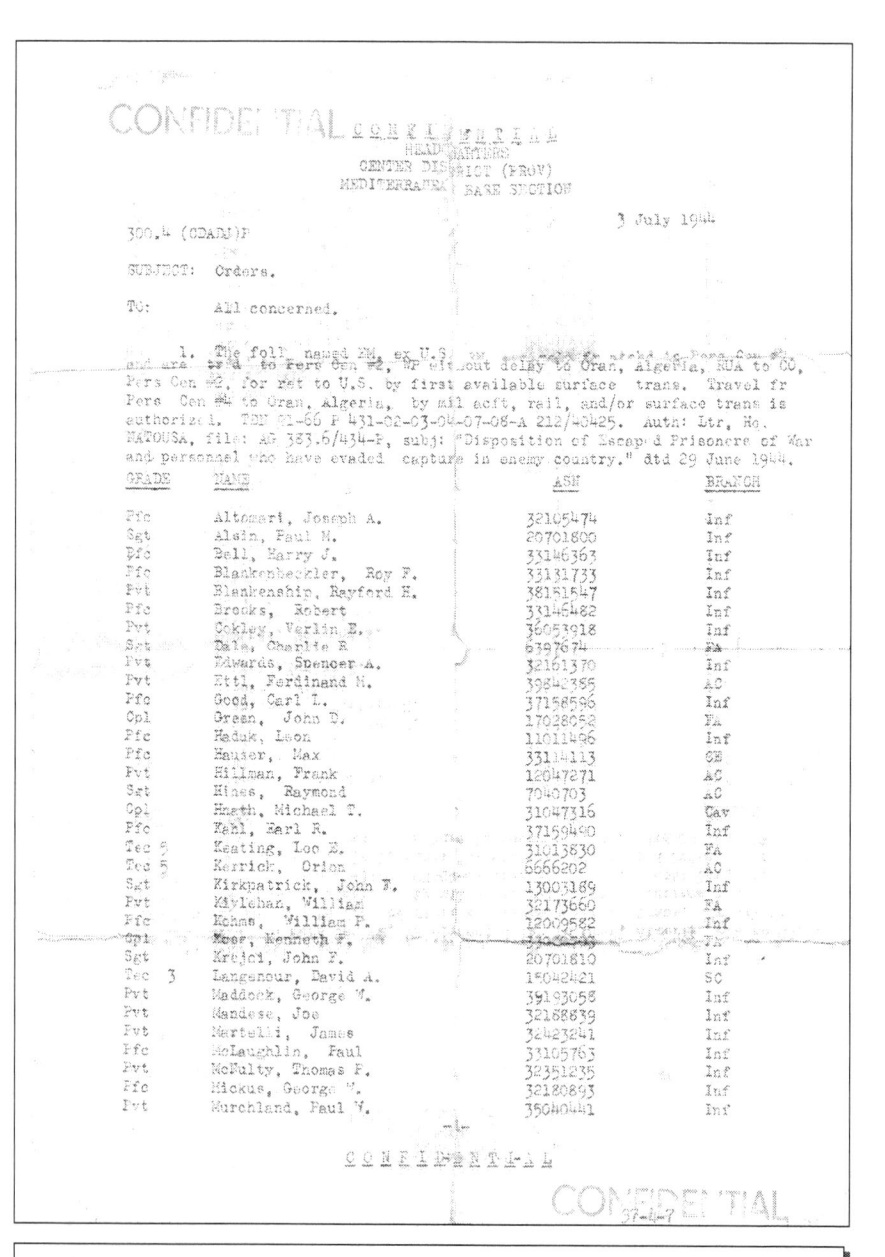

```
                    CONFIDENTIAL  CONFIDENTIAL
                              HEADQUARTERS
                          CENTER DISTRICT (PROV)
                         MEDITERRANEAN BASE SECTION

     300.4 (ODARJ)P                                    3 July 1944

     SUBJECT:  Orders.

     TO:       All concerned.

              1. The foll  named EM, ex U.S. PW, are atchd to Pers Con #2
     and are tfd to Pers Con #2, WP without delay to Oran, Algeria, RUA to CO,
     Pers Con #2, for rst to U.S. by first available surface trans.  Travel fr
     Pers Con #4 to Oran, Algeria, by mil acft, rail, and/or surface trans is
     authorized. TDN 01-66 P 431-02-03-04-07-08-A 212/40425. Auth: Ltr, Hq.
     NATOUSA, file: AG 383.6/434-P, subj: "Disposition of Escaped Prisoners of War
     and personnel who have evaded capture in enemy country." dtd 29 June 1944.
     GRADE      NAME                           ASN              BRANCH

     Pfc        Altomari, Joseph A.            32105474         Inf
     Sgt        Alsin, Paul M.                 20701800         Inf
     Pfc        Bell, Harry J.                 33146363         Inf
     Pfc        Blankenbeckler, Roy F.         33131733         Inf
     Pvt        Blankenship, Rayford E.        38151647         Inf
     Pfc        Brooks, Robert                 33146482         Inf
     Pvt        Cokley, Verlin E.              36053918         Inf
     Sgt        Dale, Charlie R                6397674          FA
     Pvt        Edwards, Spencer A.            32161370         Inf
     Pvt        Ettl, Ferdinand M.             39842356         AC
     Pfc        Good, Carl L.                  37158596         Inf
     Cpl        Green, John D.                 17028052         FA
     Pfc        Haduk, Leon                    11011496         Inf
     Pfc        Hauser, Max                    33114113         CE
     Pvt        Hillman, Frank                 12647871         AC
     Sgt        Hines, Raymond                 7040703          AC
     Cpl        Hnath, Michael T.              31047316         Cav
     Pfc        Kahl, Earl R.                  37159490         Inf
     Tec 5      Keating, Leo E.                31013830         FA
     Tec 5      Kerrick, Orion                 6666202          AC
     Sgt        Kirkpatrick, John F.           13003169         Inf
     Pvt        Kivlehan, William              32173660         FA
     Pfc        Kohns, William P.              12009582         Inf
     Cpl        Koor, Kenneth F.                                TX
     Sgt        Krejci, John F.                20701610         Inf
     Tec 3      Langenour, David A.            15042821         SC
     Pvt        Maddock, George M.             39193056         Inf
     Pvt        Mandese, Joe                   32158839         Inf
     Pvt        Martelli, James                32423241         Inf
     Pfc        McLaughlin, Paul               33105763         Inf
     Pvt        McNulty, Thomas F.             32351235         Inf
     Pfc        Mickus, George M.              32120893         Inf
     Pvt        Murchland, Paul V.             36040441         Inf

                                     -1-

                              CONFIDENTIAL
                                                    CONFIDENTIAL
```

Figure 44: First page of two on which Carl, Jim, and Altomari are listed to be sent back to Oran along with many others, Snodgrass was listed on the second page

Chapter 15

HEALING

CARL SAT UP wide-eyed and wiped his sweaty forehead on his sleeve as he looked around his room. The calendar was still neatly hanging on the wall with 1944 boldly typed across the top. Absolutely nothing was out of place. There was only a small dresser pushed against the wall and an old, creaky closet door with his clothes hanging neatly inside. The bag with the clothes he had been issued a few weeks earlier hung nicely on a brown, wooden chair to the side of the one small window. He didn't have much, but everything was right where he had left it the night before. Even the small, white feathers from the pillow he had shredded were still scattered across the floor.

He tried to shake the feeling of dread that lingered from his dream. He took a deep breath—it was so real. Somehow, he was home, but the memories were going to haunt him, not only throughout the day, but also throughout his dreams.

The last part of his dream replayed in his head. They were trying to get to safety in a plane that was flying too low and had been struck by shrapnel. Although he woke up as the plane was going down, in reality the pilot was able to gain control and land them safely. They got a quick meal, the plane was repaired, and they were back in the air and on their way to Oran.

He rubbed his arms where the sting of needles had poked through his bare skin. In order for him to be allowed back in the United States, he had to be quarantined, checked over, and his immunizations updated. It had taken almost three weeks[163] before Jim and he were approved to leave those dreadful shores of northern Africa—the place where his nightmare had begun and ended.

He didn't plan to go back there ever again. After all, he didn't *choose* to go there in the first place, he was *sent* there. Now, he was stuck with the devilish nightmares left relentlessly to replay in his mind forever.

He leaned forward, rested his head in his opened hands, and thought back a few weeks to when Jim and he had arrived in the States. They had pushed through the Atlantic waters aboard the troop carrier *USS Mariposa* and made it to the Boston Port on August 2. It was a day of mixed emotions, but it turned out to be a brutal one for Jim. His thoughts slowly drifted back to that day:

The hottest month in Boston had ended, and even with an ocean breeze, tiny beads of sweat rolled off his body onto the new material of his khaki uniform. They were like a silent reminder that the nightmares of his past would vanish into a new reality. Greeted by a blur of surreal noises, colors, and smells, they combined to form memories he was sure he wouldn't experience again. He had been positive that he wouldn't step foot on American soil again, but somehow, he had, and it was a feeling he would never forget!

Quickly sent to a welcoming area[164] *in Camp Myles Standish, they were given a small booklet on what to expect. He opened it up and skimmed through the index. Across from the index, two small white notes positioned on bright red background thanked returning soldiers for their service and promised a short stay—some good news. Then he noticed a section at the bottom of the index and whispered to Jim, "Did you see the telephone information?"*

"Sure did. Let's drop our stuff off at the barrack and head ova' to one of them phone centers around here," he said. When he was excited, his Brooklyn accent slurred even more than usual.

---

[163] Until July 23, 1944
[164] An organized camp prepared for returning soldiers. It was a brief stay (24-48 hours) where soldiers could call home, eat American food, and get some American entertainment. From this camp, Carl was sent to Jefferson Barracks in Missouri so he could get his furlough and go home before reporting for further duty in Texas.

Chapter 15 – Healing

"That's what I was thinking. Maybe we can get to one before the rush," he said still in a whisper. He wasn't sure why they were whispering. They could talk now, but for some reason, it didn't feel safe.

They found the white bus and within minutes, they were standing in front of a wooden building. It was good to see the slatted, wooden benches outside of the building empty—no long lines to get an available operator who could make the call out. If they were lucky, they would even get their call through without having to leave a message with an operator to send later.

The anticipation of hearing the voice of a loved one after so long made his stomach twist into a tight ball. After a strong suggestion not to call their parents because of the shock, he wondered whom to call as they walked in.

"I'm goin' to call my wife," Jim said with a slight smile as he quickly found an empty operator behind the counter in the corner.

Carl sat on a black bench nearby and waited his turn, but he could hear Jim as he gave the number to the operator in a hushed voice. Jim intently watched as she rang in the number and handed him the receiver. After a few seconds, he looked down and shook his head sadly, "Hmmm, that numba' don't work nomore. I guess I'll have to call my fatha'."

He knew Jim's heart must have been pounding harder with each number as the gum-chewing operator calmly rang in the new number and handed the receiver to him once again. He was nervous for Jim as fear and excitement churned relentlessly together. What would he say? What would THEY say? Questions bombarded his mind until Jim's voice broke through his thoughts, "It's me, Jimmy... What?... When did that happen?"

Silence.

Jim's face turned deathly white. He looked crumbled and beaten. What could go so wrong after living the nightmare they had just endured? What could be worse than that?

The conversation died, and Jim slowly returned the receiver to the operator after saying his traditional, "Fuggedaboutdit." The operator tried to act as if she didn't notice anything wrong. Maybe she had become oblivious to the pain she saw every day.

Carl hesitated before asking, "What happened?"

There was a new tone of defeat in his voice as Jim declared, "I got no home to go to!"

Vaguely, Carl remembered hearing something about Jim's mother dying before he left for war. It seemed odd, but even though they were together all that time, they hadn't talked much about home. It had been much too dangerous hardly to talk at all. However, he did know Jim had a little boy who he couldn't wait to see. He probably wasn't a baby anymore—maybe two or three by now.

Jim's next words stopped his thoughts dead in their tracks, "I got no motha', no wife, no son, no life!" His body collapsed defeated onto the empty bench as he buried his head in his hands and sobbed, "My little boy is dead! He was only two and I didn't even get to see him before he died! What kind of life is this? How could God take him? Why didn't He take me instead? I was there... standin' at the door of death, and He took him instead? I wouldn't of tried so hard if I woulda known..." He wiped his eyes on his shirt sleeve before spurting out the last part, "And what do ya know, my wife left me, and my dad said I might as well not go home cause I got no home to go to!"

Deep sorrow and pain penetrated through Carl like a dark bladed knife. For a brief moment, he was transported back to when he was thirteen years old and the bitter pain he had felt when seeing his father for the last time before family members took him back to Kansas to be buried. Death was an old enemy and the stench of it pierced his soul. Words escaped him as he watched his friend weep in pain.

Jim looked up at him and stuttered, "My life... My life that I worked so hard to keep is ova'! I have nottin' left."

Not sure what to say, he softly put his hand on Jim's shoulder, "You're wrong. You can build a new life. You can't give up now—you've come too danged far for that."

Jim hung his head, "I can't... I just can't!"

"Well, what are you going to do? Give me an address so we can keep in touch when we leave here."

Jim stood up and looked at him with deep sadness penetrating across his tear-stained face. There also was a hint of anger that radiated from his dark eyes as he snappily replied, "No, I got no address, and not for nottin', but I just want to forget this whole thing."

What could he say to that? He understood the forgetting about the war part, but he didn't want to lose contact. He gave it one more try, "You sure? I'll give you mine and we can keep in touch."

Jim slowly turned the other way and yelled out a spew of curse words to nobody in particular. He ended by looking back at him and adding, "No, my life is ova'! I want to forget this whole thing eva' happened!" Then, with his head down, he stumbled toward the door in an obvious daze.

The grief Jim left behind was overbearing. It hung low in the air, almost making it difficult to swallow or even breathe. Skinny, weak, and mentally exhausted, Jim was not in good physical condition, and he wondered if this would take its toll and do him in.

It didn't make sense to him. Why would Jim's father tell him not to come home? Could it be that his father considered home a place that consisted of more than only him? Perhaps with all the devastation and loss, the term home had lost its meaning. The one spark that had kept Jim alive had been completely extinguished in a matter of minutes.

A friendship built on survival and support had ended, and now worry crept its way in. Maybe he didn't want to make his call home anymore. What news would speed across the phone lines to him? It had been over a year since any news could get to him at all. So much could have happened in that year. For sure, his family thought he was dead. Had his mom received the notification from the Army saying he was still alive? He didn't know and he certainly didn't know what to expect after seeing what happened to Jim.

With the thought they might not know he was alive, he overcame the dread and took the black receiver from the operator. He gave the number and waited. Jim's numbing grip on the receiver left it feeling warm, and he silently prayed someone would answer from the other end. It rang once and then twice before a familiar voice picked up.

"Hello?"

He hesitated a moment to gather his thoughts, "Is this Linnie Strouts[165]?"

"Yes… Yes, it is," came the reluctant reply.

---

[165] Linnie Strouts is Carl's aunt

"I've been advised not to give any personal information over the phone, but you should probably sit down." He paused. "This is Carl and I need you to go tell my mother that I'm alive. I'm coming home."

There was a moment of silence on the other end, "Hello? Aunt Linnie, are you still there?"

"Carl, is that really you? They told us you were missing in action and you were probably dead. Oh, Carl is that really you?"

"I wanted to talk to mother, but I couldn't call her because of the shock."

"Of course, but talk about a shock! You about made my own heart stop beating! We thought you were dead, Carl." A sob broke through the line, "I'll go into town right now and tell her. She moved into town, you know. She probably didn't get the notice that you were alive. We prayed this day might come, thanks to the good Lord above. This is such great news! Oh, I'm so thrilled to hear your voice, Carl!"

That was it. He handed the heavy receiver back to the operator, who dropped it on the phone hooks and looked back down at the magazine she was reading. Although a small weight was lifted from his shoulders when he called his aunt, Jim's pain still hung close around him.

Chapter 15 – HEALING

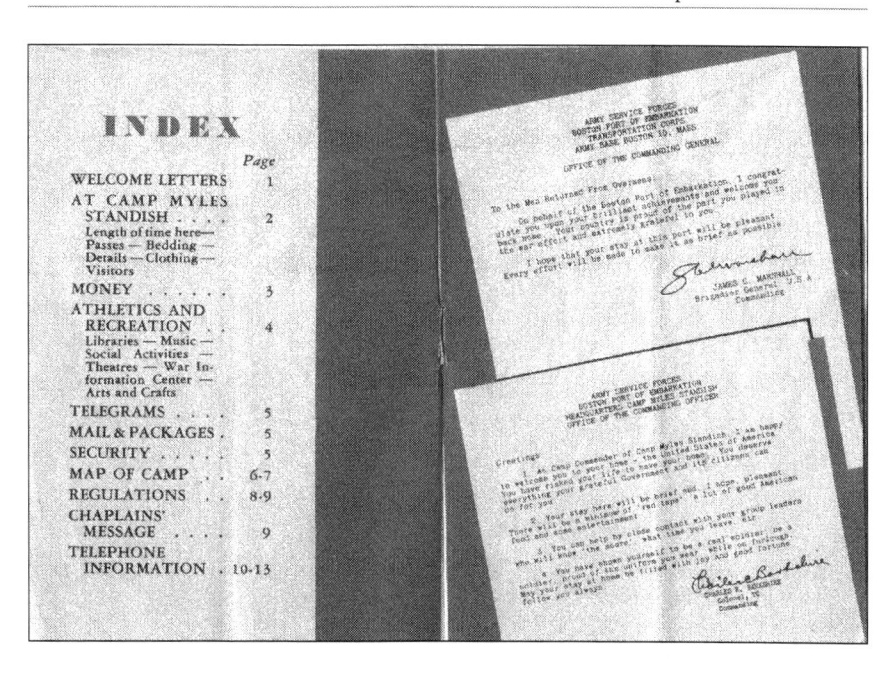

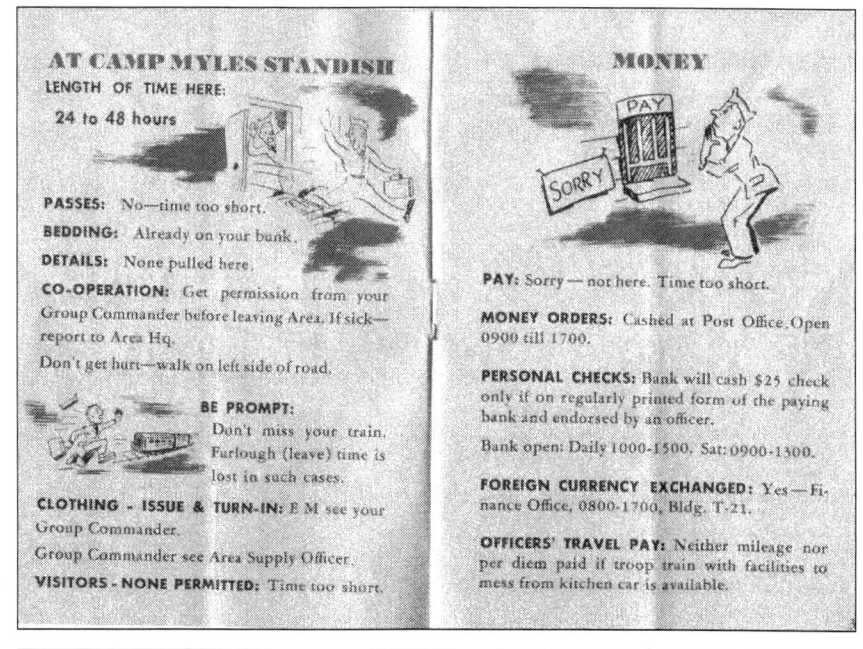

Figure 45: Scanned pages of booklet for Camp Myles Standish (Public domain)

289

He wondered about Jim[166]. Did he go back to his home state of New York? Would he stay a broken man and drink his woes away, or build a new life? Was he strong enough to survive the emotional pain?

There was no way to know the answers. Life was moving on, and he was only home for two more weeks before he'd have to report for duty in Fort Sam Houston in San Antonio, Texas, on September 4. He was done reliving the war for today. Maybe a brisk walk would help clear his mind.

He left the house and walked a few blocks to Main Street. Crossing the Main Street Bridge over the Neosho River, he stopped and looked down at the water. When he saw someone coming from the opposite direction, he quickly moved on and crossed the street. He hated being so nervous, but it had become a way of survival.

He passed the post office and stopped in front of Kling's Ben Franklin Store. He didn't really need anything, but it was a little five-and-ten-cent store, and he thought he might get a small treat while he was out. He opened the front door and walked in to be greeted by Mr. Kling, "Hey there, Carl. Boy, it's a hot one out there this morning. I'm glad it's almost fall."

It was hot and he could feel a bead of sweat rolling down the side of his face from his brief walk. He gave a half smile and said, "Yes, sir, it is."

This heat was nothing compared to the heat in Sicily, but he didn't say that as he quietly looked behind the counter at the glass containers full of colorful candies, little toys, and household necessities. He scanned through the rows of candy that he usually knew as Christmas treats when he was younger. The choices were endless: BB Bats, Candy Buttons, Dots, Dum Dums, Long Boys, Red Hots, Root Beer Barrels, Salt Water Taffies, Chocolate Covered Peanuts, nuts, and gum to name a few. Something with peanuts sounded good, he didn't care for anything too sticky. Mr. Kling broke through his thoughts, "Well, you know what you need, don't you?"

Looking up, he said, "No, what's that?"

---

[166] Carl never heard from Jim again and never knew what happened to him.

"Why, an ice cream. You should go across the street to the Hays Tavern and there's a sweet, pretty girl who works there named Nadine Hughes. She'll help you."

Although Carl hadn't expected Mr. Kling to suggest ice cream, it did sound good on such a hot day. He figured Mr. Kling was really trying to get his mind off what had happened with Helen. News sure flew fast in a small town and apparently, everyone knew it hadn't worked out between them.

"That don't sound like a half bad idea, Mr. Kling," he said. "But I think I'll take a half pound of them chocolate covered peanuts there first."

"Go on over and get your ice cream, and I'll have them ready for you when you get back," Mr. Kling said with a wink.

The Hays Tavern was across the street. He went out and looked at the two-story, wooden structure nestled between two brick buildings with its noticeable flat roof[167]. It had been there in Council Grove for as long as he could remember. In fact, Daniel Boone's great grandson, Seth Hays, started it in 1857 after going along the Santa Fe Trail for several years to trade with the Kaw (Kansa) Indians and realizing that Council Grove was a bustling wagon train stop.

Since then it had been used for a variety of reasons, but serving food was always part of it in one way or another[168]. Now, a dark sign stood out from the light building trimmed in white as it hung from the middle of the balcony announcing CAFÉ. The top floor housed sleeping rooms and the curtains were hanging nicely in the four windows that surrounded the two wooden doors.

He wondered if he should really go. He had heard Nadine's name before from his sister, Ruby. They had become good friends since his family had moved to Council Grove. Her father was a local police officer, and he was a tall man with a kind heart and quick temper. Sometimes, he patrolled the street on foot when the town's one patrol car was being used for something else.

---

[167] Originally it was built with a peaked rook, but after a fire in 1886, the roof stayed flat

[168] Note - The Hays House is still serving food and drinks in Council Grove, KS (2015)

Then Carl remembered having received a Christmas card from the Hughes family his first Christmas away. They seemed like decent folks and he hadn't met Nadine yet. It wouldn't hurt to entertain Mr. Kling's suggestion. Besides, ice cream and pie were his favorite.

He crossed the street and walked under the white balcony supported by six thin pillars before pulling the front door open and walking in. It didn't take him long to see who Nadine was when she came to take his order. She smiled as he ordered a piece of homemade pie with a scoop of vanilla ice cream.

Her dark brown hair curled around her pale face, and he wondered if she knew who he was. When she came back, she placed the pie and ice cream in front of him. Right away, he noticed the serving was larger than usual. She flashed a smile before walking away, and he couldn't help but notice she sure was pretty—Mr. Kling had been right about that.

He left an extra tip near his plate and walked back across the street to pick up the peanuts he had ordered. Mr. Kling smiled up at him when he walked in the door and held up a small bag saying, "I see you're back. So what did you think about Nadine?"

"Well, you were right. She is beautiful," he answered with a smile.

"She comes from a nice family. Good, hard-working people," Mr. Kling added.

"Thank you, Mr. Kling," he said as he paid for the peanuts and turned to leave.

Before he reached

Figure 46: Picture of the Hays Tavern from 1943 (Permission granted by the Hays House Restaurant and Tavern)

the door, Mr. Kling called out, "How about you coming on a little boat ride with us tomorrow? We're just going over there to the Council Grove Lake."

He didn't have any plans, so he said, "That sounds nice. Thank you."

"Okay, we'll pick you up at your house tomorrow," Mr. Kling said as Carl pushed the door open.

He was glad to have something different planned—something to help keep his mind off the war. A day at the lake would be relaxing with the August heat. He waved at Mr. Kling through the side window as he passed and headed back toward his house.

That night he slept a little better—at least he didn't retrace every step across the African desert, into Sicily, and around the hills of Italy. Not sure what time to expect the Klings, he got up early and got ready. When they pulled up mid-morning, he went out to get in the car and smiled when he saw Nadine was already sitting in the back seat. Her hair was pulled away from her face with a cloth headband, and she smiled shyly as he sat down beside her. Mr. Kling had set them up once again—sending him to the restaurant must not have been enough.

It was another hot day and the moving air from the boat felt good. It had been a long time since he had gone out like this, and it was a much needed break from the memories that held him hostage so much of the time. Nadine's sweet, fun, and carefree personality made the day enjoyable as they talked. It was even a little easier to breathe the fresh air as she actually made him laugh. He hadn't truly laughed for ages it seemed. By the end of the evening, he was pretty sure she liked him. Although he thought she was beautiful and outgoing, he didn't want a serious relationship while he was still enlisted in the Army.

However, as the next few days passed, they spent more time together. Her vibrant personality kept his spirits up. She was quite a bit younger than he was, but he didn't know by how much. When he asked, she said, "Well, I'm old enough to get married. How about that?"

"Well, you'll have to wait until I finish in the service," he said with a smile. "Then, if you wait, I'll think about it."

Lunch at the Hays Tavern became an every day event. Not only did he have the valid excuse of needing to gain back some of the nearly fifty pounds he had lost in the last year, but he got to see her too. Since making it to Allied lines, he had already gained five of those pounds back. He was able to eat a little more each day. Plus, the food at the

Hays Tavern was really good and one hundred percent American—a plate of beef, potatoes, corn, and a roll was his favorite.

This day was no different as his stomach rumbled in anticipation. He looked down at his plate when Nadine brought it and smiled. There was an extra pat of butter on his plate—again. It was funny to him because he didn't put butter on his food—he didn't like it. War rations had limited butter to one pat per roll and most people sought after a way to get extra. In fact, some went as far as to order an extra roll to be left uneaten just for the second pat of butter. He didn't want to be rude or wasteful, so he left both pats on his plate when he was done.

Within a few days, the second pat of butter stopped showing up on his plate, but the pie and ice cream servings were still larger than normal. He watched her as she took and delivered orders with her brown curls bouncing around her shoulders with every step she took. When business was slow, she sat down and talked with him as he drank his coffee. Captivated by her contagious smile, her bright red lipstick, and her sparkling eyes that were full of jokes and laughter, he felt comfortable around her. She didn't ask about what had happened to him in war, and he liked that.

Unfortunately, the time was coming for him to leave. He'd tried to stay reserved and protect himself from falling in love and then risk losing that love while he was away, but it hadn't worked. For the last two weeks, he had seen and talked to Nadine every single day. She had opened a small window to his heart and somehow managed to massage a soft spot through the hardened, protected layers with her beauty and charisma. They had become inseparable. Although it sounded crazy, there was an aroma of love floating ever so gently through the air that heightened his darkened senses to a brighter tomorrow.

Come what may, he had to leave for Texas the next day. He would let the pieces of life fall where they were supposed to fall. He knew better than to try to place the pieces himself. When that final thought crossed his mind, a flame of anger lit up and began to burn within him over all the things that had gone so wrong.

In those moments—when a small, innocent thought could cause sudden anger, pain, and hate—he wondered if it would be possible to live a normal life again. Why would anyone want to be with a person who had to learn to live and love again? Those thoughts consumed him as he tried to fall asleep in vain. Not that it mattered much, for even sleeping left him wandering through the darkest corners of night while searching for a nonexistent light.

It was hard to say goodbye the next day as he got on a bus and headed for an overnight trip to San Antonio, but he did it. In exchange, he was greeted at Fort Sam by the early morning Texas humidity and mosquitos the size of flies. Under those conditions, he impatiently waited in line. Luckily, it was quick moving and before long, he was standing in front of a 1st sergeant. "Good, reporting for duty, sir," he said.

"Charles?" the sergeant asked.

"No, Carl, sir," he said in surprise that his name was not on the list.

"Well, Good, it looks like we have no record for you yet," the sergeant said, rescanning through his lists. "Report for reveille[169] and you're on your own 'til something comes in."

What? He had known he was headed there for three weeks. Surely, the Army had time to have his papers in order. Now he would be stuck in limbo until then. "Yes, sir," he grumbled as he headed in the direction the sergeant pointed.

The first note sounded into the early morning light and lightened his mood as he stood saluting the flag. Its bright white stars floated in the deep sea of blue and its red and white stripes flowed with the breeze. His frustration momentarily was replaced with pride. He had done his part in defending that flag and everything for which it stood! Nothing else mattered at that moment.

A couple weeks passed, and he was classed 1-A.[170] It didn't make sense to him. He had asked to return to his company when he was in Italy, but they had denied his request saying he wasn't fit. Now two months later, they listed him in a military classification for draftees meaning he was available and fit for general military service! Unbelievable! He hoped his papers would hurry in and get everything straightened out.

---

[169] Reveille is the morning bugle call on base usually around sunrise
[170] Story of what happened in the Army from this point forward as recorded by Carl. Details and conversation have been added.

In the meantime, he was being sent unassigned to an infantry in Camp Chaffee[171] in Arkansas—a camp adjacent from Fort Smith. A month later, his papers still had not arrived. Frustrated with his day, he walked through the falling leaves as the trees prepared for winter. *At least the trees know what's going on*, he thought.

He had no idea things were about to get better, but when he saw Nadine's face, they did. "What are you doing here?" he asked in shock. Never in a million years had he expected her to show up at his camp in Arkansas. Her beautiful, bright smile made him melt inside as she said, "I guess Ruby got tired of me talking about you all the time, so we headed over here to surprise you."

"By gosh, you definitely did that," he said as he gave Ruby a hug and kissed Nadine. When their lips touched, he knew she was the one for him. "Let's get married," he said. "You said you wanted to get married... let's do it now."

"Right now? How are we going to do that?" she asked, but he could tell by the twinkle in her eye that she was playing with the idea.

"We'll go to the court house in Fort Smith," he answered. "I'll get a buddy to be my witness and Ruby can be yours." Even as he spoke, he couldn't believe the words coming from his mouth, but he wanted to be with her.

She stood twisting her hair, but didn't think long before saying, "Okay. I'll marry you."

It was getting late and he wasn't sure he could pull it off. Maybe if they hurried, they could still make it yet today. Nadine quickly changed clothes, and he ran to find a buddy who could be his witness. They all hurried over to Fort Smith and ran up the steps of the red brick courthouse. "We want to get married," he blurted out to the first person he saw who worked there.

The man kindly pointed them in the right direction before looking down at his pocket watch saying, "Y'all better hurry. We'll be closin' in about ten minutes."

Luck was on their side. They made it in time to get married with only minutes to spare. When they signed and dated the marriage

---

[171] Renamed to Fort Chaffee in 1956

Chapter 15 – HEALING

certificate, it was October 5, 1944—only six weeks after they first met. For a brief moment, he didn't feel the familiar numbness of war. With only 36 cents in his pocket, he was happy and he'd work hard to provide.

Nadine broke the unexpected news to her parents and moved to Fort Smith as an Army wife. She hadn't ever been away from home for long, and it was a new life for them both as they adjusted to the changes.

In the Army, Carl was still unassigned to an infantry and his papers had not come in yet, but he got

Figure 47: Picture of Carl and Nadine on their wedding day

the medals he had earned while fighting overseas. He sat down and carefully looked them over. Nadine stood behind him and looked over his shoulder. There wasn't much he wanted to say, and she respected his quiet stare as he picked up the medals representing his time overseas. There was a European-African-Middle Eastern Theater Ribbon with four bronze stars, a good conduct medal, and three overseas service bars. He'd pin them onto his uniform along with his Expert Machine Gun medal and infantry badge.

He should have received the Purple Heart from his injury in the prison camp, but the Army couldn't even find his papers, let alone prove he had been injured overseas. It didn't matter to him at that moment—he only wanted to put it all behind him and move on. Now if only his records would come through so he could get assigned to an infantry. He had asked several times to return to his infantry still fighting in

Figure 48: Medals Carl earned in WWII

297

Europe, but he was denied every time. There was nothing he could do but wait.

As he waited, the big news of an upcoming dance passed through the camp. It sounded fun, and Nadine begged him to take her. He was an okay dancer, and it would break up the monotony of an ordinary night at home.

The day of the dance, his sergeant came up to him and said, "Good, I'm goin' to the dance tonight and I want somethin' to impress my girl. You already married, so let me borrow your blouse."

In unbelief, he repeated, "You want to wear my medals tonight to impress your girlfriend?"

The sergeant uncomfortably shifted his feet as he tried to make it sound better, "Well, I was just thinking since you're married and—"

"No way!" he interrupted, looking the sergeant straight in the eye. "Go get them the way I did!"

He could feel the hot stare of the sergeant on his back as he turned and walked away, but honestly, he didn't care. Those medals nearly had cost him his life as he endured hell and earned every one of them through sweat and blood. Flashbacks, nightmares, memories—those were the prices he paid for wearing the medals. He wasn't about to let his sergeant undeservingly wear them to impress some girl.

That night when he got home, Nadine was dressed up and waiting—she looked beautiful. He kissed her forehead and went to the bedroom to change. The thought of going to the dance with lots of other people made his mind spin. *I can do this*, he thought as he saw his freshly ironed uniform set out on the bed.

This was a big night for her, and although he would rather stay home, he wanted to go for her. Things like this had never overwhelmed him before and he wished the anxiety would leave. His life may have been changed by the war, but hers hadn't—so he got ready.

When they got there, he watched the music run through her body as she lightly swayed with the rhythm. He also noticed everything else in that room—the people, lights, smells, actions, and noises. He closed his eyes and took a deep breath. They'd only stay for a while. By the second song, she grabbed his hand. "Come on. Let's dance."

Her laugh, the glimmer of happiness in her eyes, the way she moved—he could tell she was enjoying every minute. He tried to let go and dance the night away, but the atmosphere of the dance was overwhelming his senses. When the music slowed, he tightly held her in his arms and silently breathed through it.

He didn't want her to know because he didn't really understand it himself—it was just the way he had returned from the war. It was as if the traumas had stayed in the active part of his brain instead of being shelved away as a memory, and then they were linked with his present situation. He couldn't relax. Yet the worst part was he knew it was irrational, but it didn't stop his thoughts from racing.

Already tense from being there, he spun around when he felt a hand touch his shoulder. "I'll take this dance," said an unknown soldier as he tried to move around him and grab Nadine's hand.

Nadine pulled back and Carl pushed the soldier back saying, "Oh no you won't."

It didn't matter the soldier was several inches taller than he was and weighed a good 100 pounds more than him. When the soldier tried to grab at Nadine again, his limbs vibrated with adrenaline as his mind went into a fight or flight response. He stepped in front of Nadine to block her and yelled at the soldier, "What do you think you're doing? Can't you see she's with me?" He tried hard to control it, but as the words came out of his mouth, the adrenaline ripped through every muscle in his body, and he punched the soldier in the face. "Leave my girl alone."

The soldier staggered back with red blood trickling from his nose. Carl was ready for more, but Nadine grabbed his arm. "Come on. Let's go," she said as she walked him to the door. "He's not worth the fight. We had a good time anyway."

Their night had been cut short and he thought about what happened at the dance as he lay in bed. The war had changed him—there was no doubt about that. He couldn't shake the mental demands of the anxiety that spread inside him like deadly spores of mold—growing and showing up at the most inopportune times. He would have to work harder than ever to move forward, but with Nadine at his side, he had a reason. She was his better half and created balance.

Even so, every day was a challenge. It didn't help his sergeant was geared toward making his life miserable for not letting him borrow his decorated shirt for the night of the dance. Since then, he had pulled weeds, cleaned the shower rooms and latrines, and had K.P. duty[172]. He knew that the sergeant was giving him all the dirty work as a way of punishing him, and there was nothing he could do about it.

He was still unassigned and he was under their control until he had enough points to get discharged from the Army. Until then, he would have to hold it together and wait it out. It must have bothered the sergeant that he wasn't getting to him because it wasn't too long before the sergeant called him out from peeling potatoes and said, "Good. We still haven't received your papers, so I'll be sendin' you to seven weeks of basic trainin'."

That was the last straw. He was fed up with the sergeant and his stupid tactics. Before he could stop himself, he answered back, "You can go to hell. I've had thirteen weeks of basic training, amphibious training for combat, and almost two years of combat and POW Camps. I wanted to go back to my outfit in Italy and I was denied. Now you come up with seven weeks of basic training? Screw you!"

"Well then, you can come with me to the Orderly Room and state your refusal there," the sergeant exploded back.

That was fine by him. He was so furious his head felt like it was going to explode. He had done all the senseless duties unfairly assigned to him, and he wasn't about to go back to basic training. He absolutely wouldn't do it.

When he got to the Orderly Room, a 2nd lieutenant sat behind a large wooden desk. He was probably in his early thirties, muscular, and had short, blond hair. At first glance, the lieutenant looked like an arrogant jerk, but Carl knew looks could be deceiving. As long as the lieutenant and sergeant weren't buddies, he might stand a chance.

However, as his refusal was stated, the 2nd lieutenant leaned towards him and said, "You're here unassigned. You could be a spy for all we know."

---

[172] Kitchen duty, often associated with peeling potatoes and other such work

Chapter 15 – Healing

Did he really just call me a spy? he thought as he blood rushed to his head. There was no controlling the words he had bottled inside as they shattered through the air around them like sharp shards of exploding glass. He didn't care who they were or what rank they held, they weren't going to call him a spy! He had risked his life for his country. It wasn't his fault the Army had messed up his papers and he was still waiting for an assignment.

The two men remained speechless as he was dismissed. He was sure he would have to pay for it later, but he didn't care. The next day after eating lunch, he decided to clear up things himself and went up to the Inspecting General's (I.G.) office. After knocking on the door, he was told to go in. Two steps away from the desk, he halted and saluted the I.G. before saying, "Sir, Private Good reports."

The I.G. was possibly in his late fifties with graying hair. He sat behind his desk looking down at a stack of papers. He looked gruff and after what happened with the 2nd lieutenant yesterday, Carl nervously waited. When his salute was returned by the I.G., Carl told him why he was there.

To his surprise, the I.G. pushed his glasses on top of his head and listened before calmly asking, "So, Private Good, what is it that you would like?"

"I'd rather go back to my old outfit than be here like this, sir."

"And what outfit would that be?"

Glad he was hearing him out, he said, "Cannon Company, 7th Infantry, 3rd Division, sir."

The I.G. shook his head, "Well, I can tell you one thing—we won't be sending you back overseas."

"Then let me be a guard over the German Prisoners of War here in Camp Chaffee," he said with hope of getting a chance to be on the other side of the fence for the nearly 3,000 Germans being held there.

"Can't do that either," the I.G. said, sitting forward in his chair. "Let me tell you something. I fought in the Pacific. My outfit came back to the States, but most of them ended up going back."

"I see you're still here, sir," Carl said as the I.G. blankly stared ahead obviously lost in thought.

The I.G. looked up with his arms folded as he leaned back. "Yes, one of the lucky ones I suppose. Well, that is what I hope to be." Then stalling for a moment, he rubbed his chin before asking, "So you were with good ole Patton, huh?"

"Yes, sir. We received the warm reception of the enemy on November 8. After hitting the beaches at Fedala, Africa, we moved into Casablanca. Then we gradually headed for Tunisia. Once there, we trained for a short period and then loaded up to root those devils out of another trough. They were hogging, and I do mean hogging, sir. It was Sicily we hit there, full force at high speed on July 10. Not long after that, I was captured and moved through POW camps until I escaped one in Italy. I lived in the mountains of Italy for over nine months until making it to Allied lines and here I am. Papers or no papers—that is my story, sir."

When Carl had said the enemy had been hogging, the I.G. smiled and when he finished, the I.G. asked, "What did you do before going into the Army? You got farming background?"

"Yes, sir. Farming runs through my veins. I worked on a ranch before I left and I plan on getting back to it as soon as I get done with my time in the service."

The I.G. pulled a picture out of his billfold and handed it to him. It was a picture of grazing horses. "Beautiful animals, sir."

"I could have guessed you were a farm boy," the I.G. said with a smile. "I love farming and ranching myself."

This was going much better than he could have ever imagined. "Well, sir. Looks like we have several things in common. I want to thank you for hearing me out, sir."

"You did a good job stating your complaint. I'll see want I can do," the I.G. said as Carl gave the final salute. The I.G. returned the salute and Carl turned and left the room. It felt good to be heard for a change.

However, the next day, when he saw the sergeant, he braced for the chewing out he knew was coming. Sure enough, the words spewed out of the sergeant's mouth, but he only half listened. He wasn't surprised because he was well aware he hadn't gone through the necessary channels to meet with the I.G., but he also knew the sergeant wasn't going to do anything to get his complaint there because he was most of the problem.

He looked the sergeant square in the eye and boldly replied, "Well sir, if you would of had everything cut and dried before I got here, I wouldn't of had to go see him in the first place."

"Private Good, I've heard enough from you. You've got K.P. today," said the sergeant with a smirk.

Big surprise, he thought as he went to the kitchen. After working the long, hot day, he took a Class A pass and went to Fort Smith to see Nadine. One look at her and his troubles dissipated into the cool, fall air. With her around, things could only get better. She talked about what they would do when he was out of the Army and about having a family… and he tried to listen.

He still couldn't quite focus on the future after spending so much time trying to avoid it. He knew he wanted to try his hand at farming, but he also knew he'd be starting out from scratch. There'd be some Army loans, but that was it.

After reveille the next morning, he saw the sergeant coming toward him. *Great, what does he want now*, he thought.

"Good, Commanding Officer Davids[173] wants to see you in his office now," the sergeant said.

Not sure what to expect, he figured he would be further punished for not following the order of command. He went to the commander's office, knocked on the door, followed procedure, and reported. There was silence.

When the commander spoke, he introduced himself, "I'm Captain Davids. I see by what little record we have of yours that you're out of Cannon Company, 7th Infantry, 3rd Division. I'm out of the 7th Infantry also. I too was wounded and sent back to the States. I don't like the way they done you and are doing me. I have an order from the Personnel Office that you're to do eleven weeks of K.P. for not going through the correct channels to see the I.G. As your commander, I have to enforce this order. Report to the kitchen and I'll see what I can do for you."

---

[173] Name changed

There was nothing for him to say in return except for thank you, and he was quickly dismissed. After an hour or so, the sergeant came to the kitchen and said, "Good, the commander wants to see you again."

Once again, he followed procedure and reported to the commander's office. Upon stating with a salute, "Sir, Private Good reporting," the commander returned the salute and said, "Private Good, I think I can help you. Are you married?"

"Yes, sir, I am. My wife is staying in Fort Smith."

"That's what I thought," Captain Davids said sympathetically. "You work the rest of today and tonight I'll have a three-day pass on my desk. Leave and be back for reveille at the end of those three days. Work K.P. that day and I'll have you another three-day pass ready. In the meantime, I'll do some more thinking."

He couldn't believe what he was hearing—the top brass were on his side. It didn't matter how miserable the sergeant and lieutenant tried to make him—he was one step ahead. Once again, he was dismissed and headed back to the kitchen. Picking up where he had left off, the mess sergeant told him, "You're to do what you want. If any brass comes in, act busy until they leave."

Sounded good to him, but he planned to work anyway—it helped pass the time. When the sergeant returned for the third time that day, he already knew to report to the commander. "I figured out something else," Captain Davids said with a smile when he got to the office. "Tonight you pick up your three-day pass like we talked about. When it's up, come in and I'll have another one ready for you. At the end of that one, you'll have to stay with me that day. Then we'll do it again. Promise me you won't let me down."

It didn't take a rocket scientist to know what the commander was offering him. If he didn't do it exactly as outlined, that time would have to be counted as furlough, and they'd both get in trouble. "Yes, sir. I understand. You can count on me. Thank you, sir."

The setup worked as planned, and he was able to spend quality time with Nadine—almost like a honeymoon that was occasionally interrupted. When he was around, it wasn't so hard and lonely for her. She had spent a lot of time sewing, but now they could both relax a bit.

After eleven weeks like that, he finished off his time and got reassigned into the 174th Infantry. Since the 174th had moved on to Camp Gruber, near Braggs, Oklahoma, on December 9, they would relocate to Oklahoma and finish out the winter there. Although he appreciated everything the I.G., Captain Davids, and the mess sergeant had done for him, he was none too sad about leaving.

In Oklahoma, they moved the few things they had into a lightly furnished apartment on the second floor. It wasn't long before he was chosen as Soldier of the Month and received a three-day pass to enjoy the city of Muskogee, Oklahoma—all expenses paid. Excited to take his wife on a trip to the city, he asked about her expenses. No, the expenses would only cover him. Slightly disappointed, he knew they couldn't afford it, so he turned the trip back in.

His next transfer came at the beginning of April. They were headed to Camp Howze in Texas where he would be driving for headquarters there. They moved on base and the living quarters were not nearly as comfortable. A sheet was all that covered the open window hole and Nadine felt exposed. She was also sad from having an earlier miscarriage and getting more homesick by the day. Carl agreed that it wasn't the nicest place to live, but they'd only be there for about six months before he met the required eighty-three points he needed to be honorably discharged, and then they'd go back to Kansas.

She agreed, but every night she reminded him it was dangerous to live in such a place. Tired of hearing her complaints, he mostly tuned them out. *This is nothing*, he thought as he remembered the cold nights that he spent sleeping on the ground half starving. However, one night he was hit by a flying pebble. Confused, he sat up thinking he was in the mountains of Italy and looked around for a weapon. His heart pounded.

Nadine sat up beside him. "What was that?" she asked, finding a small white pebble on the blanket.

"What the…" He sat for a minute trying to calm his racing mind and figure things out. Nadine looked at the window and feeling justified she said, "I told you. It's not safe here."

This happened for several nights in a row, and he began to wonder if she was right. Even though he didn't have the money to send her home, maybe he'd have to find a way. But why would someone be throwing rocks at them? It didn't make sense.

A couple nights later, he was getting ready for bed and saw something out of the corner of his eye. He lifted up a small section of the thin mattress on her side and saw a small pile of pebbles—exactly like the ones hitting him in the middle of the night. It didn't take but a few seconds to piece the story together—in her desperation to go home, she was throwing the pebbles at him and saying they were coming in from outside.

When he asked about the rock pile, tears rolled down her face as she apologized, "I'm sorry. I just wanted to go home for a few days."

"That's no excuse," he tried to explain without exploding. "Do you know that every night you hit me with a pebble, my body went into danger mode and kept me awake for hours? No? You probably didn't because you went right to sleep. You can't do that. You don't understand that my body can't relax anyway, and I don't need you adding to it. I understand you're homesick—I do, but trying to trick me into sending you home is crossing the line. You'll just have to wait a few more months."

She nodded her head.

"Why don't you write a letter home instead," he suggested. "I'm going to lie down, and I don't expect to wake up to any rocks tonight."

When he got in bed, he could see her sitting at the small, kitchen table writing a letter home. He hoped it would make her feel better since there were no chances he would be sending her home now. It must have been a short letter because he felt her slip into bed before he could fall asleep.

In the next few days, things smoothed out, and she seemed to be feeling better. He didn't think much about it, until he got home one day and saw her dad, Oscar, sitting in the living room. "Hello, sir," he said in surprise, shaking his hand. "What are you doing here?"

Nadine was unusually quiet as her dad sent her a sideways glance and said, "Florence[174] and I got a letter from Nadine in the mail a few

---

[174] Nadine's mother

days ago that said she was extremely ill. It said she needed us to come. I got on the first possible train and got in today."

Carl wasn't even sure what to say. No wonder her spirits had been lifted after she wrote the letter to her parents the other night—she figured if she couldn't go to them, she'd get them to come to her. "Well, she was very homesick... I can vouch for that."

"From the sound of her letter, we thought she was on her deathbed," her dad said. "But after all the worry, I was certainly glad to see she was up and healthy."

Carl was certain he had missed some choice words when her dad realized he had spent money on a ticket just because she was homesick. But honestly, what could he do at that point besides blow off some hot-tempered steam. He was there and that was what she needed. Her plan had worked and it was enough to get her through the next couple of months in Texas.

Before his time in the Army was permanently up, there was one thing he needed to do. He grabbed a notebook and a pen and began to write, "My Prisoner of War Story in Italy." Under that, he wrote, "This is a true story."

Memories scattered around his mind. The words were all jumbled in his head, but slowly dates, names, and places popped forward with exact preciseness. It had been over two years since it had all begun, but the ghostly images of war were in his memory forever like careful etchings of glass—deep and fragile. The nightmarish details crept forward, but he boldly pushed them back as he thought of what he needed to write from the beginning. He was ever cautious to leave the worst memories tightly locked away.

For his sanity, he needed to balance the past and live in the present. He needed to heal. He couldn't pretend it didn't happen because with God as his witness, he knew it did! *Keep it simple and straightforward*, he told himself in an effort to rid himself of the dizzying pain and overwhelming hardness that had made it possible for him to survive and endure to this point in time.

He looked down at his watch and stared at the time as he nonchalantly leaned back in his chair, effortlessly balancing on two legs. He had been sitting—thinking—much longer than he realized.

Gently putting his chair back down on all four legs, he lightly tapped his pen against the wooden table. He only wanted to get back to a normal life, and if by writing this he could rid himself of some of the pain—some of the deadening hurt, he would do it. He wasn't worried about the grammar being perfect, but his story was true and he needed to release it, at least part of it. Maybe with time he would be able to tell more, but for now this was a beginning to a fresh future.

He had already discovered his future was going to be different than he had planned, but looking at his beautiful wife as she stood by the small kitchen sink with a homemade flowered apron over her dress and her curly hair dancing around her shoulders as she moved, he knew it was going to be all right. After a long drink of hot, dark coffee, he looked down at his paper. Like his future, he wanted to start over on a new page—get a fresh start where his thoughts could easily flow onto the empty page before him. At the top of an unmarked page, he began again:

Chapter 15 – Healing

My Prisoner of War Story in Italy
This is a true story.

By Pfc Carl L Good
A.S.N. 37158596
Camp Houze, Texas

Prisoner of War in Sicily and Italy
True Story
By Pfc Carl L. Good

1942, April 20 I left home for Ft. Leavenworth, Kansas, there I was inducted into the United States Army...

It took him several days, but upon writing his final lines, he felt a release. It was as if a heavy burden had been removed from his soul. Even though the war had ended, he still didn't want to talk about what had happened or the things he had seen, but he felt relieved to write some of them on paper.

Of course, there were some memories he would have to suffer through alone when they came to visit him in his quietest moments, but by some miracle, he had been one of the lucky ones to make it home. He was given a second chance. He didn't know what was to come, but he knew he could survive whatever was thrown at him... thanks to the Good Man Upstairs.

Epilogue

A LIFE WELL LIVED

CARL HAD MADE it home and was readjusting to life. After the war, he went on to have a family and lived life to the fullest. The war memories still haunted him, but he was able to work hard and not let them overtake him. The following is a brief summary of what happened next in his life.

He finished earning the last points he needed to be discharged from the United States Army and headed to Camp Wolters[175] so he could officially end that chapter of his life and begin a new one. Although hardened by the war and nervous as a cat, he was ready to face life head-on with Nadine by his side. An Army loan of $5,000 helped him get back to Kansas and start farming in Wilsey—the one thing he really wanted to do. He rented 170 acres and bought a tractor, five cows, three sows, drill/disk, cultivator, and chickens. Clyde also gave him a team of black Percheron horses as a wedding gift. With one hired man, he got started and planted corn. However, it was tough making ends meet.

It was even tougher when a little over six months after returning, his mother died, leaving his youngest brother, Johnny, parentless at the age of fifteen. Johnny decided to travel to California and joined the Air Force as soon as he could. Carl stayed in the area.

Due to his injuries from war, Carl was diagnosed with a nervous condition in 1947. It was something he had to deal with so he could lead as normal a life as possible. Fortunately, he did not turn to alcohol

---

[175] Army camp near Mineral Wells, Texas used from 1925-1946

or drugs and worked hard through the ups and downs of life—pain, heartbreak, happiness, and success.

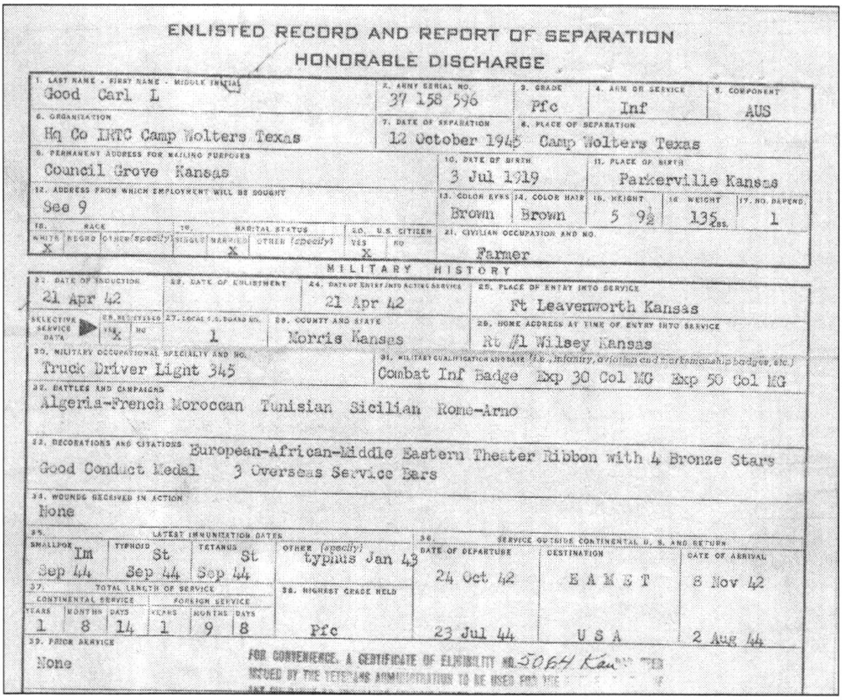

ENLISTED RECORD AND REPORT OF SEPARATION
HONORABLE DISCHARGE

1. LAST NAME - FIRST NAME - MIDDLE INITIAL: Good Carl L
2. ARMY SERIAL NO.: 37 158 596
3. GRADE: Pfc
4. ARM OR SERVICE: Inf
5. COMPONENT: AUS
6. ORGANIZATION: Hq Co IRTC Camp Wolters Texas
7. DATE OF SEPARATION: 12 October 1945
8. PLACE OF SEPARATION: Camp Wolters Texas
9. PERMANENT ADDRESS FOR MAILING PURPOSES: Council Grove Kansas
10. DATE OF BIRTH: 3 Jul 1919
11. PLACE OF BIRTH: Parkerville Kansas
12. ADDRESS FROM WHICH EMPLOYMENT WILL BE SOUGHT: See 9
13. COLOR EYES: Brown
14. COLOR HAIR: Brown
15. HEIGHT: 5 9½
16. WEIGHT: 135 LBS.
17. NO. DEPEND.: 1
18. RACE: WHITE X
19. MARITAL STATUS: MARRIED X
20. U.S. CITIZEN: YES X
21. CIVILIAN OCCUPATION AND NO.: Farmer

MILITARY HISTORY

22. DATE OF INDUCTION: 21 Apr 42
23. DATE OF ENLISTMENT:
24. DATE OF ENTRY INTO ACTIVE SERVICE: 21 Apr 42
25. PLACE OF ENTRY INTO SERVICE: Ft Leavenworth Kansas
SELECTIVE SERVICE DATA 26. REGISTERED: YES X
27. LOCAL S.S. BOARD NO.: 1
28. COUNTY AND STATE: Morris Kansas
29. HOME ADDRESS AT TIME OF ENTRY INTO SERVICE: Rt #1 Wilsey Kansas
30. MILITARY OCCUPATIONAL SPECIALTY AND NO.: Truck Driver Light 345
31. MILITARY QUALIFICATION AND DATE (i.e., infantry, aviation and marksmanship badges, etc.): Combat Inf Badge Exp 30 Cal MG Exp 50 Cal MG
32. BATTLES AND CAMPAIGNS: Algeria-French Moroccan Tunisian Sicilian Rome-Arno
33. DECORATIONS AND CITATIONS: European-African-Middle Eastern Theater Ribbon with 4 Bronze Stars Good Conduct Medal 3 Overseas Service Bars
34. WOUNDS RECEIVED IN ACTION: None
35. LATEST IMMUNIZATION DATES: SMALLPOX Im Sep 44; TYPHOID St Sep 44; TETANUS St Sep 44; OTHER (specify) typhus Jan 43
36. SERVICE OUTSIDE CONTINENTAL U.S. AND RETURN:

DATE OF DEPARTURE	DESTINATION	DATE OF ARRIVAL
24 Oct 42	E A M E T	8 Nov 42
23 Jul 44	U S A	2 Aug 44

37. TOTAL LENGTH OF SERVICE:

CONTINENTAL SERVICE YEARS	MONTHS	DAYS	FOREIGN SERVICE YEARS	MONTHS	DAYS
1	8	14	1	9	8

38. HIGHEST GRADE HELD: Pfc
39. PRIOR SERVICE: None

FOR CONVENIENCE, A CERTIFICATE OF ELIGIBILITY NO. 5064 Kan
ISSUED BY THE VETERANS ADMINISTRATION TO BE USED FOR THE

Figure 49: Carl's discharge paper from the United States Army on October 12, 1945

Nadine and he had one girl and then five rambunctious boys (the last two were twins) to keep them busy. They needed more money than he could make with the farm alone so he kept renting the farmland and moved into Council Grove where he worked a full-time job. The older boys helped him take care of the farm. On top of all that, he volunteered at the Council Grove Fire Department.

He didn't have a lot of time to dwell on the past, and he certainly didn't talk about it. Nadine learned to live with his night terrors and flashbacks, but anything that might trigger an attack was forbidden—the war was never to be mentioned—period. He was a good husband and father, but demanded hard work and respect from his children.

When he unexpectedly received a package in the mail nearly ten years after the war, he found the Army had sent him his bag that was left behind when he was captured. He opened it up with Nadine at his side and found the flag armband he had worn when landing in Fedala, rocks he had collected, foreign coins, the goat-skinned billfold, the pen/pencil he had bought in Casablanca, and a few other memories, including letters he hadn't received from his mother. They showed it all to the kids and safely tucked everything away in the attic, but he noticed those memories didn't hurt as much.

Although married life came with challenges, they made it work—even with the nine-year age difference. He worked hard and believed in passing on strong values to his children while Nadine stayed home to provide a loving atmosphere with home cooked meals, fashion sewed clothes, and organization. There was never a dull minute with five boys running around.

Carl couldn't pass up a good deal when he stopped at auctions and frequently bought boxes of "stuff" that Nadine usually deemed unnecessary. Rather than letting it become a problem as it built up in the garage, she would have two annual garage sales and sell what she could. He would come home, get mad, and then it was over… until the next sale. Then, she would take her garage sale money and use it for the two things she loved—vacation and Christmas.

Nadine loved everything about Christmas and decorated the house from top to bottom. Every year, she pulled out rolls of brightly colored garland and looped it over doorways, around the windows, and onto open shelves. She setup the chimney scene, tree, and lots of lights, making the house bright and cheery—no matter how bad the weather got outside.

The kids grew older, but their relationships with Nadine didn't fade. Whether it was getting together for Sunday coffee or a huge Christmas gathering, she lived every day to the fullest and loved her family. All but two of her children stayed in Council Grove with one living next door and one raising his family there with them.

It was shortly after such a wonderful holiday celebration in 1987 that life decided to take an unexpected twist for him. The decorations were still shining through the night a couple days after Christmas when Nadine went to bed. Sometime during the night, she woke up and went to the bathroom—her stomach was bothering her a bit. Early that morning on December 30, he reached over and felt her body next to him—she was cold and lifeless. He jumped out of bed and checked for any signs of life. There were none and there was nothing he could do to save her.

There were no words—only tears. He was completely lost and devastated. In a million years, he wouldn't have expected her to go first—his companion and best friend for forty-three years. How could that happen? He was older, he had a weakened heart from the stress of the war—he was supposed to go first! How could a wonderful and healthy person so full of love and life be alive one minute and gone the next? However, a blood clot in her leg had quickly ended her life, leaving behind not only Carl, but their six children, twenty-five grandchildren, her parents, and her two sisters—Irene Sherrer and Connie Neal.

Her death cut his soul in half and he began to visit the memories they had avoided for so many years. Things were different now and although he always supported the American Legion, war related funding projects, and POW groups, he was finally able to share some of the memories that still hung so vividly in his mind. He talked to local schools, interested newspapers, and answered questions. He wasn't going to keep his story hidden any longer. It felt good to share it, but he never undermined the true heroes who gave their lives. It wasn't uncommon for him to be asked by grandchildren if he could be interviewed—one more time. After all, that's how this story came about.

It was also while sharing his story at an event in 1991 that Carl met Katherine McDiffett. She was a Southern woman who had also lost her spouse, and they were married later that year. They were married until she passed away and joined her husband in February 2010.

Carl lived to be 92 years old, and then as a surprise to Nadine, he joined her on Christmas Eve 2011. Most likely, he galloped to heaven's gate on a white horse to the yodel of Gene Autry's, *The Last Round-Up*. They say a picture speaks a thousand words, so here are some favorites from a life well lived.

Epilogue – A Life Well Lived

Carl and Nadine as their children were growing up.
Children oldest to youngest—Carla, Danny, David, Dennis, and twins, Ron and Don

315

Carl loved the country life!

Epilogue – A Life Well Lived

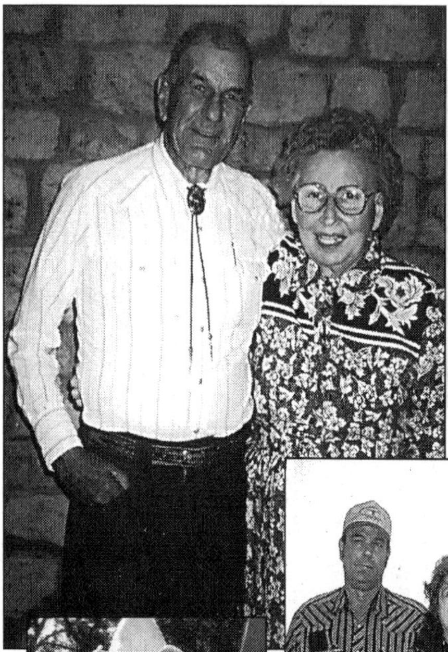

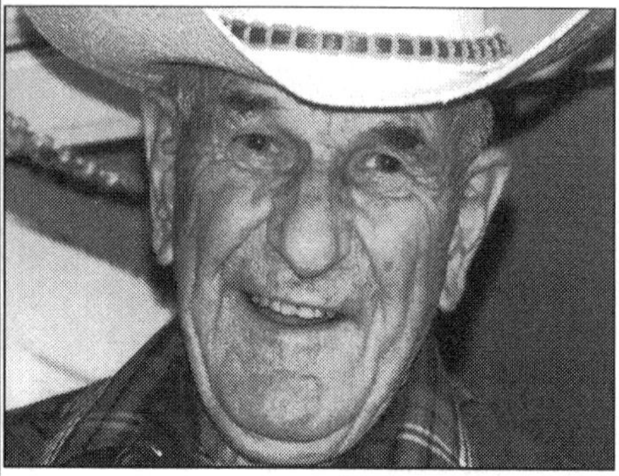

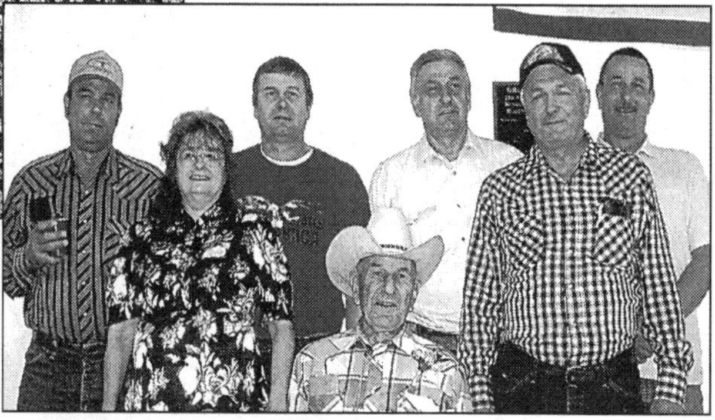

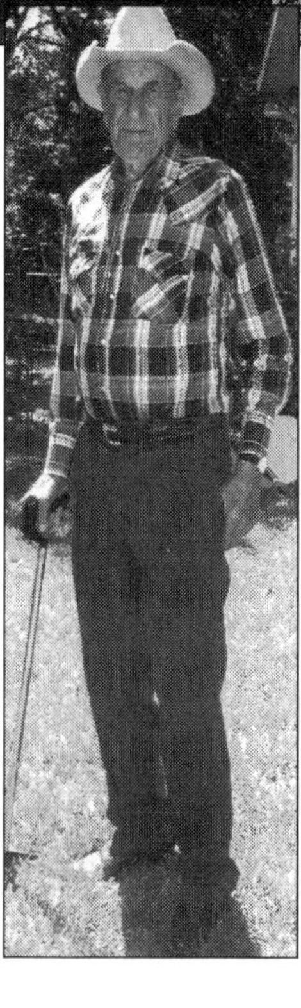

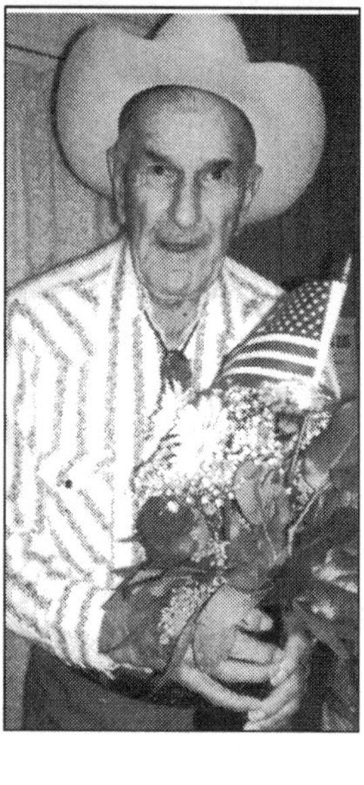

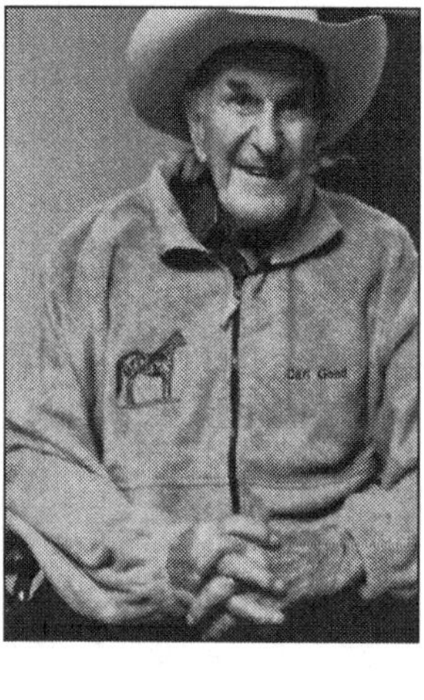

Epilogue – A Life Well Lived

Carl died on December 24, 2011, but his memory will live on.

The taps were played for him on December 29, 2011, and he was honored one last time.

Photos taken by CJ Good—grandson with the same birthday and name

In honor of all the men and women who fight for our country. Thank you!

319

WORKS CITED

174th Armored Infantry Battalion. (n.d.). Retrieved from Military.com Unit Pages: http://www.military.com/HomePage/UnitPageFullText/0,13476,702730,00.html

Anderson, C. R. (2003, October). *Algeria-French Morocco, The U.S. Army campaigns of World War II*. Retrieved from U.S. Army Center of Military History: http://www.history.army.mil/brochures/algeria/algeria.htm

Bliven, B. J. (1965). *From Casablanca to Berlin*. New York: Random House.

Blumenson, M. (1974). *The Patton papers: 1940-1945*. Boston: Da Capo Press.

Carpenter, A. E., & Eiland, A. A. (2010). *Chappie World War II diary of a combat chaplain*. Mead Publishing.

Censorship! War letters. WGBH American experience PBS. (n.d.). Retrieved from PBS Public Broadcasting Service: http://www.pbs.org/wgbh/americanexperience/features/general-article/warletters-censorship/

Cork oak (quercus suber) rainforest alliance. (n.d.). Retrieved from Rainforest Alliance: http://www.rainforest-alliance.org/kids/species-profiles/cork-oak

Customs and courtesies. (n.d.). Retrieved from Army Study Guide: http://www.armystudyguide.com/content/army_board_study_guide_topics/customs_and_courtesies/customs-and-courtesies-st.shtml

Dixon, S. (2010, January 9). *Trailblazers file archives*. Retrieved from 70th Infantry Division Association: http://www.files.trailblazersww2.org/

Dorney, R. (2005). *An active service: the story of a soldier's life in the Grenadier Guards and SAS, 1935-1958*. England: Helion & Company.

Ells, M. D. (2005). *Haunted*. Retrieved from America in WWII: http://www.americainwwii.com/articles/haunted/

Featured artifacts: Hispanic American heritage month. (n.d.). Retrieved from The National WWII Museum: http://www.nationalww2museum.org/see-hear/collections/artifacts/hispanic-american-heritage-month.html

Forties slang (40s). (n.d.). Retrieved from 1940s: http://1940s.org/history/on-the-homefront/forties-slang-40s

Fox, R. (2014, May 11). Information on the LCT. (C. G. Aceves, Interviewer) Retrieved from http://ww2lct.org/main.htm

Funari, R., & Funari, V. (2014). Information about Riccardo Funari.

Garland, L. C., & Smyth, H. M. (1965). *United States Army in World War II: The Mediterranean Theater of Operations: Sicily and the surrender of Italy*. Washington D.C.: Office of the Chief of Military History Department of the Army.

Good, C. L. (1945). My prisoner of war story in Italy (Memoir). Camp Houze, Texas.

Good, C. L. (2007, April). Experiences in WWII. (C. G. Aceves, Interviewer)

Good, C. L. (2007-2011). Interviews with Carl L. Good. (C. G. Aceves, Interviewer) Council Grove, Kansas.

Hill, D. (2008, February 1). *Recollection of camps 98 and 59 from Armie Hill*. Retrieved from Camp 59 Survivors: http://camp59survivors.wordpress.com/2008/02/01/recollection-of-camps-98-and-59/

Hill, D. (2011). *Captain Millar—valor in the hour of crisis*. Retrieved from Camp 59 Survivors: https://camp59survivors.wordpress.com/2011/03/25/captain-millar%e2%80%94valor-in-the-hour-of-crisis/

Hill, D. (2011). *Giuseppe Millozzi on the "stay put order"*. Retrieved from Camp 59 Survivors: https://camp59survivors.wordpress.com/2011/03/25/giuseppe-millozzi-on-the-stay-put-order/

Hill, D. (2014). Retrieved from Camp 59 Survivors: Experiences of the Allied Servicemen who were Prisoners of War at Servigliano, Italy: http://camp59survivors.wordpress.com/

History. (n.d.). Retrieved from Hays House Restaurant and Tavern: http://hayshouse.com/history/p205314

Howe, G. F. (n.d.). Retrieved from U.S. Army in World War II Mediterranean, Theater of Operations, Northwest Africa: seizing the initiative in the west: http://www.ibiblio.org/hyperwar/USA/USA-MTO-NWA/index.html#index

Infantry, C. C. (1942-1943). *Company Morning Reports.*

Interviews with Carl L. Good. (2007-2011). On *Carl L. Good*. Council Grove, Kansas.

Iommi, F. (2009). *La storia di Riccardo Funari: eroe antifascista di Monte San Martino.*

January 1944 - Mediterranean Theater of Operations (MTO). (n.d.). Retrieved from Combat Chronology US Army Air Forces Mediterranean - 1944, Part 1: http://www.milhist.net/usaaf/mto44a.html

Lane, T. A. (n.d.). *John O. Williams.* Retrieved from West Point Association of Graduates : http://apps.westpointaog.org/Memorials/Article/8454/

Lescastreyres, R. (2001). *1942.* Retrieved from War Memories of a Young Frenchman 1939-1945: http://www.duhamel.bz/memories/index.htm

Macky, I. (n.d.). Retrieved from PAT maps : http://ian.macky.net/pat/

McSpirit, J. (n.d.). *13 things to remember if you love a person with anxiety.* Retrieved from LifeHack: http://www.lifehack.org/articles/communication/13-things-remember-you-love-person-with-anxiety.html

Millozzi, A., & McCarthy, I. (2014). *Information on Giovanni Straffi and Monte San Martino.* Monte San Martino.

Millozzi, G. (2014). *Expert on Camp 59.*

Morison, S. E. (1959). *History of the United States naval operations in World War II, volume IX, Sicily-Salerno-Anzio January 1943-June 1944.* Boston: Little, Brown and Company.

Morison, S. E. (1984). *History of the United States naval operations in World War II, volume II, operations in North African waters October 1942-June 1943.* Boston: Little, Brown and Company.

Pearson, J. L. (2005). *Brooklynisms*. Retrieved from http://www.lampos.com/brooklyn.htm

Province, C. M. (2002). *The unknown Patton*. CMP Publications.

PTSD. (n.d.). Retrieved from Make the connection: http://maketheconnection.net/conditions/ptsd?gclid=CKO75L_0qcUCFZGDaQod4kMA6Q

Rendering honor to the flag. (n.d.). Retrieved from Army Study Guide: http://www.armystudyguide.com/content/Prep_For_Basic_Training/Prep_for_basic_customs_and_courtesies/rendering-honor-to-the-fl.shtml

Roberts, S. S. (2007, June 5). *ShipScribe*. Retrieved from http://www.shipscribe.com/

Simkin, J. (n.d.). *George Patton*. Retrieved from Spartacus Educational: http://www.spartacus.schoolnet.co.uk/2WWpatton.htm

Simkin, J. (n.d.). *Spartacus Educational*. Retrieved 2010, from Spartacus Educational: http://www.spartacus.schoolnet.co.uk/2WWpatton.htm

Simkins, J. (2014). Retrieved from Monte San Martino Trust: http://www.msmtrust.org.uk/

Slee, G. (2001). *Combined operations*. Retrieved from Operation TORCH - North Africa - 8th to 12th Nov 1942: http://www.combinedops.com/Torch.htm

Swanson, R. (2009, August 24). *USS Augusta (CA-31)*. Retrieved from http://www.internet-esq.com/ussaugusta/index.htm

Taggart, D. G., & Marshall, G. C. (1947). *History of the Third Infantry Division in World War II*. Washington D.C.: Infantry Journal Press.

The darkest hour - 5th Northamptons (part 2). (2003, November 8). Retrieved from WW2 People's War: http://www.bbc.co.uk/history/ww2peopleswar/stories/26/a2060326.shtml

Vey, W. D., & Elliott, O. J. (n.d.). *The beach boys*. Retrieved from 1st US Naval Beach Battalion: http://www.1stbeachbattalion.org/beach_boys.htm

Vogel, H. W. (2006, February 26). *World War II experiences - good grief sir, we're in trier!* Retrieved from Military History Online: http://www.militaryhistoryonline.com/wwii/accounts/hansvogeltrier.aspx

Wagner, B. (2000). *And there shall be wars.* Twig, MN: Wilmer Wagner and Lloyd Wagner Press.

Westerman, B. (2006, August). *The evolution of deep water fording and the jeep.* Retrieved from The CJ-3A Information Page: http://www.cj3a.info/sibling/cjv35u/evolution.html